# List of Tables and Charts

## Tables

## Charts

The U.S. Economic Recovery

# The U.S. Economic Recovery

## GFC Economics

2QT Limited (Publishing)

First edition published 2014

2QT Limited (Publishing)
Lancaster, United Kingdom LA2 8RE
www.2qt.co.uk

Cover images: shutterstock.com

Printed by Lightning Source UK

A CIP catalogue record for this book will be available
from the British Library

ISBN 978-1-910077-20-7

# Contents

# Glossary

**Accumulation** - Refers to the tendency for company profits to be reinvested, increasing the total quantity of capital.

**Bretton Woods Agreement** - The Bretton Woods system of monetary management was established in 1944. Participating countries were obliged to adopt a monetary policy that maintained exchange rates by tying their currency to the US Dollar. The Bretton Woods agreement also led to the establishment of the International Monetary Fund, which was charged with overseeing the international monetary system to ensure exchange rate stability and encouraging members to eliminate exchange restrictions that hinder trade.

**Calendar guidance** - The commitment of a central bank to maintain interest rates at a certain level until a specified date.

**Cheap, but tight money** - A monetary framework where credit or lending is cheap [i.e. available at low short- and long-term rates of interest], but the growth in credit or lending is simultaneously constrained.

**Classical school** - An economic school of thought that emerged in the 18th century, led by Adam Smith, David Ricardo and John Stuart Mill. It advocated free markets and self-regulation of the economy.

**Complex of interest rates** - Refers to the rate of interest on all kind of borrowing: long and short, safe and risky.

**Core consumption deflator** - This is a chain-type price index from the US Bureau of Economic Analysis that measures the rate of inflation, excluding food and energy, for personal consumption. The Federal Reserve uses this as an inflation target.

**Core inflation** - Inflation excluding food and energy. [See also *core consumption deflator*.]

**Credit crunch** - A sudden downturn in lending precipitated by distress at financial institutions. Credit crunch was the name widely given to the sub-prime mortgage crisis in the US and the run on UK banks, from 2007 onwards.

**Credit multiplier** - Lower interest rates [short- and long-term] reversing the impact of a contraction in the availability of credit.

**Crowding-in** - A restrictive fiscal stance leading to lower bond yields, reinforcing the potency of a loose monetary policy.

**Dear money** - Monetary policy that leads to higher rates of interest, to control the pace of borrowing.

**Debt deflation** - High level of debt leading to falling asset prices. It may also lead to falling consumer prices or negative inflation.

**Debt management** - Policies referring to the issuance of debt by governments.

**Debt trap** - Attempts to pay off outstanding loans leading to a higher real debt burden, as a result of the negative impact on prices.

**Dotcom recession** - Collapse of the speculative bubble in the Internet and technology sectors from early 2000 onwards.

**Easy money** - Credit or lending growing rapidly, due to lack of constraint over banks and other financial institutions.

**Easy, but dear money** - A combination of loose lending standards but higher interest rates, prevalent since the early 1970s across many countries in the West, notably the US and the UK.

**Exit Strategies** - Exiting from quantitative easing.

**Federal funds rate** [or target for the federal fund rates] - Interest rate at which a financial institution lends money held at the Federal Reserve to another institution [overnight]. The Federal Reserve announces a target for the federal fund rates at its monthly policy meetings.

**Financial capital** - The accumulation of financial assets [and cash reserves] by firms in contrast to accumulation of real assets.

**Fiscal cliff** - Restrictive fiscal stance due to the expiration of tax breaks and simultaneous spending cuts, which came automatically into effect on 1 January 2013.

**Fiscal multiplier** - Change in Gross Domestic Product in response to a change in government expenditure or tax rates.

**Foreclosed homes** - Properties are foreclosed when borrowers default and banks repossess the asset.

**Forward rate guidance** - A monetary policy tool where the central bank provides guidance for the likely future path of short-term interest rates.

**Glass-Steagall Act** - US banking act passed in 1933 separating investment from commercial banking.

**Great Depression** - Economic collapse in the US from 1929 onwards.

**Great Recession** - Economic recession starting with the failure of the investment bank Bear Stearns in March 2008 and accelerating after the collapse of Lehman Brothers in September 2008.

**Hysteresis** - Deterioration in the skills of workers that have been unemployed for long periods of time. This can potentially increase the natural rate of unemployment.

**International Clearing Union** - A global bank managing the clearance of trade between nations. This was proposed by Keynes and put forward as the official proposal of the British Government at the Bretton Woods Agreement in 1944.

**Income velocity of money** - The ratio of income divided by money.

**Large-scale asset purchases** - Used synonymously with quantitative easing [see *quantitative easing*].

**Large-scale open market purchases** - Used to describe asset purchases or quantitative easing during the Great Depression.

**Liquidity Preference/Liquidity Preference Theory** - The aversion of investors to holding long-dated bonds, particularly at low levels of interest due to the potential losses when interest rates rise.

**Liquidity premium** - The benefit extracted from holding liquid assets [cash] rather than investing in less liquid assets, i.e. assets with longer maturity.

**Liquidity trap** - When long-term government bond yields stop falling, reaching a point of resistance due to investors' risk aversion.

**M2** - A measure of money supply that includes M1 [i.e. cash and checking deposits] as well as near money [savings deposits, money market mutual funds, and other time deposits - which are less liquid than M1].

**Marginal efficiency of capital** - Formally, this is the rate of discount which makes the present value of the series of annuities given by the returns expected from the capital asset during its life equal to its supply price. Less formally, it is the gross rate of return on investment less the cost of replacement.

**Marginal propensity to consume** - Change in consumer spending in response to a change in disposable income.

**Monetary policy tools** - Tools available to central banks to influence borrowing costs including conventional tools [such as short-term interest rates and reserve requirements] and non-conventional tools [such as quantitative easing]. [See *non-conventional monetary policy tools*].

**Money illusion** - Investors or consumers suffer from money illusion when they overemphasise the nominal return on assets, nominal interest rate or nominal wages, failing to take into account sufficiently either falling inflation or deflation.

**Money-rate of interest** - The risk-free or pure rate of interest. [See *risk-free rate.*]

**Mortgage Backed Securities** - A pool of mortgages bundled together into a security that is sold to investors.

**Natural rates of interest** - The theoretical risk-free rate of interest for credit determined by supply and demand from private investors. Formally, the natural rate of interest is 'The rate of interest at which saving and the value of investment are exactly balanced, so that the price level of output as a whole exactly corresponds to the money rate of efficiency earnings of the factors of production'. [See G. Tily, *Keynes's General Theory, The Rate Of Interest And 'Keynesian' Economics*, Palgrave Macmillan, 2007, p. 54]. Less formally, it should be thought of as the rate of interest where the demand for funds and the supply of savings exactly agree.

**Non-accelerating inflation rate of unemployment [NAIRU]** - Rate of unemployment above which inflation tends to slow and below which inflation tends to rise.

**Non-conventional monetary policy tools** - Includes quantitative easing [see *quantitative easing*], extending the maturity profile of assets held by the central bank [see *Operation Twist* for example] and forward guidance of short-term interest rates. [See *forward rate guidance*.]

**Operation Twist** [maturity extension programme] - A central bank changing the average maturity of its holdings of securities [bonds]. This typically has involved a central bank selling bonds with shorter maturities and buying bonds with a longer maturity.

**Overinvestment** - Usually refers to an economy where capital spending in real terms is thought to have reached a high and unsustainable proportion of the economy. Keynes suggested this term was overused.

**Portfolio balance effect** - Describes the impact of a central bank's asset purchases on asset allocation of investors. When a central bank purchases assets [such as government bonds] from private investors, the latter will rebalance portfolios away from government bonds and into other assets. This is the first stage of the portfolio balance effect. The rationale for the rebalancing is two-fold. First, the supply of government bonds available to private investors is lower [since the central bank has effectively taken a share off the market]. Second, investing in government bonds is - in theory - less desirable given the low[er] rates of interest resulting from the central banks' actions. [This impact can be overstated.] A second stage of the portfolio balance effect follows logically from the analysis of Keynes, where low rates of interest persuade investors and savers to move funds from deposit accounts or other assets with a low rate of return into real investment.

**Post-war Keynesians** - Post-war Keynesians typically called for greater fiscal stimulus to counter business cycle fluctuations. In reality, the bulk of Keynes's work focused on monetary policy. Keynes only called for more fiscal action in the event that all monetary policy actions had been tried. It is hard to argue this was achieved in the aftermath of the 2008 recession. Furthermore, the limited settings in which Keynes [hypothetically] called for greater fiscal action [only if all requisite monetary action had been taken] occurred when government debt burdens were significantly lower than they are today.

**Printing money** - Quantitative easing involves central banks printing money - creating bank reserves - to buy government debt and other assets.

**Profit rates** - The net rate of return on investment.

**Pure Rate of interest** - See *risk-free rate.*

**QE infinity** - Nickname given to the open-ended characteristic of the third round of quantitative easing [QE3] announced by the FOMC on 13 September 2012.

**QE1** - First round of bond purchases announced by the Federal Reserve on 25 November 2008, and completed on 16 March 2010.

**QE2** - Second round of bond purchases announced by the Federal Reserve on 3 November 2010, which ended on 22 June 2011.

**Quantitative easing** - A monetary policy weapon where a central bank buys assets - normally government bonds, but can also include agency debt and mortgage backed securities - to influence the yield and borrowing costs across the economy.

**Quantitative targets** [with respect to forward rate guidance] - Setting quantitative targets [e.g. unemployment rate] that need to be met before the FOMC will hike the target for the federal funds rate.

**Rate targeting** - An alternative description of forward rate guidance.

**Reaching for yield** - Investors' seeking higher returns from higher yielding and riskier assets. This has the effect of pushing down the yields on riskier assets and lowering spreads, for example, between investment grade and junk bonds.

**Reflation** - Rising asset prices. Sometimes used to describe a rebound in inflation.

**Reverse tap** - A monetary policy tool where a central bank buys government bonds at a fixed price, which is announced to investors. The central bank would stand ready to buy any amount of securities required to ensure a target for bond prices [and thus yields] is secured.

**Risk premium** - Minimum amount of money or yield that an investor is willing to accept to compensate for the risk of holding assets that may default.

**Risk-free rate** - The theoretical rate of return on an investment with no risk of default.

**Savings & Loans crisis** - Failure of savings & loan associations [specialised banks created to fund and promote homeownership in the US after the Second World War] from 1986 to 1995. The number of failures accelerated sharply from 1989 onwards.

**Short sales** - Sales of a property where the net price falls short of the balance of debts secured against the property.

**Signalling channel** - Impact of quantitative easing on interest rate expectations [and therefore bond yields].

**Supply channel** - Impact of quantitative easing on bond yields by changing the supply of bonds outstanding.

**Tap issue** - Where a government offers debt at a fixed price, across a range of maturities.

**Treasuries** - US Government debt.

**Yield curve** - A curve reflecting the yield of debt or bonds across different maturities.

**Zero Lower Bound** - Zero interest rates. Called the Zero Lower Bound, as it is assumed that interest rates by and large cannot be negative.

The U.S. Economic Recovery

# GFC Economics

**'Rigorous, independent macro-economic research, with a strong track record'**

GFC Economics was established as a small research consultancy by Graham Turner in 1999. It has since grown to be a well-respected and highly regarded source of quality, independent research.

The research team consists of four economists:

**Graham Turner** has over 28 years experience as an economist. Prior to founding GFC Economics, he worked in the City and established himself as an expert on the Japanese economy. Since starting his own consultancy he has written four books and produced consistently accurate research on four of the major global economies: US, Euroland, Japan/Asia and UK. His focus is now on guiding the strategic view of the research, supported by the rest of his team.

**Brian Davidson** has more than six years' experience in financial markets including equity research, credit research, investment strategy and financial journalism. His focus is the US economy, alongside Brazil, Mexico and South Africa. He is currently completing his MSc in Finance at Birkbeck University, London.

**Johanna Aigner** worked in the Economics research department at The Bavarian Regional Bank (Bayern LB) before joining GFC Economics and has an MSc in

Economics from the University of Edinburgh. Her focus is Euroland and UK.

**Guillaume Derrien** worked in the department for Business Innovation and Skills (Regional Growth Fund) at the Civil Service for a short period before joining GFC Economics and has an MSc in Economics from Nottingham University. His focus is Japan and Asia.

Under the leadership of Graham Turner, GFC Economics accurately predicted the collapse of the dotcom bubble in 2000 and in 2006 warned that the US (and the West) was heading for a hard landing. Nevertheless, it has been relentlessly bullish on equity markets since the summer of 2011, forecasting that the S&P 500 would surpass the highs of 2007. The strong team of economists has developed a rigorous framework for analysing the economy which has been used both to predict financial crises and successfully forecast the sustainability of the current economic recovery. GFC Economics is heavily focused on data analysis, demonstrated through the effective use of charts, to show clear underlying trends that are important to the institutional investor. The objective has been to call the major turning points in the economic cycle for the US, Euroland, the UK and Japan.

There is a clear emphasis on understanding policy responses in a historical context, with a strong focus on how monetary policy can drive a recovery and the associated risks. GFC Economics was one of the first to advocate quantitative easing during the final months of 2007 and subsequently, in the summer of 2008, GFC Economics was invited to explain the rationale for a radical Japanese-style monetary policy for the UK at a meeting with an MPC member at the Bank of England.

The company has continued to grow despite the credit crunch of 2008, attracting interest from a wide range of asset managers and hedge funds.

If you would like to know more about GFC Economics, please contact: info@gfceconomics.com

## Books

*Solutions to a Liquidity Trap: Japan's Bear Market and What it Means for the West.* Published by GFC Economics (June 2003).

*Solutions to a Liquidity Trap* is an in-depth analysis of Japan's long bear market and examines in detail the policy mistakes made by the Japanese authorities as they battled against more than a decade of deflation. It contains a strong historical narrative of all the financial crises that erupted from 1990 onwards, including a detailed record of all the key bankruptcies that wreaked so much havoc.

It also contains retrospective simulations, carried out with Oxford Economic Forecasting, which show how different policy outcomes from the Bank of Japan may have averted deflation.

To order a copy of *Solutions to a Liquidity Trap* please send a cheque for £25 (includes postage and packaging) to GFC Economics, Unit 501, 7 Whitechapel Road, London, E1 1DU.

The U.S. Economic Recovery

# Acknowledgements

First and foremost, I would like to record my huge thanks to my wife Jackie and my family. This is the fourth book I have written in eleven years. That would not have been possible without their encouragement.

I would also like to put on record my thanks to Liz Bright, finance director at GFC Economics for her support, which culminated in the publication of this book. I would like also to thank Johanna Aigner, Brian Davidson and Guillaume Derrien, economists at GFC Economics for their contributions to this book, from proofing, editing, research, re-writing sections and providing a rigorous intellectual review. Thank you also to Emily Somerville at GFC Economics for working diligently on the book.

In addition, I would like to acknowledge the contribution of Geoff Tily, economist at the UK Treasury and author of *Keynes's General Theory, the Rate of Interest, and 'Keynesian' Economics*. Geoff is one of a handful of economists to truly understand the work of John Maynard Keynes and the significance of his analysis of monetary policy. As Geoff would argue, Keynes has been misunderstood, and we are all poorer for it. By digging deeper into the work of Keynes, it is possible to see how the current economic recovery can endure.

Graham Turner, March 2014.

# Introduction

This book is about the economic recovery underway in the US. Much of the analysis can equally be applied to the UK, Euroland and Japan. It draws upon the lessons of the Great Depression and the cycle of relentless boom and bust witnessed since the early 1970s. It outlines the rationale behind a policy of *cheap, but tight money* needed to underpin the current upturn and secure a full employment that will endure. The economic upswing of 2013 can be sustained. The economic cycle can become less volatile. The key is investment in the real economy and not a consumption-led boom with debt as the primary agent for growth. This will allow productivity to rise, helping to embed low inflation. It will in turn reinforce the ability of central banks to persist with a secular policy of low short- and long-term interest rates, critical to a long economic recovery.

This is an optimistic book. There is already convincing evidence that real investment can lead an economic recovery in the US and drive a long cycle of expansion. Investment is strong and rising in areas such as information technology, which will accelerate the potential growth path of the US economy. The policy of cheap, but tight money is working in the US, and can succeed in the

UK and Euroland. It may take time to reverse the fallout from the recession that followed the turmoil of 2008, as households, governments and financial institutions repair the damage inflicted on their balance sheets. Nonetheless, if the authorities persist with the current policy mix of cheap, but tight money and do not deviate, they can avoid another unnecessary financial crisis.

This book also offers a critique of the policy mistakes made since late 2008 in response to the sub-prime debacle. A full economic recovery is far from certain. The Federal Reserve has not always completely understood the full array of policy tools at its disposal. It made tactical mistakes in its implementation of *quantitative easing* from late 2008 onwards. We argue that a policy of reverse taps - fixing long-term interest rates - could have delivered a much swifter economic recovery. In the summer of 2011, the US central bank stumbled upon a policy aligned more closely with the prescription set out by the monetary analysis of John Maynard Keynes. However, at times, the Federal Reserve has seemed uncertain of its optimal policy and has been too timid in the application of cheap, but tight money. Fundamentally, the Federal Reserve remains a reluctant convert to a policy that can work and could prove more effective than many realise.

The biggest mistake the Federal Reserve has made since late-2008 is not to understand the significance of Keynes's Liquidity Preference Theory. This remains the most significant contribution of *The General Theory* to the current economic debate. Many *post-war Keynesians*, such as Lawrence Summers and Paul Krugman, have concluded that fiscal policy had an important if not decisive role to play in securing the economic recovery. This is wrong. A closer reading of Keynes's work, and not just *The General Theory*, shows that fiscal policy should not be used in the way advocated by so many politicians and economists in response to the crisis of 2008. The Obama fiscal stimulus enacted in February 2009 was misconceived and contrary to the true analysis of Keynes.

Indeed, we go further. The logic of the Liquidity Preference Theory suggests there is a strong case for governments aiming for budget surpluses to bring down the level of government debt. This would make it easier for central banks to implement the policy of cheap, but tight money and ensure real investment continues to drive the economic recovery. For too long, excessive government debt burdens have been allowed to compromise central banks in their critical task of delivering a stable economic cycle.

It should be stressed: this rebuttal of the post-war Keynesian interpretation of *The General Theory* should not be seen as vindication of fiscal policies that penalise the less fortunate. There are many ways to aim for budget surpluses that do not increase inequality. The question of a fairer distribution of income is completely independent of the fundamental point that central banks will find it harder to deliver a strong recovery so long as governments continue to run budget deficits. Indeed, allowing central banks the latitude to implement a policy of cheap, but tight money offers a better prospect that the decade or more-long decline in the median wage can be reversed. Loose fiscal policies are not the answer to a sustainable rise in living standards for the majority.

This book is divided into four chapters. The first describes how and why investment can drive economic recovery and outlines the case for a secular shift to lower interest rates under a cheap, but tight monetary policy framework. It is a positive message: the Federal Reserve can secure full employment and reverse the decline in the median wage. The second chapter reviews US monetary policy since late 2008, evaluating the initial mistakes made by the Federal Reserve and the belated conversion to a more successful policy. The third chapter is a close look at the work of Keynes and argues that much of his work has been misunderstood. His analysis of monetary policy remains supremely relevant for central banks today and needs to be embraced. If the Federal Reserve and others are ready to acknowledge Keynes's critical contribution to monetary theory, the economic recovery can continue for longer than perhaps many expect. The last chapter looks at real lessons of the Great Depression. It argues that the monetary policy advocated by Keynes -

quantitative easing - played the decisive role in securing a turnaround in the US economy from 1932 onwards. This has important lessons for today.

GFC Economics.

# Chapter 1

# The Potential for an Investment-Led Recovery

By the end of 2013, growth expectations were being revised higher in a number of countries that had suffered heavily during the credit crunch. In the US, *non-conventional monetary policies* had helped push real GDP up by an average annualised rate of 3.3% during the second half of 2013.[1] The UK economy was also recovering strongly despite the government's tight fiscal policy.[2] Employment had hit record highs, rising at the fastest rate since current records began in 1971.[3] In the eurozone, the combination of *cheap money*, lower government spending

---

[1] Source: Bureau of Economic Analysis [BEA]. Real Gross Domestic Product [GDP] expanded by an annualised rate of 4.1% in Q3 2013 and by an annualised rate of 2.4% in Q4 2013.

[2] Source: Office of National Statistics [ONS]. Real GDP rose 2.7% y/y in Q4 2013, the fastest increase since Q1 2008. Source: Organisation of Economic Cooperation and Development [OECD]. According to the OECD, the Government primary balance as a share of GDP, UK, [i.e. excluding interest payments] fell from -9.7% in 2009 to -3.4% in 2012. The cyclically adjusted Government primary balance dropped from -8.6% of GDP in 2009 to -2.2% in 2012.

[3] Source: ONS, Labour Force Survey. Employment [aged 16+] rose 193,000 between October to December 2013 over the previous three months. This followed a jump of 280,000 for September to November over the previous three months, the biggest since current records began in May 1971.

and higher taxes had eventually secured a turnaround. The European Central Bank had eschewed conventional quantitative easing. Nevertheless, a number of peripheral countries, notably Spain, Ireland and Portugal, were pulling out of recession. Unemployment was endemic, but it was starting to fall.[4] House prices were rising again.[5] European Commission President José Manuel Barroso had declared an end to the crisis in the single currency.[6]

This chapter will consider whether the improvements can be sustained. The focus will largely be on the US. However, it will evaluate the new policy paradigm that is required to deliver a less volatile and enduring recovery across the West. Indeed, there is already convincing evidence that a policy of *cheap, but tight money* [low rates of interest and control of borrowing] can provide

---

[4] Source: Eurostat. In Spain, the number of unemployed fell by 180,000 [seasonally adjusted] in the six months to January. In Portugal, unemployment dropped by 51,000 [seasonally adjusted] over the corresponding period. In Ireland unemployment was down 24,000 over this period. Greek unemployment declined 22,000 in the six months to December [one month lag].

[5] Source: Eurostat. The House Price Index covers all residential properties purchased by households [flats, detached houses, terraced houses, etc.], newly built and existing, independent of final use and independent of their previous owners. In Spain, the house price index rose 1.3% q/q [seasonally adjusted] in Q3 2013, the first increase since Q2 2010. The y/y rate fell at the slowest pace since Q2 2011. In Ireland, house prices climbed 2.8% q/q [seasonally adjusted] and 3.7% y/y in Q3 2013. The house price index was up 0.5% q/q [seasonally adjusted] in Portugal, although this was still down 2.9% y/y.

[6] See *Portugal, Europe and the World,* José Manuel Barroso, 7 January 2013, p. 4. Mr Barroso declared that 'the existential threat to the euro is essentially over'.

the right backdrop for an investment-led recovery. In the US, UK and across Euroland, capital spending is turning higher.[7] The turnaround witnessed in 2013 could be the start of a long economic expansion. However, this will depend upon central banks and governments fully digesting the true meaning of Keynes's work.

## Dissecting the Crisis

It is important not to lose sight of the underlying causes of the financial crisis in 2008. In March 2013, FOMC member Sarah Bloom Raskin became one of the first central bankers to acknowledge that the deep recession of 2008 was not just a result of excessive, poor quality lending and a liberalised financial system.[8] The median

---

[7] Source: ONS, Eurostat and BEA. According to the ONS, gross fixed capital formation [GFCF] in the UK rose 2.4% q/q, up from 1.7% q/q in Q3. The y/y rate climbed to 8.7%, the sharpest increase since Q1 2012. Eurostat reported that GFCF across the eurozone increased by 1.1% q/q in Q4 and added 0.2 percentage points to overall quarterly GDP growth. The y/y rate was 0.1%, the first positive growth rate in three years. In the US, private fixed non-residential investment was rising by a y/y rate of 3.0% in Q4 2013, but had risen at a much quicker pace over the last three quarters of 2013, up by an annualised rate of 4.7% in Q2, 4.8% in Q3 and 7.3% in Q4 2013.

[8] See *Aspects of Inequality in the Recent Business Cycle*, Sarah Bloom Raskin, 18 April 2013, p. 6-7. 'The question then arises as to why households with poor income prospects sought out levels of mortgage debt that would ultimately prove so problematic. Putting aside the practice, in the run-up to the crisis, of lenders steering households to mortgage debt products that were more costly than what such households may have otherwise qualified for, one reason may have been that many households in the middle and lower end of the income distribution, whose wage earnings were stagnant, did not recognize the long-run and persistent trends underlying their lack of income growth'. Furthermore, Ms Raskin noted 'In a separate line of inquiry on the social dynamics of spending, Bertrand and Morse [2013] find that moderate-income

wage had been trending down for more than a decade in the US, playing a critical, but unrecognised role in driving debt levels higher. [See Chart 1a] Loose credit filled a gap left by rising inequality. From the perspective of policymakers, this may or may not have been intentional. However, the accumulation of a record debt burden in the personal sector cannot be divorced from the 9.0% drop in the real median wage witnessed between the peak of 1999 and 2012.[9]

The rise in inequality can be traced back to the early 1970s. The share of GDP taken by wages & salaries in the US peaked at 51.7% in Q1 1970 and began a long slide.[10] Persistent inflation through the 1970s eventually ushered in restrictive monetary policies, accompanied by legislation designed to reform labour markets and curb the power of unions. As the share of GDP accruing to workers fell, profits began to rise quickly.[11]

---

households spend more if they live in states with rapid spending growth among high-income households, which suggests another channel for inequality to increase debt'. See *Trickle-Down Consumption*, M. Bertrand and A. Morse, National Bureau of Economic Research, Working Paper series, March 2013. Note: Ms Raskin left the FOMC after the committee meeting in 31 July 2013.

[9] Source: Federal Reserve, Flow of Funds [FoF], Financial Liabilities - Households & Non-profit Institutions and Bureau of Labor Statistics [BLS], BEA, GDP, current prices and Bureau of Labor Statistics, Real Median Household Income. The ratio of financial liabilities for households & non-profit institutions [personal sector] to GDP rose from 73.7% in Q3 2001 to a record 99.0% in Q1 2008. The Real Median Household Income fell from $56,079 in 1999 to $51,017 in 2012, a drop of 9.0%.

[10] Source: BEA, Wage & Salary accruals and GDP, current prices.

[11] Source: BEA. Profits with inventory valuation and capital consumption

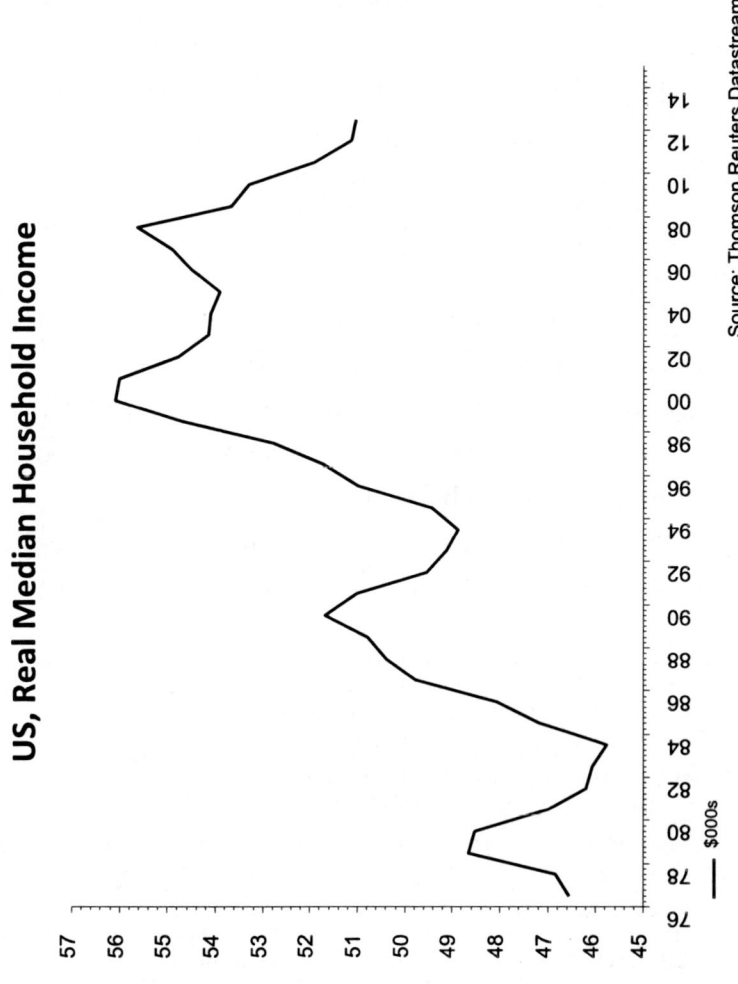

**US, Real Median Household Income**

Source: Thomson Reuters Datastream

Chart 1a

The turmoil of 2008 widened the imbalance between labour and capital. The share of GDP taken by wages & salaries in the US had fallen to 47.5% by the time Paul Volcker took over as chair of the Federal Reserve in 1979, ushering in a new era of *dear money*. The ratio of wages & salaries to GDP subsequently fell to 43.4% in Q3 2005 - the peak of the US housing market.[12] [See chart 1b] It then tumbled to a fresh post-1945 nadir of 42.1% in Q4 2011 in the aftermath of the *Great Recession*. At first glance, the subsequent recovery has been limited, with wages & salaries still only accounting for 42.3% of GDP by Q4 2013.[13] By contrast, corporate profits have soared to new highs.[14] [See chart 1c]

The impact of globalisation and technological change in accelerating the downward trend in wages was subject

---

adjustments [before tax] hit a post-1945 low of 6.7% of GDP in Q4 1982. It rose steadily, hitting 12.6% in Q4 2011 and 12.6% in Q3 2013.

[12] Source: National Association of Realtors [NAR]. The median price of existing one-family homes sold [seasonally adjusted by Thomson Reuters Datastream] hit a peak of $230,200 in October 2005.

[13] Source: BEA. As we shall argue, there is evidence that wages were starting to rise more quickly by early 2014. See footnote 103.

[14] Source: BEA. Profits, after tax, with inventory valuation and capital consumption adjustments, rose 8.6% y/y in Q3 2013, extending the rise from the 2008 low [Q4 2008] to 115.4%. As a share of GDP profits were 10.1% of GDP, the second highest during the post-1945 period. The post-1945 peak was 10.3% reached in Q4 2011. The Q3 2013 ratio is also significantly above the high reached in Q3 2007 [7.5%], prior to the 2008 financial crisis. Profits, before tax, with inventory valuation and capital consumption adjustments, climbed 5.7% y/y in Q3 2013, extending the rise from the 2008 low [Q4 2008] to 89.2%. As a share of GDP, before tax profits on this basis were 12.6% of GDP in Q3 2013. This compares with a post-1945 peak of 13.1% [Q4 1950].

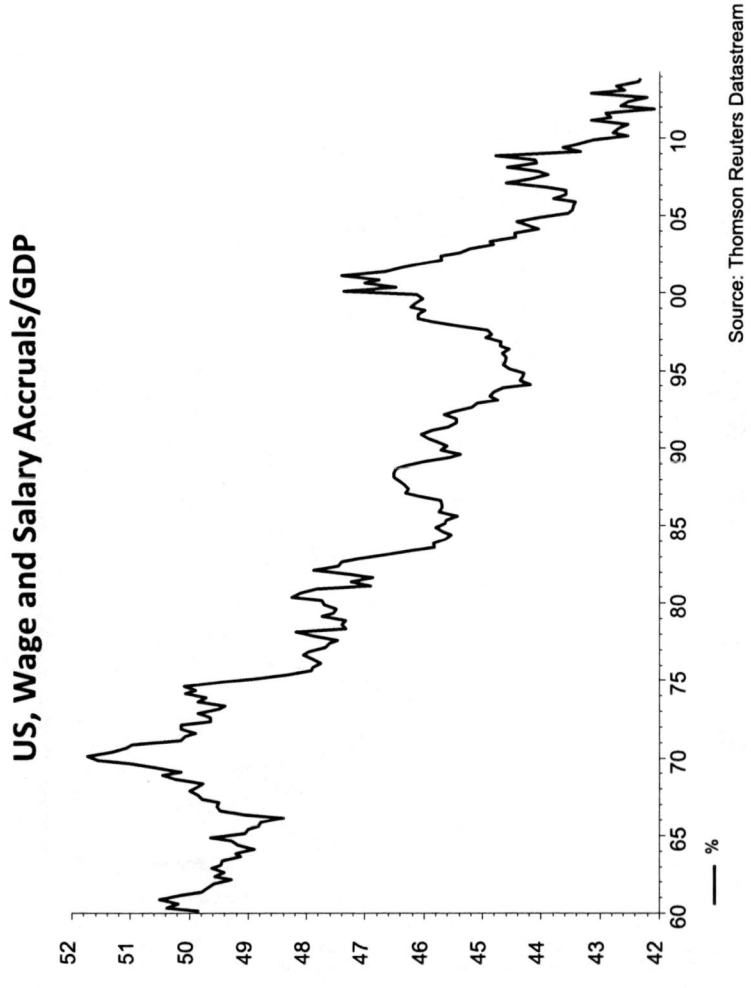

US, Wage and Salary Accruals/GDP

Source: Thomson Reuters Datastream

Chart 1b

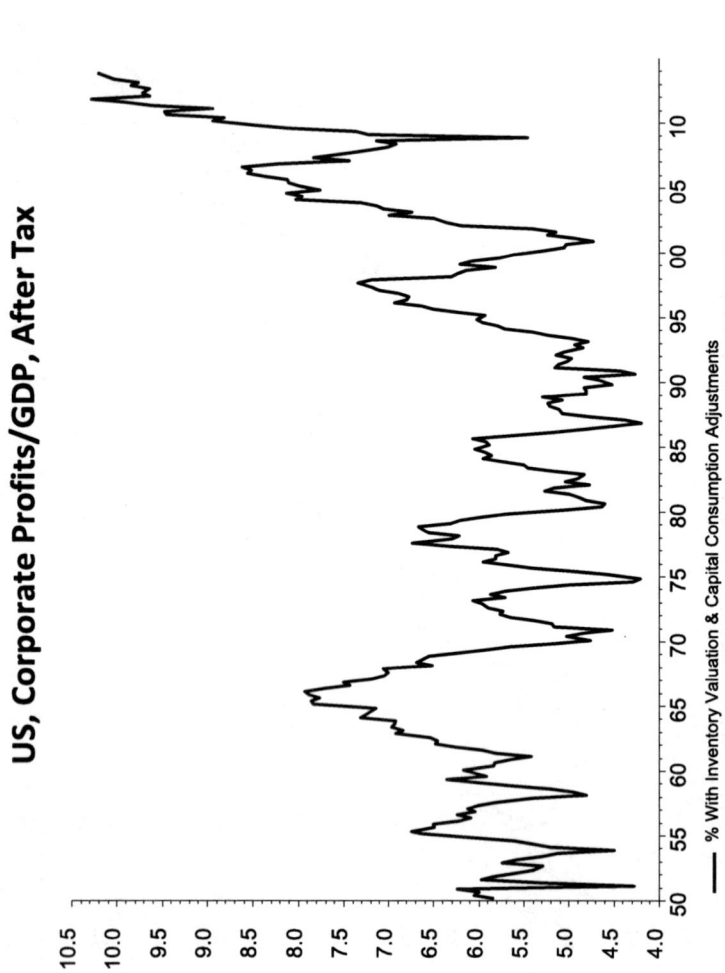

**US, Corporate Profits/GDP, After Tax**

— % With Inventory Valuation & Capital Consumption Adjustments

Source: Thomson Reuters Datastream

Chart 1c

to intense debate. Federal Reserve officials deliberated over the ramifications for workers. During the early 1990s, former FOMC chair Alan Greenspan repeatedly drew attention to the role of technology in advancing productivity and suppressing wage rates for some groups of employees.[15] The heavy loss of manufacturing jobs to countries offering cheaper wages also became a focus of Federal Reserve officials through the 1990s and during the recovery from the *dotcom recession* of 2001.[16]

However, central banks failed to draw a connection between the fall in the median wage and the housing bubble. Policymakers did not connect inequality to rising debt. The lack of bargaining power enjoyed by many workers was at least recognised and considered important, because it implied inflation would remain low. However, there was widespread failure to recognise that the control of consumer prices would not guarantee financial stability. Indeed, by framing monetary policy around the narrow target of inflation, central banks ignored the rise in house prices and consumer debt. Low inflation fuelled complacency among central banks and governments.

A prolonged squeeze on wages could, in theory, short-

---

[15] See *Technological advances and productivity*, Alan Greenspan, 16 October 1996. See also *The Level and Distribution of Economic Well-Being*, Ben Bernanke, 6 February 2007.

[16] See *Embracing the Challenge of Free Trade: Competing and Prospering in a Global Economy*, Ben Bernanke, 1 May 2007.

circuit the economic recovery under way at the end of 2013 in the US, the UK and Euroland. A lack of wage reflation has been a repeated concern in Japan too. Prime Minister Shinzo Abe has exhorted companies to award higher wages in a bid to permanently eradicate deflation.[17] A combination of tight money and limited wage gains could restrict consumer demand. The economic recovery may stall: attempts by companies to push profits relentlessly higher will become self-defeating. Profit margins may be squeezed by weak demand and competition between companies, which will intensify in response to lacklustre consumption. Stock markets will eventually fall as a result. From this perspective, non-conventional monetary policies are likely to fail if the imbalance between chronically 'weak' labour and 'strong' or 'excessive' capital is not corrected.

Keynes acknowledged that an economic recovery may need to be underpinned by policies that address income inequality. A variation in the marginal propensity to consume across different groups of individuals implies governments have the scope to influence demand, through tax policies, for example.[18] More recently,

---

[17] See *Abe asks business leaders to raise wages to help beat chronic deflation*, The Japan Times, 13 February 2013.

[18] See *The General Theory of Employment, Interest and Money*, John Maynard Keynes, Macmillan Cambridge University Press, 1973, p. 95. See page 243 of Chapter 3 for more. See also p. 38 and 41 for wider discussion on marginal propensity to consume.

US President Obama has cited inequality as a major impediment to recovery, describing the divergence in incomes as the 'defining issue of our time'.[19]

## Stimulating Investment

Nevertheless, the focus of Keynes was the application of the correct monetary policy to stimulate a recovery in investment, as the primary route to job creation. This would be underpinned by cheap, but tight money, so that investors would be obliged to focus on *real* investment if they wanted to earn a positive real rate of return on their savings. This would initially operate via the *portfolio balance effect*.

The subsequent sharp decline in corporate bond yields witnessed since December 2008, for example, has been criticised as an unjustifiable side-effect of quantitative easing.[20] [See chart 1d] This was the focus of one FOMC member, Jeremy Stein, who warned in February 2013 that investors were *reaching for yield*.[21] However, reducing

---

[19] See *Inequality is 'defining issue of our time'*, says Obama, Financial Times, 4 December 2013. We can either settle for a country where a shrinking number of people do really well while a growing number of Americans barely get by, or we can restore an economy where everyone gets a fair shot, and everyone does their fair share, and everyone plays by the same set of rules. No challenge is more urgent. No debate is more important.

[20] Source: Merrill Lynch High Yield Cash Pay ($)/Thomson Reuters Datastream. Corporate bond yields [high yield or non-investment grade] fell from a high of 22.15% on 12 December 2008 to a low of 7.06% on 25 June 2013.

[21] See *Overheating in Credit Markets: Origins, Measurement and Policy*

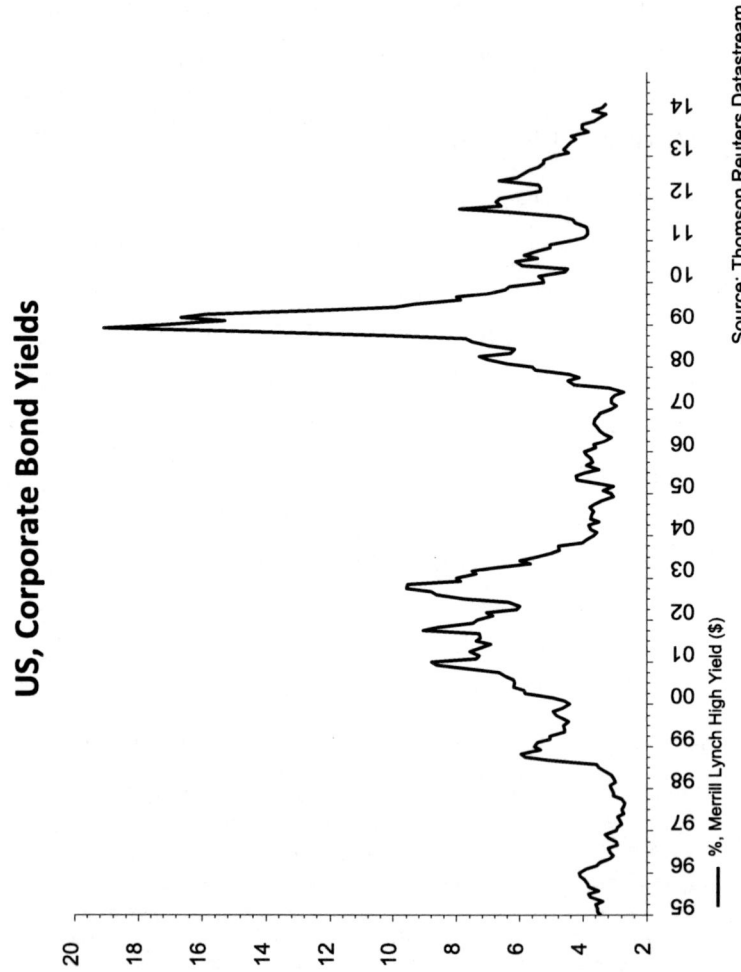

**US, Corporate Bond Yields**

— %, Merrill Lynch High Yield ($)

Source: Thomson Reuters Datastream

Chart 1d

the cost of borrowing for companies is precisely how central banks can set the stage for an investment-led recovery. Volatile long-term interest rates have been a fundamental source of instability in the economic cycle since the early 1970s. Persistently low long-term rates could reduce the targeted rate of return on capital outlays for companies. Projects deemed untenable in an environment of *easy, but dear money* may become viable. This may also increase the relative attractiveness of real investment for savers. Specifically, faced with the prospect of low deposit rates, savers will be obliged to consider alternative investments to secure a positive real rate of return. A similar incentive will apply to companies, with their historically high profits less likely to be diverted into financial capital should the authorities prevent debt levels from rising.

Correctly applied, it can thus be seen that cheap, but tight money will ensure that it is profits, not debt, that facilitates investment. This may not in itself guarantee a strong investment-led recovery in the short run. Nonetheless, it provides the correct and necessary incentives. Critically, preventing debt levels from rising materially across households and corporates would underpin financial stability, the essential second plank

---

*Responses*, Jeremy Stein, 7 February 2013. Mr Stein concluded 'Putting it all together, my reading of the evidence is that we are seeing a fairly significant pattern of reaching-for-yield behaviour emerging in corporate credit'.

of this new policy.

Stimulating investment would at first glance not alter the imbalance between weak labour and strong capital, which helped push the share of wages & salaries in GDP to secular lows in the US. Indeed, focusing on higher capital outlays seems counter-intuitive. The crisis of 2008 prompted a fall in consumption, but the decline in capital spending was more pronounced. Companies were forced to slash investment, partly because corporate borrowing costs leapt. However, the decline in consumption also exposed the rather limited rise in capacity utilisation witnessed during the housing boom. Investment had been running close to historic highs, prior to the crisis of 2008.[22] [See chart 1e] Firms were soon saddled with large excess capacity, particularly in manufacturing. This caused a swift decline in profitability. In the US, the peak for capacity utilisation across industry in 2007 was below the high point of previous economic cycles.[23] [See chart 1f]

---

[22] Source: BEA, Real private fixed investment, non-residential, and Real GDP. The ratio of real private fixed investment, non-residential, to real GDP rose to 13.4% in Q1 2008. This was higher than the previous cyclical high of 13.2% reached in Q3 2000. Following the financial crisis of 2008, this ratio dropped to 11.0% in Q4 2009. Real private fixed investment, non-residential, fell 20.0% between Q1 2008 and Q4 2009.

[23] Source: Federal Reserve, Capacity Utilisation, All Industry. Capacity utilisation reached a high of 80.8% in December 2007, prior to the financial crisis of 2008. This compares with previous cyclical peaks of 82.3% in April 2000, 85.2% in January 1989, 86.7% in December 1978, 88.8% in February 1973 and 88.5% in March 1969.

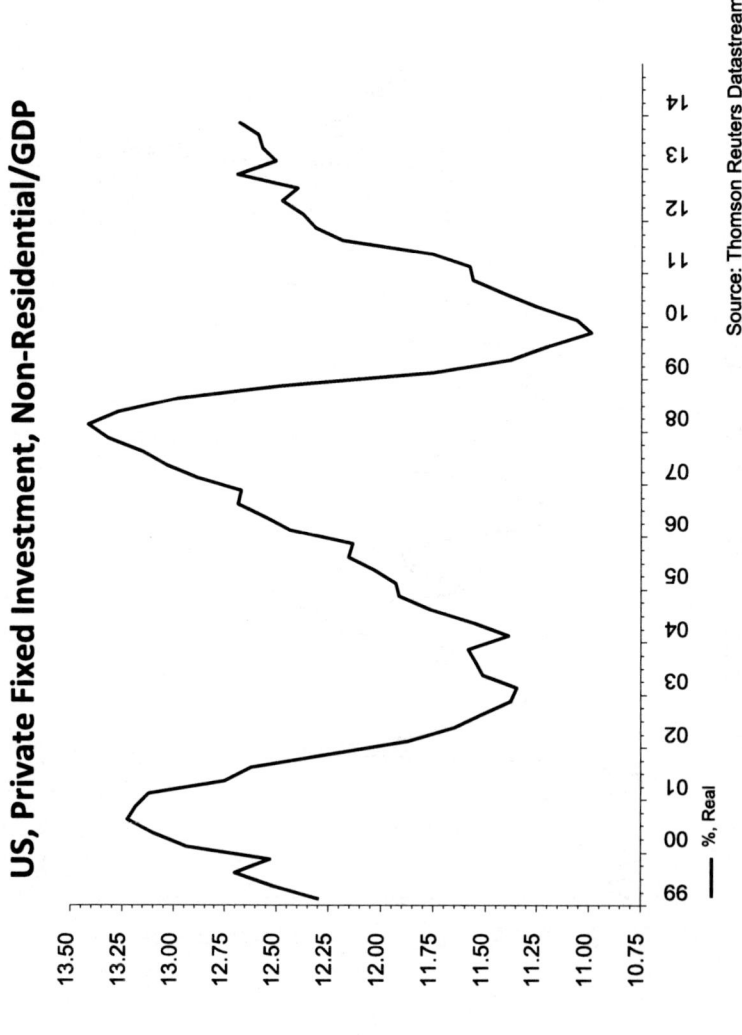

**US, Private Fixed Investment, Non-Residential/GDP**

Source: Thomson Reuters Datastream

Chart 1e

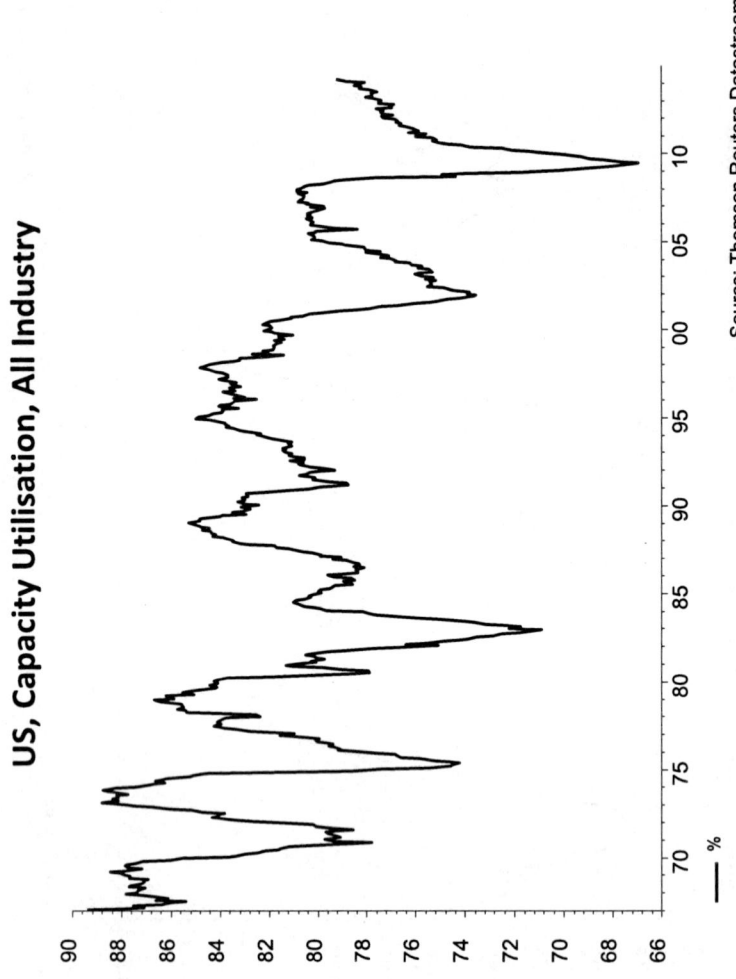

**US, Capacity Utilisation, All Industry**

Source: Thomson Reuters Datastream

Chart 1f

At face value, this implies the crisis of 2008 had its roots in overinvestment. Indeed, there is ostensibly a parallel with the economic boom of the late-1920s, when investment also rose quickly.[24] From this perspective, it would appear that the answer to a sustainable recovery in consumer demand would be to prioritise a reversal in the secular decline in wages & salaries as a share of GDP. By extension, this implies companies would have to allow wages rates to rise and accept lower profits.

However, this is too simplistic. A sustainable economic recovery does not imply profits have to shrink to accommodate a faster rise in wages & salaries. There does not have to be a trade-off between capital and labour. This counter argument applies to margins too, not just the absolute level of profits. [See chart 1g] Margins need not be eroded by a rise in wages and salaries. Any potential squeeze on profit margins [caused by higher wages & salaries] would depend critically on whether investment remains high enough to underpin productivity improvements. If that happens, this would ensure a rise in wage rates did not feed into higher unit labour costs. Technological advances can increase the marginal productivity of capital and labour.

---

[24] See *Historical Statistics of the United States, Colonial Times to 1970, Part 1*, US Department of Commerce, p. 229. The ratio of real non-residential fixed investment to real Gross National Product rose to 13.0% in 1929, before dropping to 5.4% in 1933.

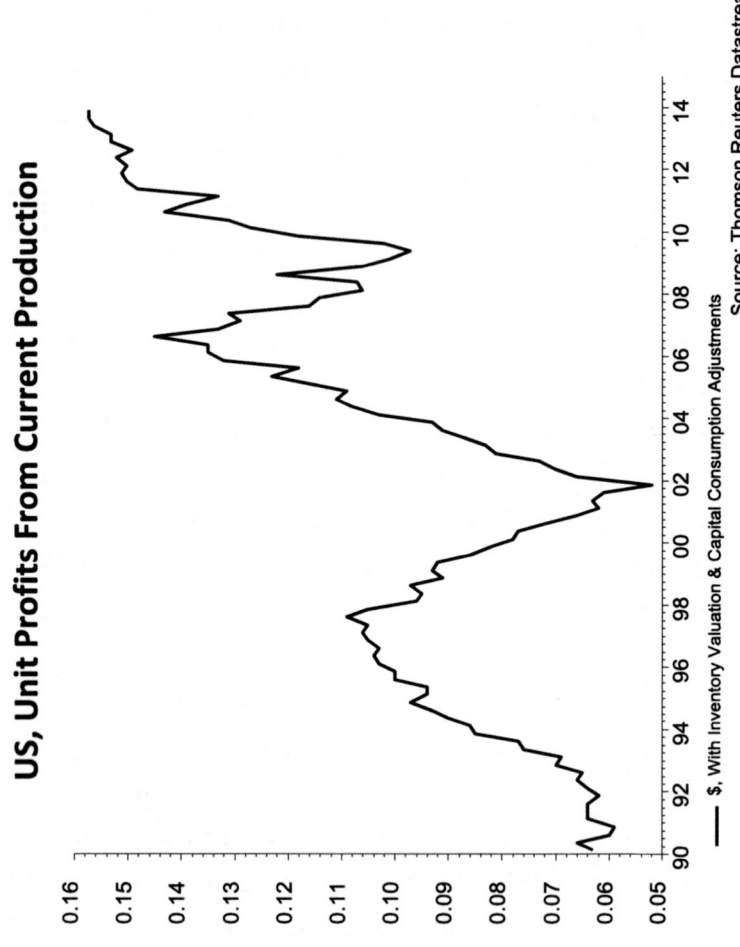

**US, Unit Profits From Current Production**

— $, With Inventory Valuation & Capital Consumption Adjustments

Source: Thomson Reuters Datastream

Chart 1g

Monetary [and fiscal] policy can thus conceivably be aligned to promote capital *and* labour, or put another way, investment *and* wages. Indeed, simply aiming for higher wages & salaries, in the short- to medium-term, at the expense of profits may not lead to a durable economic recovery. Investment might fall, undermining the productive potential of an economy and increasing the risk of a rise in inflation. That would lead central banks to raise interest rates and could short-circuit the economic recovery before full employment had been secured. Instead, the authorities need to put in place the correct monetary policy [low short- and long-term interest rates] and the appropriate framework for financial stability to stimulate investment. Once the economy starts to approach full employment, wages may well rise more quickly, without inflation picking up. The modest rise in wages & salaries during the last economic upswing did not endure, because it was predicated on a housing bubble.[25]

For some economists, *accumulation* lies at the heart of the repeated economic crises facing the West since the early 1970s. In essence, the free market is based around a system of accumulation. In a competitive environment,

---

[25] Source: BEA, Wage & Salary Accruals and GDP, current prices. In response to the housing boom, the ratio of wage & salary accruals to GDP rose from a post-1945 low [at the time] of 43.4% in Q4 2005 to 44.8% in Q4 2008, before turning down and dropping to a new secular low of 42.1% in Q4 2011.

companies are obliged to exploit every potential opportunity to maximise profits, otherwise they may not survive. They will be undercut by rivals and driven out of business. There is no middle way. Every company is forced to accumulate profits, to avoid being swallowed by a competitor. This can lead to over accumulation. Their combined actions may result in either excess capacity in the form of plant, machinery and equipment, as firms recycle their profits into expanding capacity and chasing market share. Or it can lead to the growth of *financial capital*, if firms struggle to put their profits to effective use through real investment. In some cases, this may involve share buybacks or higher dividend payments.[26] [See chart 1h] Mergers and acquisitions might also be a symptom of excess capital chasing a dwindling pool of real investment opportunities. The tendency of large technology companies to swallow small start-ups is seen as a manifestation of this 'contradiction of capitalism' and a possible threat to a long economic recovery.

Similarly, the collapse of credit spreads and risk premiums during the housing bubble prior to 2008 was cited by central banks as a manifestation of excess financial capital or a glut of global savings chasing higher

---

[26] Source: BEA, Corporate Net Dividend Payments, Current Prices. Net dividend payments rose to $902.1billion in 2013, up from $818.9billion in 2007. This increase of 10.2% is less than the comparable increase in profits with inventory valuation and capital consumption adjustments [after tax], which rose 45.3% between 2007 and 2013.

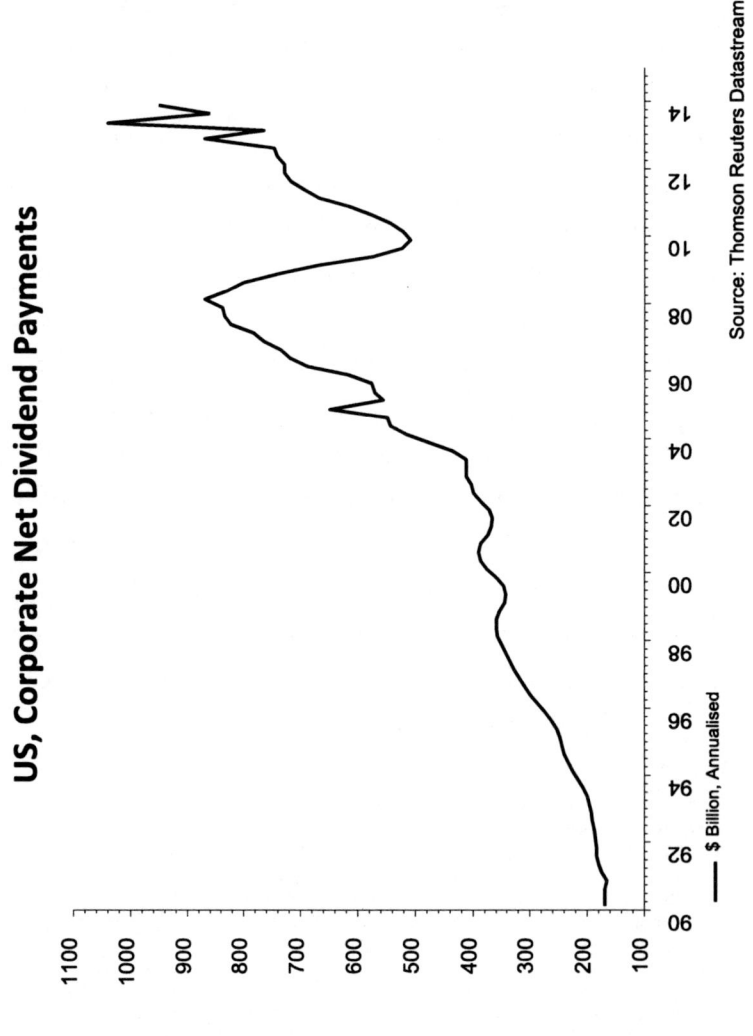

**US, Corporate Net Dividend Payments**

Source: Thomson Reuters Datastream

— $ Billion, Annualised

Chart 1h

27

returns and driving yields on riskier assets [mortgage backed securities, corporate bonds, etc] lower.[27] It is ironic: at the time, this was seen as a reflection of an increasingly stable world economy. According to this hypothesis, savers accepted a lower rate of return because the risks of investing had fallen.[28] Central banks had tamed the economic cycle and free from political interference, they could act should inflation become a threat.[29] From an alternative perspective, these low rates of return were symptomatic of over accumulation. It was not enough for central banks and regulators to respond to the crisis of 2008 with non-conventional monetary policy tools and by embracing tighter control over the financial system. The recession was symptomatic of deeper problems, namely a chronic imbalance between labour and capital.

The unwillingness of central banks and governments to acknowledge the role of debt in driving the economic cycle and propagating booms ensured their immediate

---

[27] Source: Merrill Lynch High Yield Cash Pay ($)/Thomson Reuters Datastream. Corporate bond yields [High Yield or non-investment grade] fell from a high of 14.02% on 14 October 2002 to 7.56% on 26 February 2007.

[28] See *Global Saving Glut and the US Current Account Deficit*, Ben Bernanke, 10 March 2005 and *Global Imbalances: Recent Developments and Prospects*, Ben Bernanke, 11 September 2007.

[29] See *The Conquest of Worldwide Inflation: Currency Competition and Its Implications for Interest Rates and the Yield Curve*, Randall S. Kroszner, 16 November 2006, p. 4. 'The fundamental forces I have described today - globalization, deregulation, financial innovation, and public understanding about the costs of inflation -- provided the impetus for fighting inflation and opened the political path to institutional reforms, such as central bank independence, that enhance central bank credibility'.

response to the crisis of 2008 was impaired. This materialised in the finance system first, but policymakers misread the dynamics, falling repeatedly behind the curve from early 2007 onwards. Their initial response often focussed on treating the symptoms - liquidity shortages - rather than the cause of the economic collapse - falling house prices. The authorities failed to recognise the importance of preventing defaults. The latter was a big contributor to the crisis of 2008, with the Federal Reserve too preoccupied with measures to ease liquidity shortages, when it should have been cutting interest rates more aggressively.[30] Appendix II US Monetary Policy Diary [pages 163 - 190] details the plethora of liquidity operations launched by the Federal Reserve from 10 August 2007 onwards.

Defaults typically prompt a traumatic devaluation of capital. This can lead to a reduction in the availability of credit, which feeds into a collapse of demand. The overinvestment then becomes apparent. The slide in asset prices destroys financial capital. However, it also creates surplus or redundant capital in the real economy,

---

[30] Source: Federal Reserve, Factors Affecting Reserve Balances. In the first week of March 2008, US Treasury Securities Held by the Federal Reserve were $713.4billion. By the first week of July 2008, this had fallen to $478.8billion, a drop of 32.9%. To make room on its balance sheet for the liquidity injections, the Federal Reserve sold Treasuries in April 2008. The size of the Federal Reserve's balance sheet remained broadly unchanged during the time of these 'support' operations. Total assets held by the Federal Reserve edged down from $894.0billion in the first week of March 2008 to $892.7billion in the first week of July.

with firms saddled with spare capacity. This quickly becomes idle and much of this is written down in value too.

An intense write-down in excess capital sets the stage for a recovery in the economy and the process of accumulation resumes. From this viewpoint, the depth of the destruction in capital or investment during the downturn will determine the length and intensity of the upswing. However, it will also depend on the authorities recognising the role of debt in driving the cycle.

## The Slump of 2008

The epicentre of the 2008 financial crisis lay in countries that saw house prices and personal sector debt levels rise sharply, including the US, the UK, Spain and Ireland. Nevertheless, major exporters were hit too. In Germany, for example, manufacturing production fell by 24.0% in the year to April 2009.[31] [See chart 1i] The decline was quicker than the reversal seen in the US over any comparable period during the Great Depression.[32] New orders in Germany had fallen 34.1% from their 2008 peak, led by an even bigger drop in foreign demand of

---

[31] Source: Statistisches Bundesamt.

[32] See *Historical Statistics of the United States, Colonial Times to 1970, Part 2*, US Department of Commerce, Bureau of the Census, p. 667. The biggest contraction in any one year came in 1932, when manufacturing production fell 21.0%.

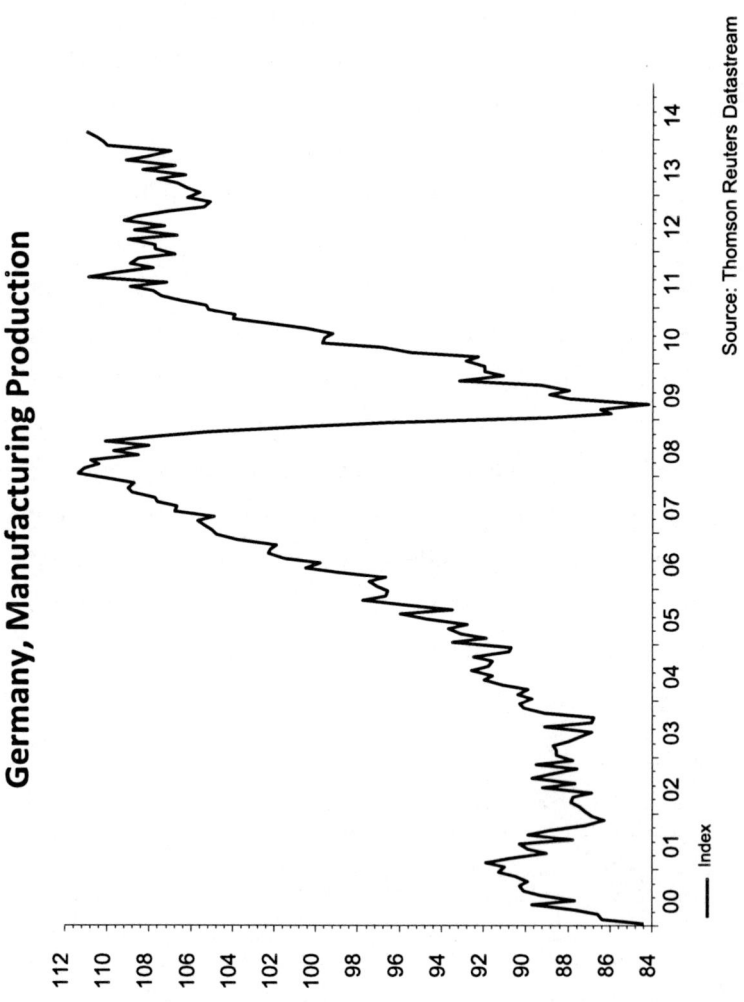

**Germany, Manufacturing Production**

Source: Thomson Reuters Datastream

Chart 1i

38.0%.[33]

One of the hardest affected countries was Japan. By February 2009, exports had nearly halved from their peak a year earlier.[34] In just four months, manufacturing output shrank by 28.7% and by the first quarter of 2009, real GDP had fallen 9.2%.[35] [See chart 1j] This nearly matched the decline in the US during the first quarter of the Great Depression, when real GDP fell 10.0%.[36] Other Asian exporters suffered, including Taiwan, South Korea, Thailand, Singapore and Malaysia.[37] These countries had been less dependent on house prices to drive growth but were still hit, because they relied upon the expansion of debt elsewhere to absorb their production. The collapse in output and the resulting excess capacity pummelled profit margins. In Japan, profits tumbled by more than two-thirds as manufacturers recorded a loss for the first

---

[33] Source: Bundesbank.

[34] Source: Ministry of Finance, Japan. Exports of Goods, Customs-Cleared Basis, fell 47.9% between January 2008 and February 2009.

[35] Source: Ministry of Economy, Trade and Industry, Industrial Production, Manufacturing and Cabinet Office (Japan), GDP, Yen Billion (2000 prices).

[36] See *Historical Statistics of the United States, Colonial Times to 1970, Part 1*, US Department of Commerce, Bureau of the Census, p. 224.

[37] Source: Ministry of Economic Affairs, Taiwan. Industrial Production fell 40.3% y/y in January 2009. Source: Bank of Thailand. Manufacturing Production dropped 25.8% y/y in January 2009. Source: National Statistics Office, South Korea. Industrial Production shrank 25.3% y/y in January 2009. Source: Department of Statistics, Singapore. Industrial Production excluding rubber processing dropped 25.7% y/y in January 2009. Source: Department of Statistics, Malaysia. Industrial Production fell 17.6% y/y in January 2009.

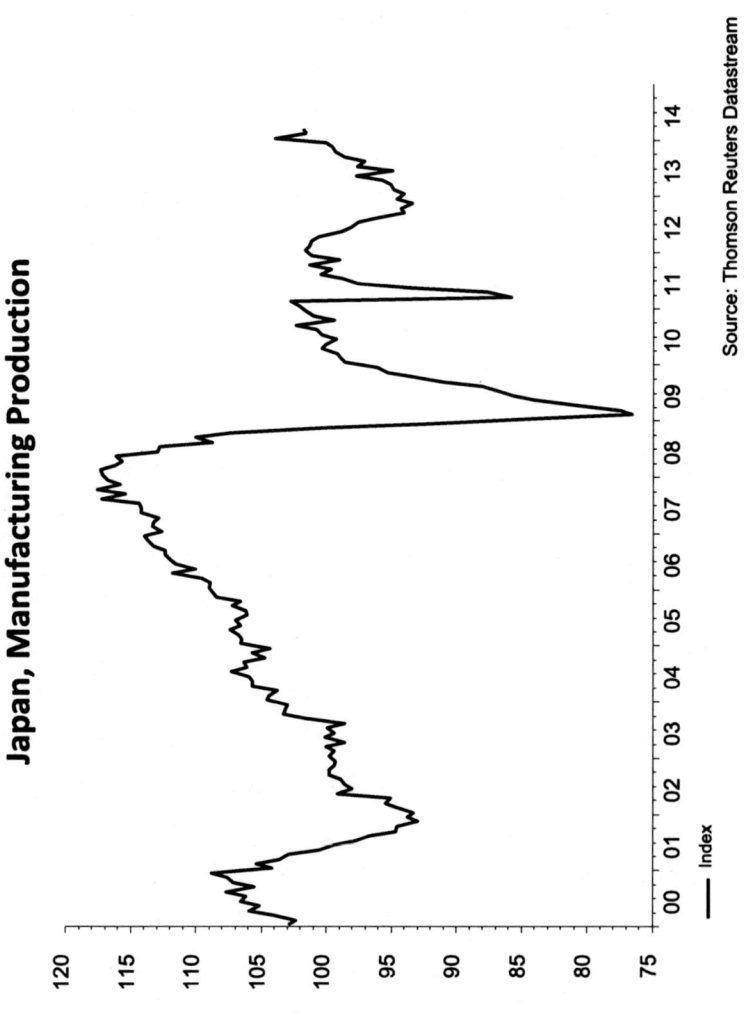

**Japan, Manufacturing Production**

—— Index

Source: Thomson Reuters Datastream

Chart 1j

33

time on record.[38] [See chart 1k]

In the US, capacity utilisation across industry fell to its lowest in the post-1945 period. Profits had already been under pressure as the economy slowed from late-2006 onwards. The decline intensified during 2008, before aggressive cost cutting stabilised margins in the first quarter of 2009. Excess capacity led to big declines in spending on capital goods. In Germany, orders from abroad for capital goods fell by nearly half between June 2007 and April 2009.[39] In Japan, machinery orders from overseas tumbled by nearly three-quarters over the course of 2008 and early 2009.[40] At first glance, these huge declines suggest investment cannot [and should not] be relied upon to drive the economic recovery on its own.

However, the collapse in production of capital goods following the 2008 financial crisis may not have been a necessary consequence of 'overinvestment'. It is possible that the boom might have been averted if governments and central banks had recognised the flaws in allowing debt levels to rise and relying upon the rate of interest to control the economy. A sustainable rise in investment,

---

[38] Source: Ministry of Finance. Incorporated Business, Current Profits - Manufacturing, fell 141.7% y/y in Q1 2009, to *minus* Y2.246trillion.

[39] Source: Deutsche Bundesbank. Manufacturing Foreign Capital Goods Orders had fallen 45.5% by April 2009, compared with the June 2007 peak. In the three months to April 2009, they were down 43.3% y/y.

[40] Source: Cabinet Office (Japan). Machinery Orders, Foreign Demand, dropped 74.8% y/y in February 2009.

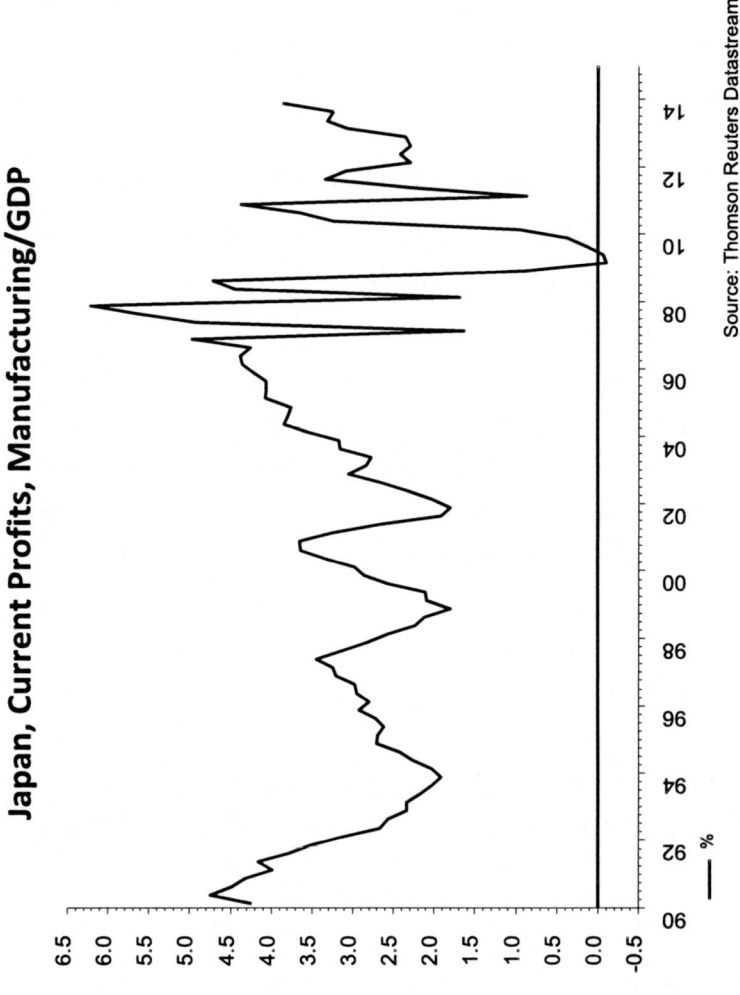

Chart 1k

one that can deliver full employment, will only be achievable if governments and central banks abandon the policies of easy, but dear money that have driven the economic cycles since the late-1960s.

## Overinvestment: A Different Perspective

Keynes understood the critical role of investment in driving the business cycle. He analysed the net return on investment through the prism of the *marginal efficiency of capital*. This is essentially the prospective yield from any capital good in relation to its replacement cost.[41] Keynes argued that the gyrations in the business cycle are 'mainly due to the way in which the marginal efficiency of capital fluctuates'.[42] Current expectations for the yield of capital goods play a critical role in influencing the marginal efficiency of capital. The point is more pertinent in the case of durable assets. However, the basis for investment expectations is 'very precarious' and 'based on shifting and unreliable evidence'. As a result these expectations 'are subject to sudden and violent changes'.[43] Rising

---

[41] See *The General Theory of Employment, Interest and Money*, Keynes, 1936, p. 135. 'More precisely, I define the marginal efficiency of capital as being equal to that rate of discount which would make the present value of the series of annuities given by the returns expected from the capital-asset during its life just equal to its supply price. This gives us the marginal efficiencies of particular types of capital-assets'.

[42] Ibid. p. 313.

[43] Ibid. p. 315.

interest rates [in response to higher inflation or higher perceived inflation] may provide the trigger for a reversal or the sudden decline in the anticipated net rate of return on investment. In the latter stages of a boom, optimistic expectations for the yield of capital goods may be enough to offset any rise in costs of production [or replacement costs]. It may also be sufficient to compensate for higher borrowing costs, but only for a short period. Indeed, Keynes argued that 'The later stages of the boom are characterised by optimistic expectations as to the future yield of capital-goods sufficiently strong to offset their growing abundance and their rising costs of production and, probably, a rise in the rate of interest also'.[44]

While the boom is underway, most new investment may show a satisfactory current yield. Disillusion may eventually set in because 'doubts suddenly arise concerning the reliability of the prospective yield, perhaps because the current yield shows signs of falling off, as the stock of newly produced durable goods steadily increases'.[45] Pushing interest rates up to avoid overinvestment may ultimately compound the fallout from any potential dip in the prospective yield, increasing the risks of [an unnecessary] economic slump.

The drop in the marginal efficiency of capital

---

[44] Ibid. p 315.

[45] Ibid. p. 317.

also tends to impact upon the willingness to spend. It is typically accompanied by a 'severe decline in the market value of stock exchange equities'.[46] The marginal propensity to consume falls just when it should be rising to absorb the stock of newly produced goods.[47] This leads to the erroneous conclusion that overinvestment is the cause of the boom and should be avoided at all costs, even if it requires higher interest rates.[48]

In mitigation, it is quite possible that particular types of assets may be produced in 'excessive abundance' and may be a 'waste of resources'.[49] Keynes was not oblivious to these risks. Indeed, misdirected investment or a misallocation of resources can happen even without a boom. However, the possibility that investors may over expand in a particular sector is not a reason to abandon a cheap, but tight monetary policy. On the contrary,

---

[46] Ibid. p. 319.

[47] Ibid. p. 320. 'Moreover, the corresponding movements in the stock-market may, [as we have seen above], depress the propensity to consume just when it is most needed'.

[48] Ibid. 'The preceding analysis may appear to be in conformity with the view of those who hold that over-investment is the characteristic of the boom, that the avoidance of this over-investment is the only possible remedy for the ensuing slump, and that, whilst for the reasons [given above] the slump cannot be prevented by a low rate of interest, nevertheless, the boom can be avoided by a high rate of interest'.

[49] Ibid. p. 321. 'It may, of course, be the case - indeed it is likely to be - that the illusions of the boom cause particular types of capital-assets to be produced in such excessive abundance that some part of the output is, on any criterion, a waste of resources; - which sometimes happens, we may add, even when there is no boom. It leads, that is to say, to misdirected investment'.

investors will be forced to become more discerning. Investors will make mistakes, but learning from these will be an important feature of this new policy framework. This would address the problem of moral hazard. Furthermore, the systemic threat posed by these 'mistakes' will be less [because of lower leverage]. By contrast, if the authorities pursue the opposite - easy, but dear money - and debt levels rise quickly, there is a higher chance that central banks and governments will be forced to intervene in a slump, at a greater cost to the taxpayer.

To reiterate, the importance of cheap, but tight money in facilitating investment is crucial. Tighter credit standards will cushion the fallout from any sudden drop in the prospective yield for capital goods. It will also reduce the potential damage from excessive debt. Should the prospective yield on capital goods fall, there will be less pressure for a deflationary and 'traumatic' devaluation of capital.

Keynes argued that there is a danger that 'investments which will in fact yield, say, 2 per cent in conditions of full employment are made in the expectation of a yield of, say, 6 per cent, and are valued accordingly. When the disillusion comes, this expectation is replaced by a contrary 'error of pessimism', with the result that the investments, which would in fact yield 2 per cent in conditions of full employment, are expected to yield less than nothing; and the resulting collapse of new investment then leads to a state of unemployment in which the investments, which would have yielded 2 per cent in conditions of full employment, in fact yield less than nothing. We reach a condition where there is a shortage of houses, but where nevertheless no one can afford to live in the houses that there are'.[50]

This leads to the somewhat unconventional conclusion that the remedy for a boom is not higher, but *lower* interest rates.[51] The key to an extended economic upswing is securing the correct combination of low interest rates [short- and long-term] and effective constraints on credit growth, to prevent a rapid rise in debt levels across households and companies. There is a danger that pushing interest rates higher would indeed deter new investment, albeit not 'in those particular directions which were under the influence of speculative excitement and, therefore, in special danger of being over-exploited'.[52] A rate of interest that is high enough to quell speculative investment would check reasonable new investment. Indeed, pushing interest rates higher is tantamount to a 'remedy which cures the disease by killing the patient'.[53] In the event that full employment is

---

[50] Ibid. p. 321-322.

[51] See Chapter 3, p. 243.

[52] See John Maynard Keynes, 1936, op. cit., p. 323.

[53] Ibid.

secured with a genuine case of over investment, it might be more appropriate to focus on policies that increase the marginal propensity to consume.[54] This would allow or ensure that the 'excessive' investment did not lead to a sharp fall in *profit rates*, which could trigger the next recession. Unless the full employment 'equilibrium' was accompanied by a rise in inflation, pushing interest rates higher could trigger an unnecessary slump.

Keynes acknowledges that there are indeed '*two* ways to expand output', namely investment and consumption.[55] He comes down on the side of investment because there are 'great social advantages of increasing the stock of capital until it ceases to be scarce'.[56] He concluded this is 'a practical judgement, not a theoretical imperative'.[57] However, in view of the central role played by the *Liquidity Preference Theory* in guiding monetary policy, there is a strong theoretical case for emphasising investment in an economic recovery [see Chapter 3 for more on the

---

[54] Ibid. p. 324. 'Furthermore, even if we were to suppose that contemporary booms are apt to be associated with a momentary condition of full investment or over investment in the strict sense, it would still be absurd to regard a higher rate of interest as the appropriate remedy. For in this event the case of those who attribute the disease to under-consumption would be wholly established. The remedy would lie in various measures designed to increase the propensity to consume by the redistribution of incomes or otherwise; so that a given level of employment would require a smaller volume of current investment to support it'.

[55] Ibid. p. 325.

[56] Ibid.

[57] Ibid.

Liquidity Preference Theory].

This point is not expanded upon in *The General Theory*. As we shall see in Chapter 2, one of the biggest difficulties facing central banks at the Zero Lower Bound - by no means the only one - is the misplaced fear of inflation. A recovery led by production of capital goods may prevent bottlenecks, raising productivity and accelerating the potential growth path for the economy. Furthermore, focusing on investment is the next logical stage of the portfolio balance effect, a key transmission mechanism between non-conventional monetary policies and a reflation of asset markets. A drop in borrowing costs and a rebound in asset prices are necessary for the rehabilitation of an economy following a financial crisis. However, the second stage of the portfolio balance effect - when savings and profits [and not debt] drive investment - determines whether policy makers have learnt the necessary lessons from the crisis of 2008.

## Inflation Risks in Perspective

The policy of quantitative easing has been controversial. The broader strategy of monetary reflation, including forward rate guidance, has been attacked repeatedly by more hawkish central bankers. When the Federal Reserve and the Bank of England embarked upon quantitative easing, inflation was cited by critics as a major risk. Some of this misapprehension reflected the experience of Germany in 1923. However, this episode had scant relevance for the economic difficulties facing the US and UK following the financial crisis of 2008. The hyperinflation experienced in Germany was the culmination of unsustainable war reparations, as forewarned by Keynes in 1919.[58] In mitigation, inflation did rebound in the US and UK following the introduction of quantitative easing in late 2008. Inevitably, protagonists seized upon the rise in consumer prices as vindication of their warnings that *printing money* was inflationary.[59] However, the Chinese government had responded to the sub-prime crisis and the collapse of Lehman Brothers by

---

[58] See *The Economic Consequences of the Peace*, John Maynard Keynes, Labour Research Department, 1920. See also *The World in Depression*, Charles P. Kindleberger, University of California Press, p. 20. According to Kindleberger, 'There is some disagreement as to when the inflation shifted from rapid to hyper: possibly May 1921 after the Reparations Commission report; January 1923 with the Franco-Belgian occupation of the Ruhr; or immediately, June 1922 with three strongly negative events - the French government's refusal to revise the reparation schedule of May 1921; the report of a bankers' committee, headed by J.P. Morgan stating the impossibility of making a loan to Germany so long as reparations were not scaled down; and on June 22, the assassination of [Germany's] Foreign Minister Rathenau. The exchange rate went down from 275 marks to the Dollar in May to 370 in June. By October it was 485 and by June 1923, 16,667'.

[59] Source: BEA, Price Index for Personal Consumption Expenditures [consumption deflator] and ONS, Consumer Price Index. In the US, the consumption deflator rose from a low of -0.8% y/y in August 2008 to a post-2008 high of 2.9% y/y in September 2011, before dropping back to 0.8% y/y in October 2013. In January 2014, it was 1.2% y/y. In the UK, the consumer price index accelerated from 1.1% y/y in September 2009 to a post-2008 high of 5.2% y/y in September 2011, before dipping to 1.9% y/y in January 2014.

unveiling its own monetary and fiscal stimulus.[60] This undoubtedly contributed to the rebound in commodity prices.

Critics of quantitative easing believed that printing money had been responsible for the surge in demand for commodities in China and other 'booming' emerging market economies, which pushed import prices up in the US and the UK.[61] According to this hypothesis, the decision of the Federal Reserve and the Bank of England to buy assets on such a large scale had triggered capital outflows to emerging market economies. This argument was misplaced.[62] [See chart 11] The emerging market growth story [and run-up in commodity prices] began well before the 2008 crisis and the introduction of

---

[60] See *China authorises 'massive' stimulus package*, Financial Times, 10 November 2008. The Chinese State Council authorised [on 9 November 2009] $586billion of investment on infrastructure and social welfare investment. This was equivalent to 12.7% of Gross Domestic Product [2008]. Source: National Bureau of Statistics, China.

[61] Source: BLS, Import Price Index, All Commodities, non-seasonally adjusted, US and ONS, Price Index Total Imports non-seasonally adjusted, UK. The import price index in the US rose from a post-2008 low of 113.0 in January 2009 to a post-2008 high of 144.2 in March 2012, a rise of 27.6%. The import price index in the UK climbed from post-2008 low of 92.4 in July 2009 to a post-2008 high of 111.9 in March 2012, an increase of 21.1%.

[62] Source: BEA, Private Assets, Foreign Securities. US gross outflows into foreign securities [bonds and equities] totalled $227.0billion in 2009, $139.1billion in 2010, $143.8billion in 2011 and $144.8billion in 2012. However, these portfolio outflows were higher before QE1 was announced on 25 November 2008. US gross outflows into foreign securities totalled $251.2billion in 2005, $365.1billion in 2006 and $366.5billion in 2007. There is no evidence from these numbers that quantitative easing materially increased gross capital outflows.

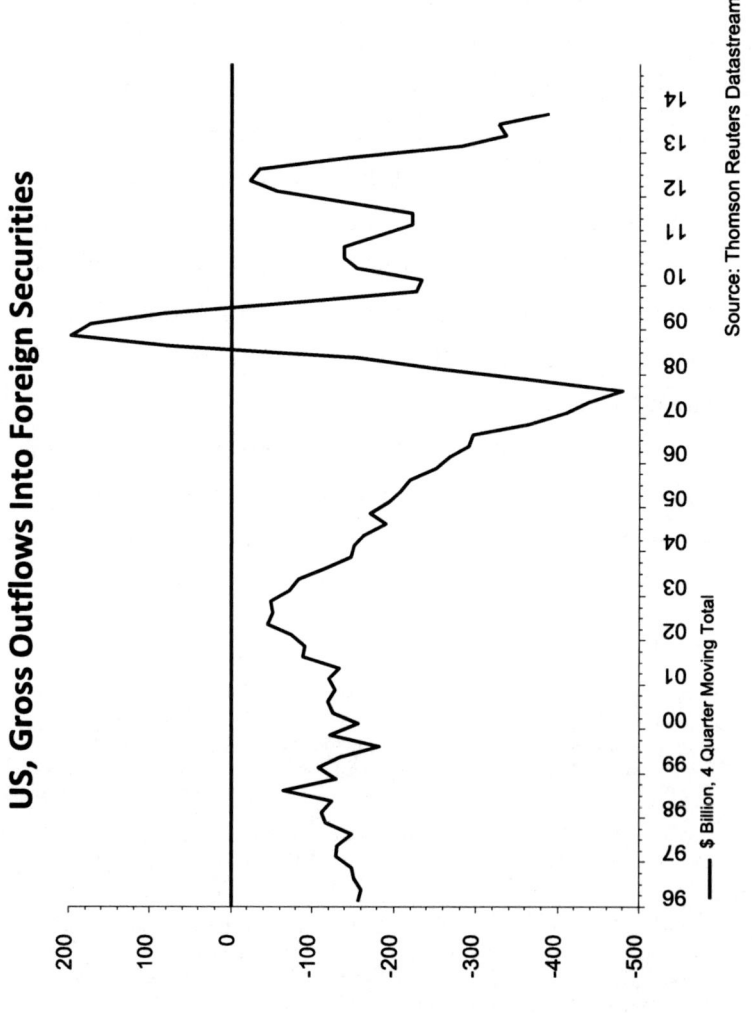

**US, Gross Outflows Into Foreign Securities**

Source: Thomson Reuters Datastream

$ Billion, 4 Quarter Moving Total

Chart 1I

quantitative easing. In addition, the introduction of QE3 in September 2012 - comparable in size to QE1 - did not lead to a rebound in commodity prices.[63]

The inflationary effects of quantitative easing were overstated. *Core inflation* never went above target in the US in response to QE1 or QE2.[64] By the time the FOMC had embarked upon QE3, inflation in the US had started to fall swiftly.[65] Indeed, the experience of the US has provided a strong counterweight to critics of quantitative easing. By January 2014, core inflation in the US had fallen to just 1.09%.[66] [See chart 1m]

Sceptics of non-conventional monetary policies had more success in the UK, where inflation was consistently above target.[67] The Bank of England's asset purchases

---

[63] Source: Thomson Reuters Datastream. The S&P/Goldman Sachs Commodity Index [spot] rose from 376.9 in 13 June 2006 to 536.6 in 4 May 2007, an increase of 42.4% and an all-time high. The same index has fallen from 388.2 in 13 September 2012 - when QE3 was implemented - to 325.4 in 13 March 2014, a drop of 16.2%.

[64] Source: BEA, Price Index for Personal Consumption Expenditures, excluding Food & Energy [core consumption deflator]. The *core consumption deflator* rose to a post-2008 high of 2.04% y/y in March 2012.

[65] Source: BEA, Price Index for Personal Consumption Expenditures [consumption deflator]. QE3 was announced on 13 September 2012: the consumption deflator had eased to 1.7% y/y. Excluding food & energy, the consumption deflator had also slowed to 1.7% y/y.

[66] Source: BEA, Price Index for Personal Consumption Expenditures, excluding Food & Energy [core consumption deflator].

[67] Source: ONS, Consumer Price Index. Inflation was above the Bank of England's 2.0% target from December 2009 until December 2013.

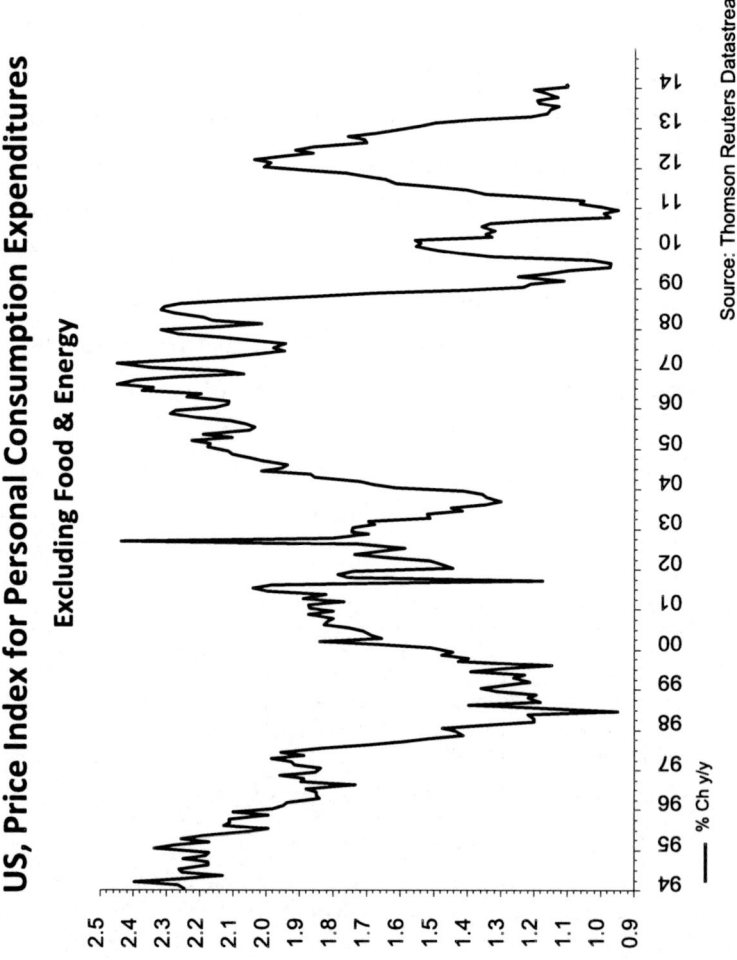

US, Price Index for Personal Consumption Expenditures

Excluding Food & Energy

Source: Thomson Reuters Datastream

Chart 1m

47

were proportionately larger than in the US.[68] Sterling also fell sharply during the credit crunch.[69] By contrast, after depreciating for much of 2008, the Dollar rose in anticipation of the announcement on 25 November 2008 by the Federal Reserve that marked the start of QE1.[70] Nevertheless, the rise in import prices in the UK was less than in the US.[71] Furthermore, the depreciation of Sterling came to an end on 29 December 2008. Thereafter, Sterling rose and eventually inflation fell below target in January 2014.[72] Even in the UK, it was hard to make the case that quantitative easing was a material threat to inflation.

---

[68] Source: Federal Reserve [Securities Held Outright], BEA [GDP, Current Prices], Bank of England, [Other Assets, Loans to Asset Purchase Facility] and ONS [GDP, Market Prices]. Securities Held Outright by the Federal Reserve rose to $3.879trillion by 13 March 2003. This was equivalent to 22.9% of Q4 2013 GDP [annualised]. Other assets, loans to Asset Purchase Facility, held by the Bank of England, were £403.6billion on 26 February 2014. This was equivalent to 24.3% of Q4 2013 GDP [annualised].

[69] Source: Bank of England, £ Broad Index, Trade-Weighted. The trade-weighted index for Sterling fell from 97.72 on 1 January 2008 to 73.43 on 30 December 2008, a drop of 24.9%.

[70] Source: Federal Reserve, $ Broad Exchange Rate Index. The broad trade-weighted index for the Dollar dropped from 99.04 on 1 January 2008 to 94.79 on 15 July 2008, before rising to 110.47 on 24 November 2008, the day before the announcement on QE1. It then rose to a high of 115.0 on 3 March 2009. It subsequently fell, reaching a low of 93.95 on 26 July 2011.

[71] See footnote 61.

[72] Source: Bank of England, £ Broad Index, Trade-Weighted and ONS, Consumer Price Index. From the low of 73.43 on 30 December 2008, the trade-weighted index for Sterling climbed to 84.52 on 30 December 2013.

## Looking Ahead

The success of cheap, but tight money will, of course, depend upon effective implementation. There are a number of risks that could prevent this dual policy from delivering a return to full employment across countries in the West. The first relates to the conduct of monetary policy. Central banks have not always appreciated the range of the tools at their disposal and their potency. Critically, they have not fully understood the significance of Keynes's Liquidity Preference Theory when trying to secure an economic recovery. Mistakes have been made since 2008. Indeed, Appendix 1 [Reverse Taps] after Chapter 2 will argue that full employment could have been secured sooner if monetary policy had been immediately aligned with the framework outlined by Keynes in the early 1930s.

On 18 December 2013, the FOMC announced that it would reduce its bond purchases. At the current pace of withdrawal, QE3 is scheduled to end before the end of 2014.[73] Scaling down quantitative easing need not derail the economic recovery. Nevertheless, the temptation of markets to extrapolate a modest rise in wages or inflation will be high. A lack of clarity in the alternative policies

---

[73] At a pace of $10billion cuts to the stimulus programme at each meeting, the FOMC would reduce its asset purchases to $15billion per month by September 2014. This could be reduced by $15billion at the October meeting or reduced by $10billion in October and $5billion in December.

needed to underpin cheap money - and an unwillingness to use them more aggressively - may be a problem. Indeed, the inclination of some central bankers to revert to interest rate hikes to affect control of the economy, instead of using *macro-prudential tools*, could short-circuit an economic recovery.

It is encouraging that some Federal Reserve officials, not least, the FOMC chair Janet Yellen, understand the importance of prioritising unemployment when inflation remains palpably low. The early critics of quantitative easing - and there were many - fretted over the risks to inflation, ignoring the huge social costs from unemployment. They have been proved wrong. The high profile admissions from a minority of central bank hawks that inflation is not a threat at the early stage of an economic recovery has also been helpful.[74]

Nevertheless, the hawks have not been vanquished. The Federal Reserve presidents for Philadelphia and Dallas - Charles Plosser and Richard Fisher - voted against the interest rate cuts in the early months of 2008.[75] Excluding New York, the Federal Reserve presidents serve one-year terms on a rotating basis. Mr Plosser and

---

[74] See Chapter 2, p 129.

[75] Richard Fisher, president of the Federal Reserve Bank of Dallas, voted against rate cuts on 30 January, 18 March and 30 April 2008. Charles Plosser, president of the Federal Reserve Bank of Philadelphia, voted against rate cuts on 18 March and 30 April 2008.

Mr Fisher returned to the FOMC in January 2014.[76] One FOMC member was already agitating for a possible rise in interest rates at the first FOMC meeting of 2014.[77]

There will be many ways for central banks to send a strong signal to markets should they continue to scale back quantitative easing. Forward rate guidance can be strengthened. The rather narrow targets for forward rate guidance initially set by the FOMC can be widened. However, the control of interest rate expectations to counter the tendency towards liquidity preference may require much more than strong guidance. The FOMC will need to articulate how a policy of cheap money, backed by a commitment to financial stability can drive investment spending, delivering a sustainable recovery *and* low inflation. As we shall see in Chapter 3, a fear of inflation is only one of the reasons for liquidity

---

[76] The Federal Open Market Committee [FOMC] consists of twelve members:- the seven members of the Board of Governors of the Federal Reserve System; the president of the Federal Reserve Bank of New York; and four of the remaining eleven Reserve Bank presidents, who serve one-year terms on a rotating basis. The rotating seats are filled from the following four groups of Banks, one Bank president from each group: Boston, Philadelphia, and Richmond; Cleveland and Chicago; Atlanta, St. Louis, and Dallas; and Minneapolis, Kansas City, and San Francisco. Non-voting Reserve Bank presidents attend the meetings of the Committee, participate in the discussions, and contribute to the Committee's assessment of the economy and policy options.

[77] See *Minutes of the Federal Open Market Committee*, January 28-29, 2014, Federal Reserve, p. 15. According to the minutes, 'One participant cited evidence that the equilibrium real interest rate had moved higher, and a couple of them noted that some standard policy rules tended to suggest that the federal funds rate should be raised above its effective lower bound before the middle of this year'.

preference. Focusing on the current low rates of inflation would provide one possible anchor for investors. To reiterate, inflation targeting was not the cause of the housing boom prior to the recession of 2008: it was the erroneous assumption that the control of inflation was enough to ensure financial stability.

However, there was precious little discussion of the dynamics [rising investment spending] that can drive low inflation among FOMC officials during 2013. On the contrary, Mr Bernanke called the low inflation rates as transitory.[78] In March 2014, at her first press conference on becoming the chair of the FOMC, Ms Yellen suggested that the 'potential growth path of the economy may be lower, at least for a time', in response to 'residual impacts of the financial crisis'.[79] As we shall see, this overlooked the significant rise in real investment spending - particularly in technology and related areas - witnessed since the final quarter of 2009. The Federal Reserve will need to offer a more convincing narrative in 2014 and beyond.

The projected date for the first interest rate hike

---

[78] See *Transcript of Chairman Bernanke's Press Conference*, June 19 2013, p. 14. Mr Bernanke claimed 'there are a number of transitory factors that may be contributing to the very low inflation rate'. He was emphasising a point made in the FOMC statement released that day: 'Partly reflecting transitory influences, inflation has been running below the Committee's longer-run objective'.

[79] See *Transcript of Chair Yellen's Press Conference*, March 19 2014, p. 5.

can be extended. The FOMC could introduce specific targets for the federal funds rate beyond the anticipated lift-off to demonstrate that any increase in short-term interest rates will be slow. It could also reduce its 'longer run' estimate for the federal funds rate, which remains incompatible with a policy of cheap, but tight money. There is much to be done to underpin cheap, but tight money. However, *quantitative guidance* may be a poor substitute for a policy that addresses the problem of liquidity preference identified by Keynes. Calendar-based guidance was an effective tool that was aligned more closely to the prescription for reflation outlined by Keynes in the early 1930s.

## Is Cheap, But Tight Money Working?

The recovery in the US housing market witnessed by early 2014 was far from complete. House prices remained below their highs of 2007.[80] [See chart 1n] The number of borrowers in serious arrears had dropped by just over half from the highs, but were well above levels prevailing prior to the sub-prime crisis.[81] [See chart 1o] Many first

---

[80] Source: NAR. The median price of existing one-family homes sold [seasonally adjusted by Thomson Reuters Datastream] had risen to $204,400 by January 2014, but this was still 11.2% below the peak of $230,200 witnessed in October 2005.

[81] Source: Mortgage Bankers Association. Residential mortgage loans, 90+ days delinquent fell from a high of 5.02% in Q1 2010 to 2.45% in Q4 2013, but this was still up from 0.98% in Q1 2007, the unofficial start of the sub-prime mortgage crisis.

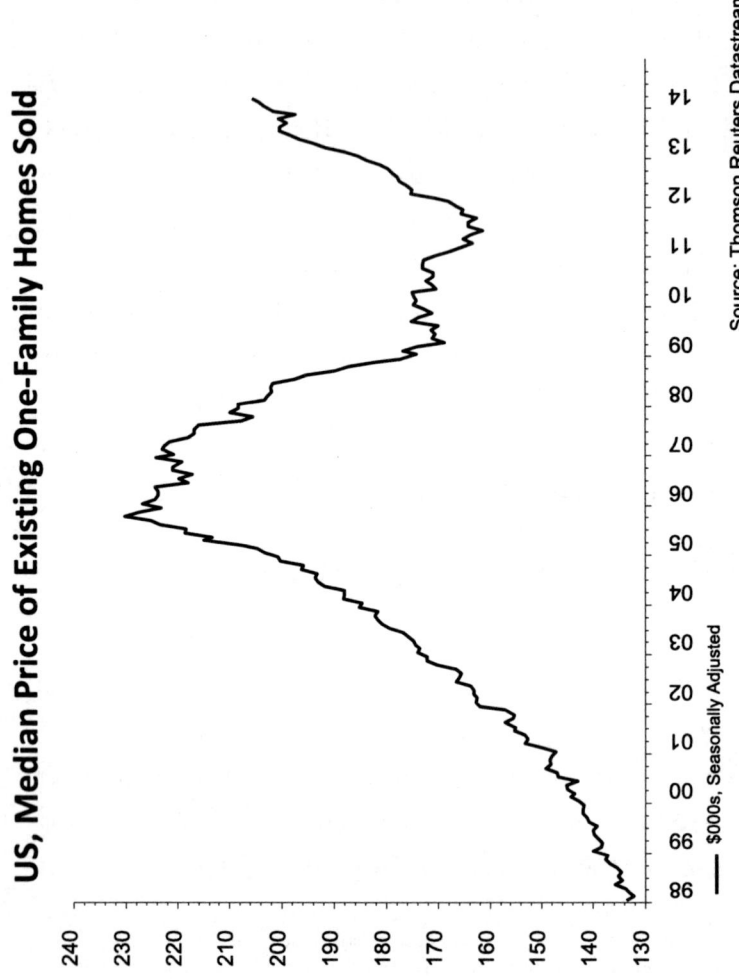

US, Median Price of Existing One-Family Homes Sold

Source: Thomson Reuters Datastream

$000s, Seasonally Adjusted

Chart 1n

54

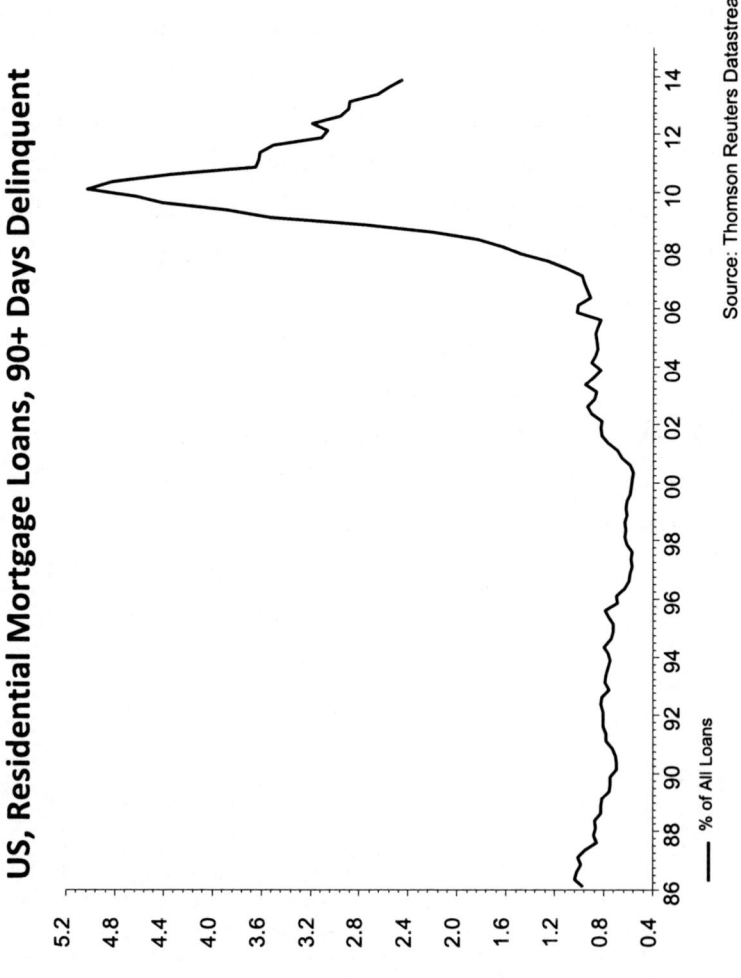

**US, Residential Mortgage Loans, 90+ Days Delinquent**

—— % of All Loans

Source: Thomson Reuters Datastream

Chart 1o

55

time borrowers were struggling to secure mortgages. Investors have largely driven the rise in house prices.[82]

However, the dependence on debt and housing to fuel previous economic cycles implies that a recovery based heavily on the property market is undesirable. Indeed, the unwillingness of banks to lend since 2008 is the flipside of a cheap, but tight money policy that may lead to a more lasting economic recovery. By holding personal sector debt levels down, the FOMC will be under less pressure to raise interest rates to quell any boom. In short, a strong upturn in the US housing market need not be a prerequisite to a return to full employment. It could be a hindrance if it forced the Federal Reserve into a premature hike in interest rates.

Indeed, the evidence available at the end of 2013 in the US shows how a policy of cheap, but tight money can work. Personal sector debt as a share of GDP has been trending down since Q1 2009.[83] [See

[82] Source: NAR. On average, sales to investors have accounted for 18% of all home sales between October 2008 and January 2014. Investors accounted for 20% of all sales in January 2014. The share of first time buyers has averaged 35% over the same period. Nevertheless, this has been trending down since mid-2012. First time buyers as a share of the market fell to 26% of all home buyers of existing homes in January 2014, the lowest since records began in October 2008. First time buyers, as a share of the whole market, have not been above 30% since November 2012.

[83] Source: Federal Reserve, Flow of Funds [FoF], Financial Liabilities - Households & Non-profit Institutions and Bureau of Economic Analysis [BEA], GDP, current prices. The ratio of financial liabilities for households & non-profit institutions [personal sector] to GDP has fallen from a high of 99.0% in Q1 2008 to 80.5% in Q4 2013. This was the lowest since Q1 2003.

chart 1p] Nevertheless, deleveraging has not stopped unemployment from falling faster than the Federal Reserve expected and has not prevented consumer spending from rising. The sluggish rise in wage rates has not derailed the economic recovery: on aggregate, wages are finally rising, partly because higher investment spending has been accompanied by faster job creation.[84]

There has been less deleveraging in the corporate sector.[85] [See chart 1q] At first glance, quantitative easing has pushed stock markets up, corporate bond yields down and created a different set of risks.[86] Corporate bond issuance has soared.[87] [See chart 1r] However, the latter has been misinterpreted. The non-bank credit

---

[84] Source: BEA, Wage & Salary Disbursements, All Industries and Price Index for Personal Consumption Expenditure [consumption deflator]. Wages & salaries adjusted by the consumption deflator rose 1.9% y/y in 2013, following gains of 2.4% y/y in 2012 and 1.7% y/y in 2011. However, there was a pick up in real wage rates [see footnote 103].

[85] Source: Federal Reserve, Flow of Funds [FoF], Financial Liabilities - Non-farm & non-financial corporate business and Bureau of Economic Analysis (BEA), GDP, current prices. The ratio of financial liabilities for non-farm & non-financial corporate business to GDP rose to 90.9% in Q4 2008. It fell to 87.1% in Q3 2012. By Q4 2013, it had edged up to 87.6%, although this was unchanged from Q4 2012.

[86] Source: Merrill Lynch High Yield Cash Pay ($)/Thomson Reuters Datastream. Corporate bond yields [High Yield or non-investment grade] fell from a high of 22.62% on 12 December 2008 to a low of 5.91% on 9 May 2013. By 28 February 2014, it was still only 6.01%.

[87] Source: Federal Reserve Flow of Funds, Financial Liabilities - Non-farm & non-financial corporates, corporate bonds. Corporate [non-farm & non-financial] bond liabilities rose to a record $6.26trillion in Q3 2013, up 11.9% y/y, the fastest increase since Q1 2002. As a share of corporate sector liabilities, this was a record 42.4%.

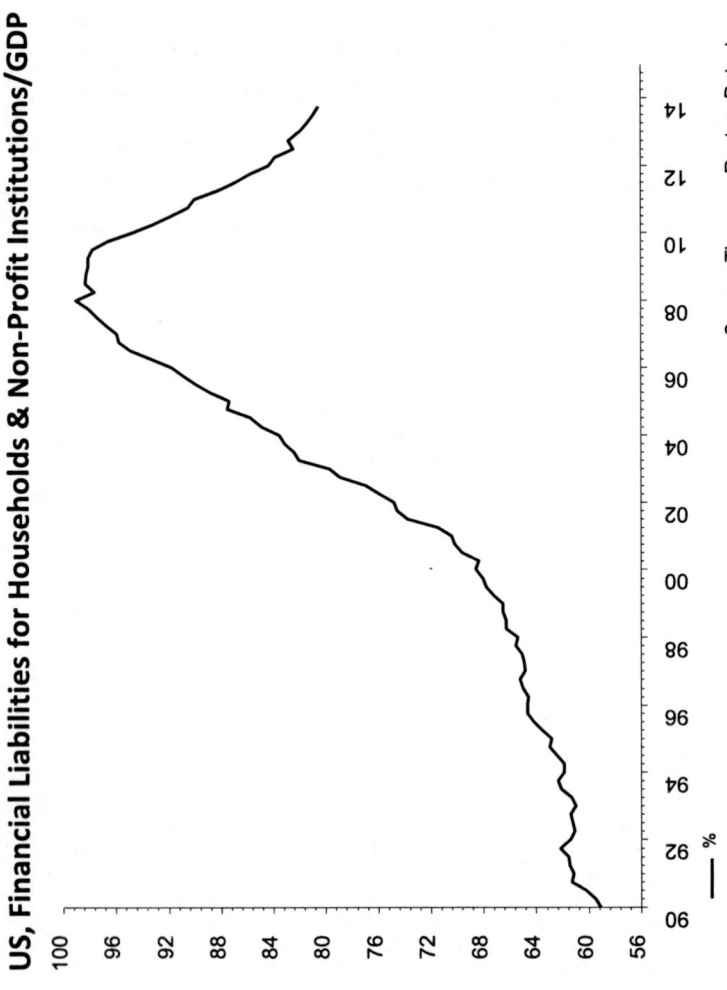

Chart 1p

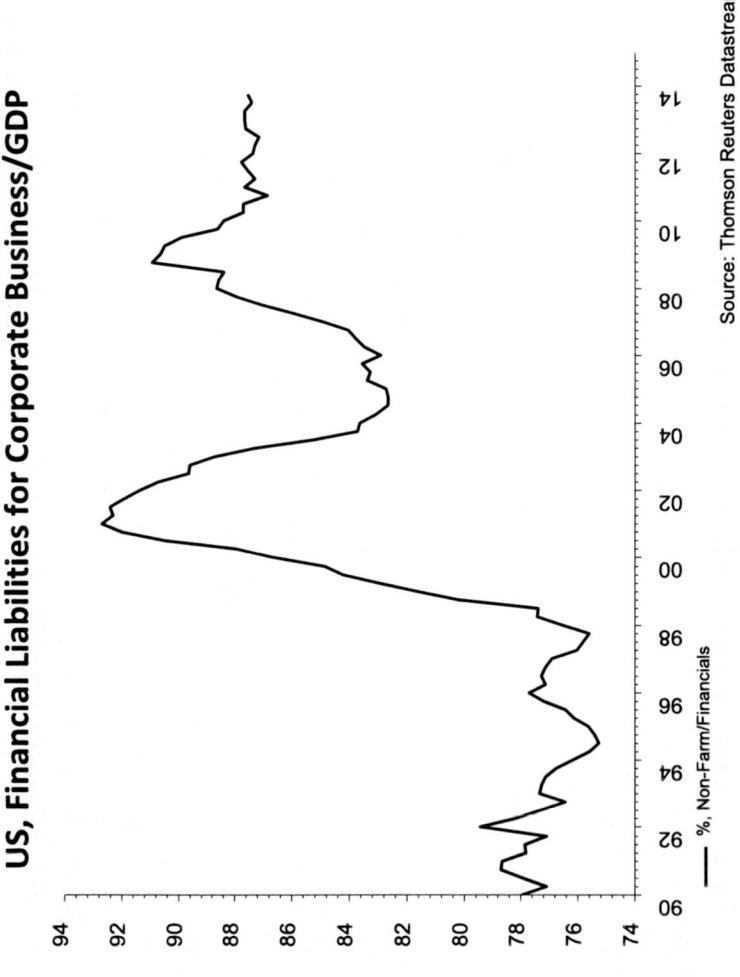

US, Financial Liabilities for Corporate Business/GDP

% Non-Farm/Financials

Source: Thomson Reuters Datastream

Chart 1q

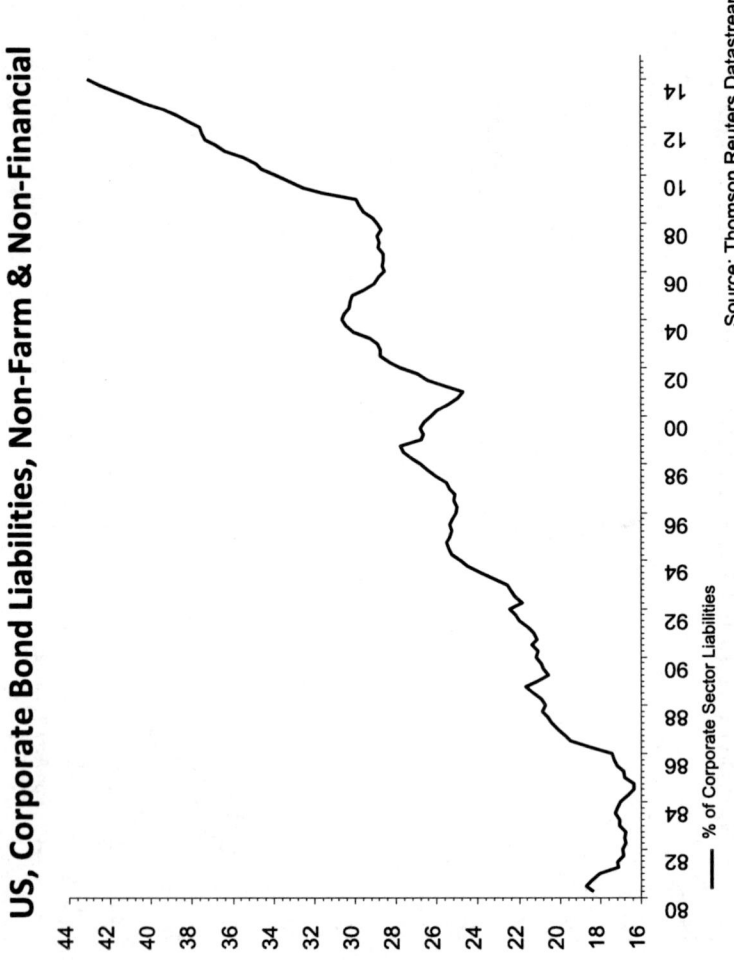

Chart 1r

channels [savers, asset managers] have offset the squeeze on lending from banks.[88] Companies are using capital markets more to finance their debt. Furthermore, many companies have been taking advantage of low long-term interest rates to issue longer-term debt in place of shorter-dated borrowing. They are adjusting their capital structure and extending their debt maturity profile, which will reinforce financial stability.[89]

Furthermore, companies are investing. As share of GDP, non-residential investment has been rising again after falling sharply in response to the crisis of 2008. On this basis, investment spending is still running below the highs of Q1 2008.[90] However, dissecting the numbers shows that the areas of investment that are more likely to drive productivity have risen to new highs. The charts on pages 62 and 63 show non-residential investment disaggregated into three components. [See charts 1s and 1t] The first line shows that investment in structures has fallen [as a share of GDP] since the financial crisis

---

[88] Source: Federal Reserve Flow of Funds, Financial Liabilities - Non-farm & non-financial corporates, corporate bonds.

[89] See *Evaluating Large-Scale Asset Purchases*, Jeremy Stein, 11 October 2012. Mr Stein noted 'that a natural response for any firm facing an unusually low-term premium is to adjust its capital structure by issuing cheap long-term debt to replace its shorter-term debt. It is therefore not surprising that the average debt maturity of large nonfinancial firms has increased notably over the past few years'.

[90] Source: BEA. The ratio of real private fixed investment, non-residential, to real GDP rose to 12.7% in Q4 2013, up from a post-2008 low of 11.0% in Q4 2009. However, this compares with a high of 13.4% in Q1 2008.

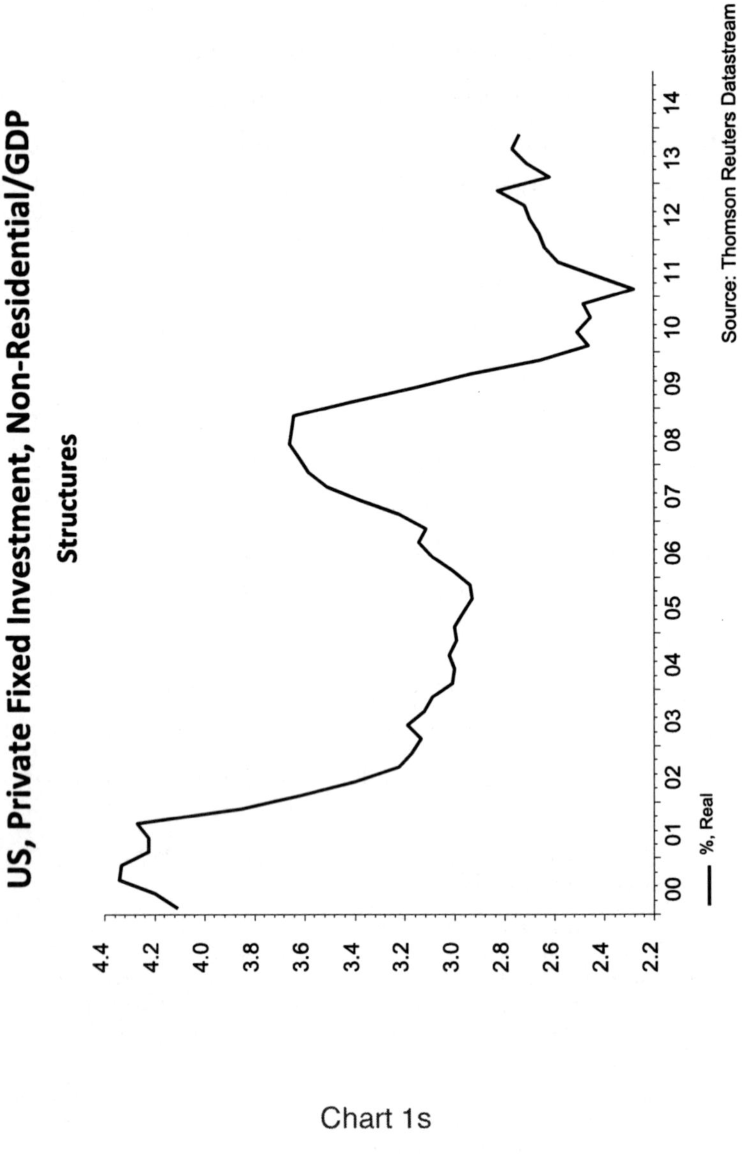
US, Private Fixed Investment, Non-Residential/GDP
Structures
4.4
4.2
4.0
3.8
3.6
3.4
3.2
3.0
2.8
2.6
2.4
2.2
00
01
02
03
04
05
06
07
08
09
10
11
12
13
14
%, Real
Source: Thomson Reuters Datastream

Chart 1s

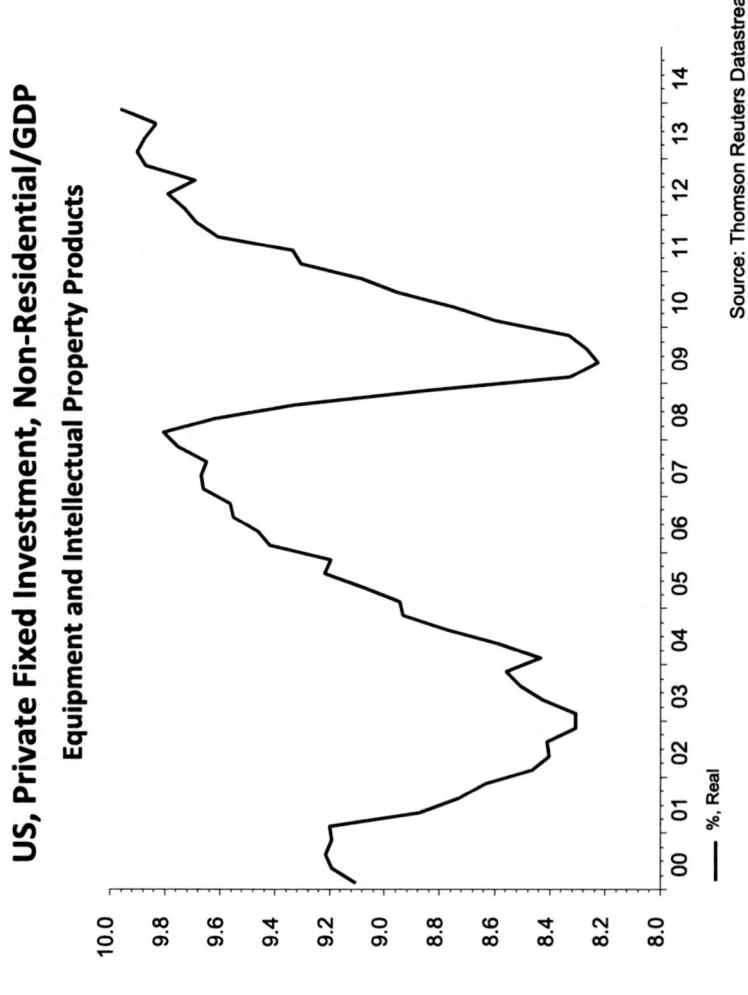

**US, Private Fixed Investment, Non-Residential/GDP**

**Equipment and Intellectual Property Products**

— %, Real

Source: Thomson Reuters Datastream

Chart 1t

of 2008.[91] Indeed, it is even lower than at the peak of the Dotcom boom.[92] The other two components of non-residential investment are business equipment and intellectual property products. As a share of GDP, these two categories of investment [combined] had risen to a new high of 10.0% in Q4 2013.[93] Spending on business equipment was close to secular highs as a share of GDP.[94] Investment in intellectual property products was running at record highs.[95] Within this broad category, spending on software had risen to an all-time high of 1.9% of GDP by the end of 2013.[96] Spending on research & development rose strongly during the housing boom, but has not fallen back and has been largely trending sideways, close to historic highs.[97] Indeed, between 2007

---

[91] Source: BEA. Real private fixed investment, non-residential, structures to real GDP fell from 3.7% in Q2 2008 to 2.8% in Q4 2013.

[92] Source: BEA. Real private fixed investment, non-residential, structures to real GDP reached 4.3% in Q3 2000.

[93] Source: BEA. Real private fixed investment, non-residential, equipment and intellectual property products, to real GDP reached a high of 9.8% in Q1 2008, before turning down sharply.

[94] Source: BEA. Real private fixed investment, non-residential, equipment, to real GDP rose to 6.0% in Q4 2013. This compares with a high of 6.1% reached in Q4 2007 and the previous cyclical high of 5.8% in Q3 2000.

[95] Source: BEA. Real private fixed investment, non-residential, intellectual property products, to real GDP climbed to 4.0% in Q4 2013.

[96] Source: BEA. Real private fixed investment, non-residential, software, to real GDP rose to 1.9% in Q4 2013.

[97] Source: BEA. Real private fixed investment, non-residential, research & development, to real GDP was 1.6% in Q4 2013. This is up from a low of 1.4% in Q1 2004, but unchanged [after rounding] from the 1.6% 'peak' reached in Q3 2011.

and 2013, spending on research & development expanded by 9.7% in real terms.[98] There have been some notable areas of strength in sectors that underline the potential for strong productivity gains. For example, spending on research & development in semiconductor and other electronic equipment product manufacturing [i.e. high technology] has jumped 52.4% in $ terms between 2007 and 2012.[99]

Furthermore, while spending on structures has fallen as a share of GDP, a number of areas in this classification have been strong. Some of these are likely to benefit the potential growth path of the economy. For example, investment in structures for the energy, mining and transportation sectors has risen sharply.[100] Other areas for investment in structures have been weak, which may have less relevance for the underlying productivity of the economy. For example, investment in structures for shopping malls has fallen sharply.[101] Technology may be

---

[98] Source: BEA, Real private fixed investment, non-residential, research & development.

[99] Source: BEA, Private fixed investment, non-residential, research & development, semi-conductor and other electronic product manufacturing.

[100] Source: BEA, Private fixed investment, non-residential, structures. For the power sector, investment in structures [in $ terms] rose 44.2% between 2007 and 2013. For mining exploration, shafts, and wells investment in structures climbed 35.4% [in $ terms] between 2007 and 2013. For transportation, investment in structures climbed 41.6% [in $ terms] between 2007 and 2013.

[101] Source: BEA, Private fixed investment, non-residential, structures. For multi-merchandise shopping, investment in structures fell 54.0% [in $ terms] between 2007 and 2013.

a partial explanation for this decline too, with the rise of Internet shopping.

The focus on over-accumulation as the cause of the financial crisis in 2008 wrongly suggests that an investment-led recovery is necessarily doomed to fail. In mitigation, profits were under pressure before the US economy slipped into recession, turning down from Q3 2006 onwards. Profits had reached historic highs as a share of GDP.[102] From this perspective, the data supports the thesis that over-accumulation was the underlying cause of the sub-prime crisis. Critics argue there were insufficient investment opportunities in the private sector to sustain these high profits, even with the housing bubble. The squeeze on the median wage implies demand did not rise quickly enough. This remains a risk: higher investment may eventually squeeze profit rates [profits in relation to investment, or the net rate of return]. Stock markets will fall. Logically, another crisis would ensue.

None of this is inevitable. Profit rates or the net rate of return could fall if investment rises more quickly than consumption, but this may not be automatic. Higher investment may protect profit margins through productivity gains that also allow wages to rise as the

---

[102] Source: BEA. Profits, after tax, with inventory valuation and capital consumption adjustments, to GDP reached 8.6% in Q3 2006, before falling steadily, as house prices dropped. The Q3 2006 ratio was the highest during the post-1945 period.

economy expands.

Either way, the possibility that the net rate of return will fall is precisely why the policy of cheap, but tight money is essential and can be effective.

Indeed, Keynes argued that any decline in profit rates may be inevitable if investment spending is to lead the recovery. This tendency should be accommodated or cushioned by a low rate of interest. Over accumulation and falling profit rates are not the underlying problems *per se*: the latter may simply be too high in relation to the *risk-free* rate and inconsistent with a long economic recovery. The expected rate of return may have to be lowered for investment to rise more quickly. The prospective yield from capital goods may well be set at levels that are too high in the first place and inconsistent with the objective of investment-led growth. The correct response to any decline in the rate of return from these exalted, unrealistic levels is a lower risk-free interest rate through the policy of cheap, but tight money.

Critics argue there is no guarantee that firms will expand their real investment enough to secure full employment. *Hysteresis*, or the erosion of workers' skills - a legacy of the 2008 crisis and the inadequate monetary policy response in the first three years - may also, they claim, reduce the central bank's latitude to drive reflation. Mature companies could choose to recycle high profits into higher dividends, or buy back outstanding shares.

Nevertheless, these share buybacks and dividend payments may be re-directed by investors towards smaller start-ups or other, faster growing sectors. Indeed, the early data in the US suggests that investment and wages can rise in tandem.[103] Furthermore, to secure higher wages, policymakers need to recognise that it is economic slumps that have inflicted so much damage on wages for the lower paid. Eliminating boom and bust, and focusing on investment to drive growth through a policy of cheap, but tight money, can eliminate the periodical busts of high unemployment, which hurt workers. Should the economy approach full employment, any reflation in the median wage is more likely to endure.

Central bank and government attempts to preserve financial stability, preventing a return to easy money, may unravel under pressure from institutions seeking a return to a less-regulated financial system. Resisting the short-term political imperative of a dash for growth based on higher borrowing will be essential. It will take time for savers and companies to become accustomed to the new framework, and the change in incentives. A return to leverage as a driver for economic growth would provide additional short run stimulus, a tempting

---

[103] Source: BLS. By February 2014, total private non-farm average hourly earnings were rising 2.5% y/y. Adjusting this by the price index for Personal Consumption Expenditures, excluding food & energy [core consumption deflator], this represented a real increase of 1.2% y/y. This compares favourably to an average increase since January 1950 of 0.8%.

prospect for politicians driven by the electoral cycle. It could shorten the time period required for countries in the West to restore full employment. However, it would increase the risks of a return to boom and bust. The return of easy money would undermine the ability of central banks to keep rates low, curtailing the rise in sustainable investment that would raise productivity and the potential growth path of the economy.

The clamour among savers for a nascent recovery to be accompanied by a rise in interest rates will have to be resisted. Deposit rates today may be less than inflation in many countries, including the US and the UK. Savers are in this sense being 'penalised'. However, the optimal policies required to deliver durable economic expansion suggests this is necessary. As already indicated high risk-free rates of return are not commensurate with an investment-led recovery. Indeed, Keynes was critical of any assumption that savers are entitled to a real risk-free rate of return suggesting 'Interest today rewards no genuine sacrifice, any more than does the rent of land. The owner of capital can obtain interest because capital is scarce, just as the owner of land can obtain rent because land is scarce. But whilst there may be intrinsic reasons for the scarcity of land, there are no intrinsic reasons for the scarcity of capital'.[104] Any political pressure for

---

[104] See Keynes, 1936, op. cit., p. 376.

a reversal in low interest rates, acquiescing to savers, is a threat to the necessary dual policy of cheap, but tight money.

All of these risks will need to be assessed carefully going forward. However, they do not constitute valid reasons for abandoning the new policy framework required in the aftermath of the crisis of 2008. The more hawkish members of central banks may start chipping away at the policy of cheap, but tight money. Should the recovery deepen, the temptation to relax the new regime needed to buttress financial stability will intensify. That will test the resolve of governments, central banks and regulators. It is incumbent upon all these groups to ensure the lessons of the 2008 crisis and Keynes's monetary theory are digested in order to avoid a repeat of the deep recession that followed the bursting of the housing bubble.

# Chapter 2

# US Monetary Policy since the Crisis

## Introduction

On 17 February 2009, President Barack Obama signed into law the American Recovery and Reinvestment Act. The $787billion economic stimulus was a textbook *post-war Keynesian* response to the economic recession that had gripped the US in the wake of the Lehman Brothers' collapse.[1] The Recovery and Reinvestment Act was criticised by some economists, including Nobel laureate Paul Krugman, for being too small because it did 'not cover even one-third of the [spending] gap'.[2] For Keynesians, fiscal policy was critical to the reflation strategy. The Federal Reserve had an important role to

---

[1] Source: http://www.recovery.gov/arra/about/pages/the_act.aspx [accessed 6 June 2014]. The American Recovery and Reinvestment Act of 2009 was passed by Congress on 13 February 2009. It was designed to: 'create new jobs and save existing ones; spur economic activity and invest in long-term growth; foster unprecedented levels of accountability and transparency in government spending'. The estimated cost of the programme was $787billion, which was subsequently revised to $840billion.

[2] See *Nobel Laureate Paul Krugman: Too Little Stimulus in Stimulus Plan*, University of Pennsylvania, 19 February 2009. http://knowledge.wharton. upenn.edu/article/nobel-laureate-paul-krugman-too-little-stimulus-in-stimulus-plan/ [accessed 6 June 2014].

play in reversing the recession. However, interest rates had been cut repeatedly in response to the decline in house prices. The target for the *federal funds rate* had dropped to just 0.0% - 0.25% by the end of 2008.[3]

Fiscal Policy, it seemed, needed to move centre-stage. This, claimed many economists, was the conclusion to be drawn from *The General Theory* and one important lesson from the Great Depression. In reality, many Keynesians misinterpreted the role of fiscal policy in driving the recovery from 1932 onwards. The importance of monetary policy and *liquidity preference* were overlooked. As we shall argue in Chapter 4, the turnaround from the Great Depression was triggered by *large scale asset purchases*, not fiscal stimulus.

This mistaken assessment of the Great Depression led to a wrong policy prescription during the immediate aftermath of the 2008 *credit crunch*. Indeed, the case for a large fiscal stimulus to end the recession has been discredited by subsequent events. Greater monetary policy action was required and would ultimately prove successful in reflating the economy, even in the face of fiscal contraction. The FOMC eventually got the policy prescription correct, although there were unnecessary and costly delays. Indeed, as we shall argue in Appendix

---

[3] See *Federal Reserve Press Release, 16 December 2008*. The committee decided to establish a target range of 0.0% - 0.25% for the federal funds rate.

I at the end of this chapter, there were more radical policy options available to the Federal Reserve such as the *reverse tap*, which could have produced a swifter recovery in the US economy.

A failure to understand the true significance of Keynes's work initially led to an incorrect application of monetary policy by the Federal Reserve. It was not until the summer of 2011 that the requisite policies were put in place. This involved relegating fiscal policy behind a primary focus on controlling interest rate expectations and thus bond yields. The introduction of *forward rate guidance* on August 2011 was closer to the prescription to be drawn from Keynes's analysis. It proved much more successful than many economists expected. By early 2014, the Federal Reserve had reversed more than half of the original slump in house prices.[4] [See chart 2a] The S&P 500 had hit new all-time highs.[5] [See chart 2b] The unemployment rate had dropped to 6.7% as the US continued to create jobs, despite the fiscal tightening

---

[4] Source: National Association of Realtors [NAR]. The median price of existing one-family homes sold [seasonally adjusted by Thomson Reuters Datastream] rose from a post-2008 low of $161,400 in July 2011 to $204,400 in January 2014. This compares with a peak of $230,200 in October 2005. The increase between the low of July 2011 and January 2014 represents 58.1% of the decline witnessed between October 2005 and July 2011.

[5] Source: Thomson Reuters Datastream. The S&P 500 composite price index reached an all-time high of 1848.4 on 31 December 2013, 18.1 per cent above the peak prior to the 2008 financial crisis [1565.1 on 9 October 2007]. The S&P 500 composite price index rose further in early 2014, climbing to 1878.0 on 7 March 2014.

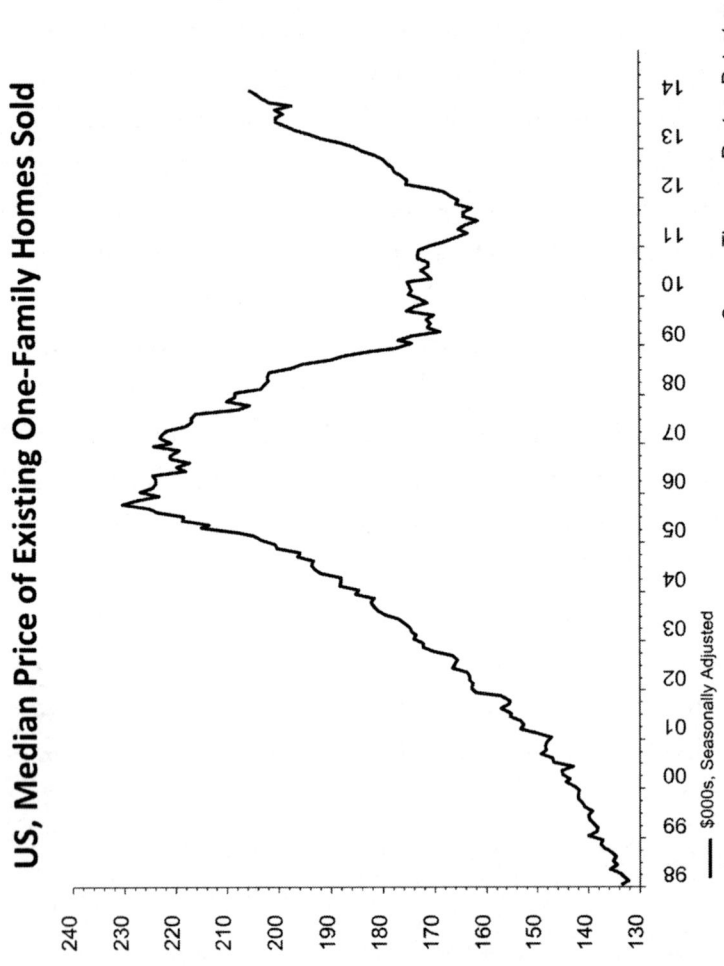

US, Median Price of Existing One-Family Homes Sold

Source: Thomson Reuters Datastream

$000s, Seasonally Adjusted

Chart 2a

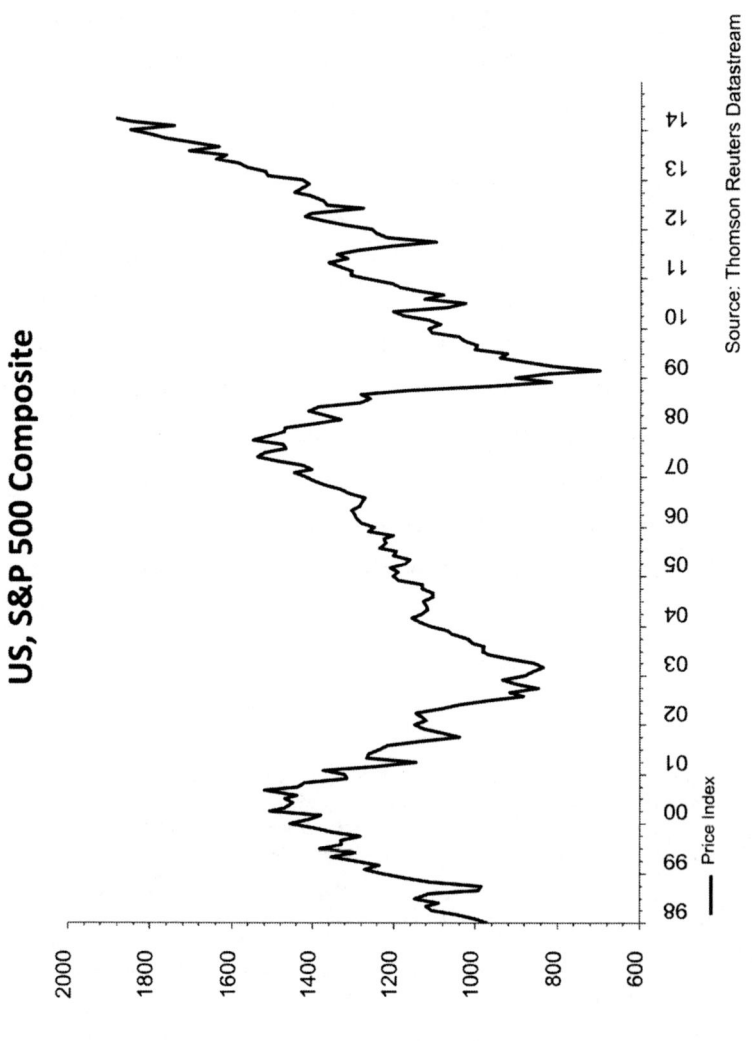

**US, S&P 500 Composite**

Source: Thomson Reuters Datastream

Chart 2b

from 2010 onwards.[6] Indeed, 2013 had seen more jobs created than any year since the start of the economic recovery.[7] The monetary reflation strategy was proving more effective than critics had predicted.

## Behind the Curve

The failure of Lehman Brothers on 15 September 2008 triggered a stock market slump and paralysis in financial markets. The epicentre of the crisis was the securitisation of sub-prime mortgages, but the collateral damage was widespread. Historically, large movements in corporate bond yields have foreshadowed big changes in unemployment: during the final weeks of 2008, corporate bond yields soared and job losses multiplied.[8] The official jobless rate carried on climbing, finally hitting a peak of 10.0% in October 2009.[9] The wider U-6 jobless rate

---

[6] Source: Bureau of Labor Statistics [BLS]. Total unemployment as percent of the civilian labour force [official unemployment rate] fell from 7.9% in December 2012 to 6.7% in December 2013. It dropped again to 6.6% in January 2014 before rising to 6.7% in February 2014.

[7] Source: BLS. Total employment for non-farm industries rose 2.331million between December 2012 and December 2013. This compares with an increase of 2.236million between December 2011 and December 2012, a rise of 2.083million between December 2010 and December 2011 and a gain of 1.058million between December 2009 and December 2010.

[8] Source: Merrill Lynch High Yield Cash Pay ($)/Thomson Reuters Datastream. Corporate bond yields [non-investment grade] jumped from 11.54% on 1 September 2008 to a high of 22.62% on 12 December 2008.

[9] Source: BLS, Total unemployment as percent of the civilian labour force [official unemployment rate].

rose to a high of 17.2%.[10] [See chart 2c] Including all the individuals that had left the labour force but still wanted work, the 'true' unemployment rate was even higher.[11]

The demise of Lehman Brothers was not the start of the credit crunch. Indeed, the deterioration in lending standards, particularly for sub-prime mortgages, had been evident through 2004 and 2005.[12] House prices had climbed remorselessly since the end of the *dotcom recession*[13] in Q3 2001, propelled higher by a rise in personal sector debt.[14] Fearful that the housing boom

---

[10] Source: BLS, U-6, Total unemployed, plus all persons marginally attached to the labour force, plus total employed part-time for economic reasons, as a per cent of the civilian labour force plus all persons marginally attached to the labour force. The U-6 rate reached 17.2% in April 2010.

[11] Source: BLS, Marginally attached to the labour force as a sub-total of total not in the labour force, persons who currently want a job. The latter rose from a 2007 low of 4.352million [October 2007, 2.8% of the civilian labour force, 16 years and over] to a high of 6.979million in August 2012 [4.5% of the civilian labour force]. By February 2014, this had dropped to 6.060million [3.9% of the civilian labour force].

[12] See *Foreclosures in the Subprime Market and Their Cost to Homeowners*, Center for Responsible Lending [CRL], December 2006. Many homeowners were running into trouble long before the target for the federal funds rate started to rise in June 2004. Based on an in-depth analysis of 1998 to 2004, the CRL found that as many as one in eight subprime loans had either ended or would end in foreclosure within five years. See *The Credit Crunch*, Graham Turner, Pluto Press, 2008, p. 59.

[13] Source: Bureau of Economic Analysis [BEA]. Subsequent upward revisions show that technically the economy did not enter a recession [i.e. contract for two consecutive quarters]. Real Gross Domestic Product fell by an annualised rate of 1.1% q/q in Q1 2001, rose 2.1% q/q in Q2 2001 and fell 1.2% q/q in Q3 2001, before expanding by 1.0% q/q in Q4 2001.

[14] Source: Federal Reserve, Flow of Funds [FoF], Financial Liabilities - Households & Non-profit Institutions and Bureau of Economic Analysis [BEA], Gross Domestic Product [GDP], current prices. The ratio of financial liabilities for households & non-profit institutions [personal sector] to GDP

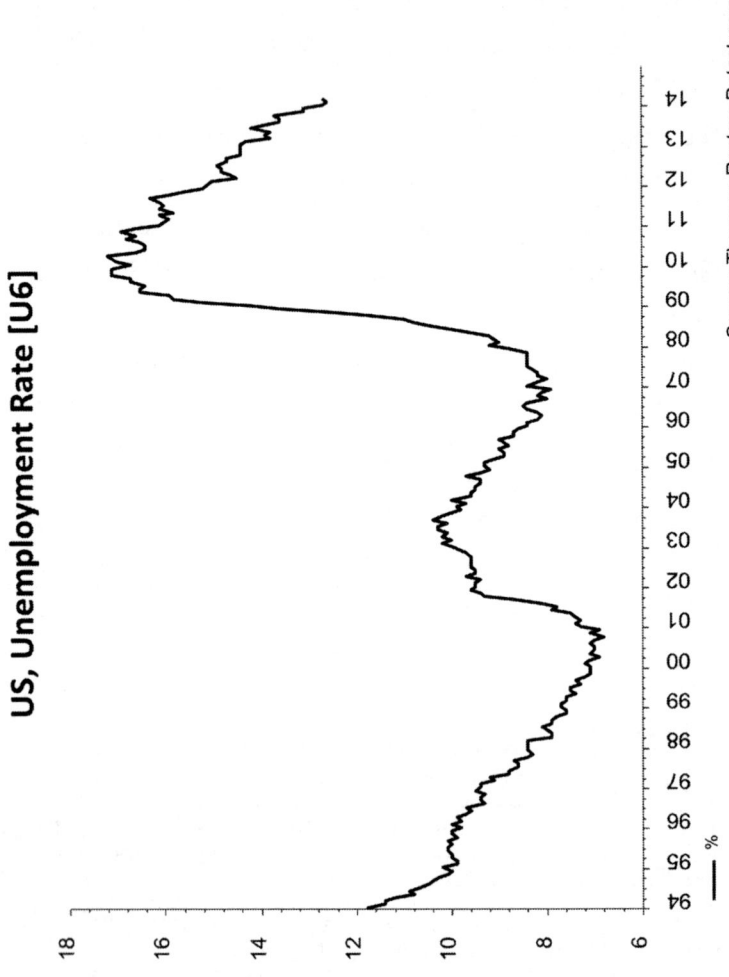

Chart 2c

might cause the US economy to overheat and push inflation above target, the Federal Reserve had been raising interest rates.[15] However, the steady rise in mortgage arrears began to take its toll. From early 2005 onwards, the number of unsold homes started to rise quickly.[16] Higher inventories could simply be a sign that more homeowners wanted to move and were putting their properties on the market. However, the number of homes listed for sale also began to rise sharply in relation to sales: the housing market was running into trouble.[17] [See chart 2d] Confirmation of the housing market peak came from a National Association of Home Builders survey in July 2005.[18] [See chart 2e] Four months later, the National Association of Realtors reported the first significant drop in house prices.[19] Other house price

---

rose from 73.7% in Q3 2001 to a record 99.0% in Q1 2008.

[15] See *Federal Reserve Press Release*, 29 June 2006. The committee decided to establish a target of 5.25% for the federal funds rate, up from 5.00%. This had risen from a low of 1.0% between 25 June 2003 and 30 June 2004.

[16] Source: NAR. Existing one-family and condominium homes available for sale climbed from 2.34million in January 2005 to 3.03million by December 2005. It eventually rose to a peak of 3.87million in January 2008.

[17] Source: NAR. Months' supply of existing family homes and condominiums for sale jumped from 3.9 in January 2005 to 5.3 in December 2005. It eventually climbed to a peak of 11.4 in November 2008.

[18] Source: National Association of Home Builders [NAHB]. June 2005 marked the peak of the NAHB housing market index. It dropped from 72.0 in June 2005 to 8.0 in January 2009.

[19] Source: NAR. The median price of existing one-family homes sold [seasonally adjusted by Thomson Reuters Datastream] fell from $230,200 in October 2005 to $227,400 in November 2005 [a decline of 1.2% m/m]. It continued to fall, dropping to $168,700 in April 2009.

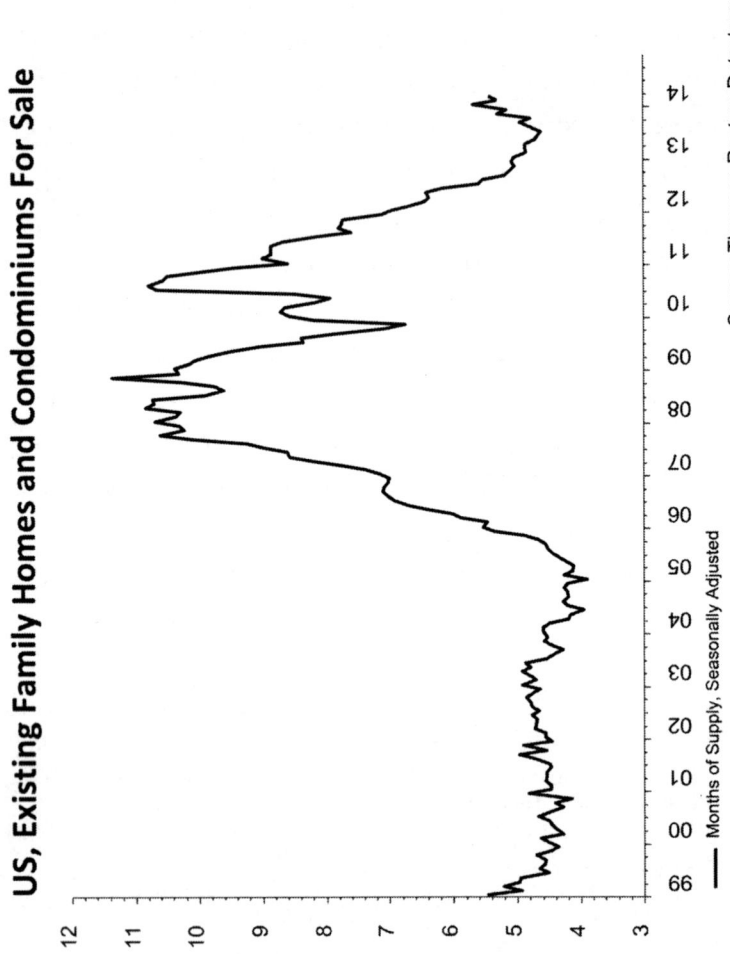

**US, Existing Family Homes and Condominiums For Sale**

Months of Supply, Seasonally Adjusted

Source: Thomson Reuters Datastream

Chart 2d

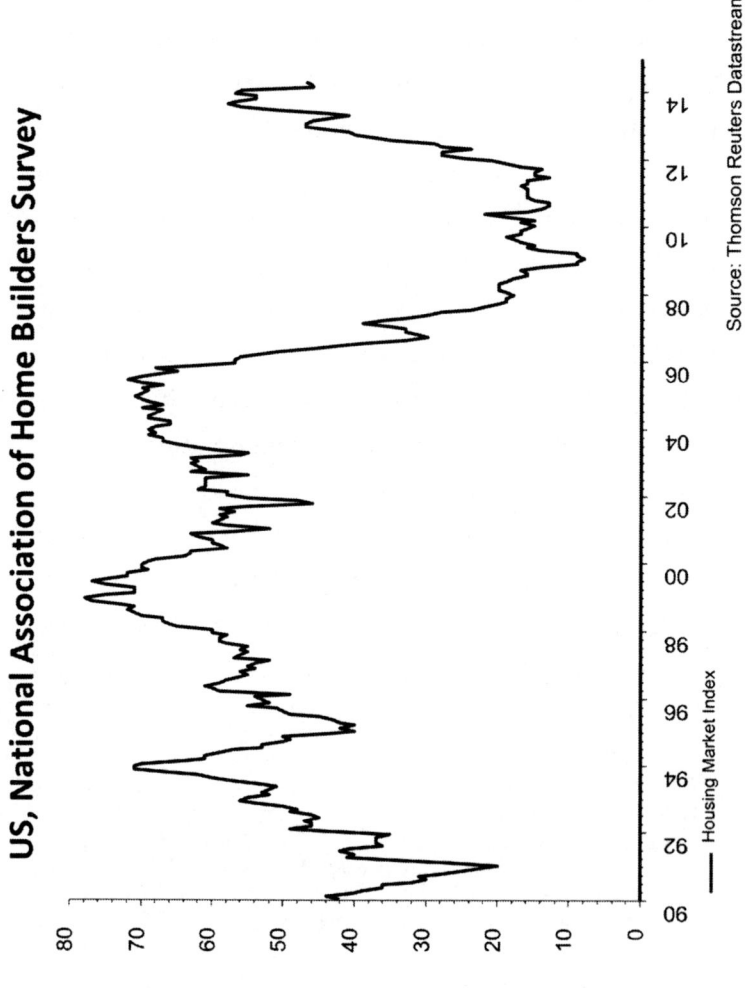

**US, National Association of Home Builders Survey**

Housing Market Index

Source: Thomson Reuters Datastream

Chart 2e

indicators began to turn down swiftly during the early months of 2006.[20]

The first interest rate cut did not arrive until 18 September 2007, when the FOMC lowered the federal funds target from 5.25% to 4.75%.[21] The FOMC was worried that the 'potential for significant further weakening in housing activity and home prices represented a downside risk to the economic outlook'.[22] Nevertheless, 'this policy decision was a close call' and the FOMC argued it was necessary to 'underscore the upside risks to inflation stemming from the recent increases in the prices of energy and other commodities'.[23] These concerns proved misplaced and were soon set aside as the FOMC cut interest rates again on 11 December 2007 to 4.25% and by a further 75 basis points to 3.5% on 22 January 2008.[24] Eight days later, the FOMC held an extraordinary meeting and pushed down the federal

---

[20] Source: S&P/Case-Shiller, CoreLogic and Federal Housing Finance Agency [FHFA]. The S&P/Case-Shiller Home Price Index, 20-City Composite [seasonally adjusted] peaked at 206.6 in April 2006 and fell to 140.8 in May 2009. The CoreLogic house price index reached a peak of 199.4 in April 2006 and dropped to 141.1 in February 2010. The FHFA House Price Index was slower to turn. The index hit a record high of 227.3 in April 2007 before dropping to 194.3 in September 2009.

[21] See *Federal Reserve Press Release*, 18 September 2007.

[22] See *Minutes of the Federal Open Market Committee [FOMC]*, October 30-31 2007, p. 6.

[23] Ibid. p. 7-8.

[24] See *Federal Reserve Press Release*, 22 January 2008.

funds target by another 50 basis points, to 3.0%.[25]

After the investment bank Bear Stearns ran into trouble in the spring of 2008, interest rates were cut twice, by 75 basis points to 2.25% on 18 March 2008 and to 2.0% on 30 April.[26] Thereafter, the FOMC sat on its hands: interest rates were left unchanged as house prices continued to slide.[27] The collapse of Lehman Brothers eventually forced the FOMC into action again. The target for the federal funds rate was slashed to 0.0% - 0.25% in three consecutive meetings as interest rates hit the *Zero Lower Bound*.[28] [See chart 2f]

The Federal Reserve then embarked upon a policy [*large-scale asset purchases*] that was central to reversing the slump in 1932 during the Great Depression [see Chapter 4]. However, the *initial* implementation of

---

[25] Ibid. 30 January 2008.

[26] See *Federal Reserve Press Release*, 18 March 2008 and 30 April 2008. On 16 March 2008, Bear Stearns was forced to sign a 'merger agreement' with JP Morgan Chase in a stock swap worth just $2 a share. The terms were subsequently changed and a final price of $10 per share was agreed. 'To help facilitate the deal, the Federal Reserve is taking the extraordinary step of providing as much as $30billion in financing for Bear Stearns's less-liquid assets, such as mortgage securities that the firm has been unable to sell'. See *J.P. Morgan Buys Bear in Fire Sale, As Fed Widens Credit to Avert Crisis*. http://online.wsj.com/news/articles/SB120569598608739825 [accessed 6 June 2014].

[27] The next reduction in the FOMC's target for the federal funds rate did not occur until 8 October 2008.

[28] See *Federal Reserve Press Release*, 8 October 2008, 29 October 2008 and 16 December 2008. The FOMC reduced its target for the federal funds rate from 2.0% to 1.5% on 8 October 2008, from 1.5% to 1.0% on 29 October 2008 and to a range of 0.0% - 0.25% on 16 December 2008.

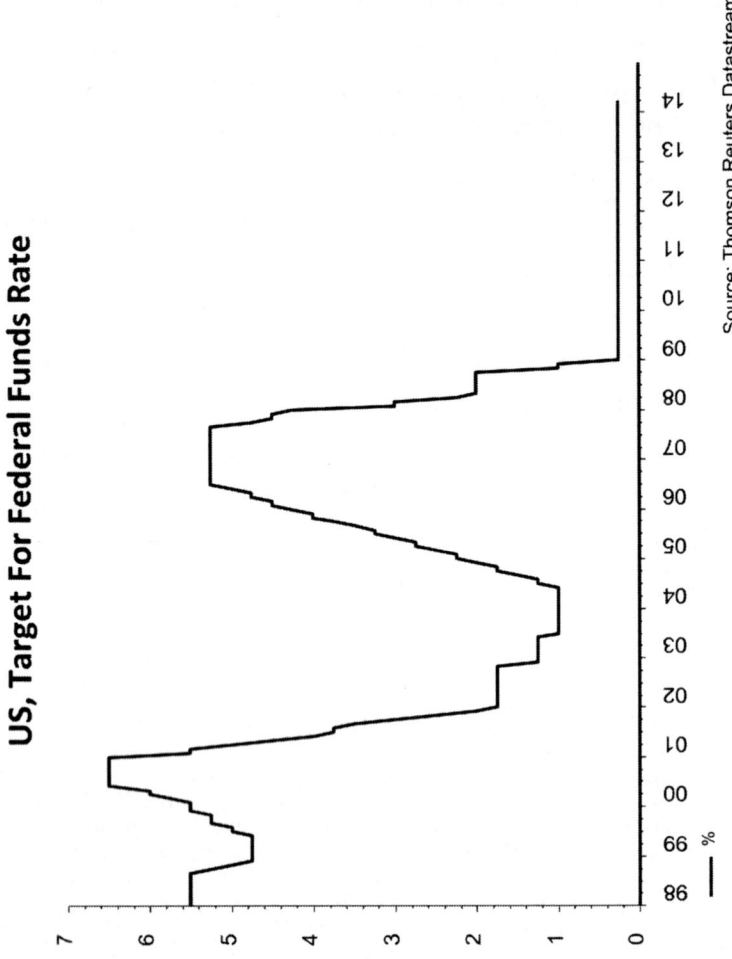

Chart 2f

quantitative easing was flawed. The economy did emerge from recession in the third quarter of 2009.[29] For Keynesians, this was vindication: higher government spending and tax cuts had, it appeared, worked. For the FOMC, the turnaround in US economy was proof that quantitative easing is *always* an effective monetary policy tool in response to a deep recession.

The subsequent recovery in the US economy did not validate either of these claims. The FOMC failed to recognise that the tactical implementation of quantitative easing was absolutely critical. It is important to dig deeper and consider whether a different approach to monetary and fiscal policy might have resulted in a faster economic recovery. Indeed, it is possible to argue that the Obama stimulus was counter-productive and undermined the efficacy of quantitative easing. Any increase in real GDP or employment as a direct result of the fiscal stimulus needed to be set against the damage inflicted by the rise in borrowing costs that occurred in the spring of 2009, following confirmation of the fiscal stimulus.[30]

---

[29] Source: BEA. Real Gross Domestic Product rose by an annualised rate of 1.4% q/q in Q3 2009, following four consecutive declines totalling 4.6%.

[30] Source: Thomson Reuters Datastream and MBA. The US Treasury Benchmark Bond 10-Year Yield climbed from a low of 2.08% on 12 December 2008 to 2.85% on 13 February 2009, in anticipation of the American Recovery and Reinvestment Act of 2009. It subsequently climbed to 3.93% on 10 June 2009. The Conventional Mortgage Contract Rate, 30-Year, rose from a low of 4.61% in the fourth week of March 2009 to a high of 5.57% in the second week of June 2009. See *Obama sets expansive goal for jobs*, Washington Post, 23 November 2008, and *Obama expands goals of stimulus*, Financial Times, 22 December 2008.

The assumption that higher government spending and tax cuts will necessarily generate an economic recovery does not follow from *The General Theory*. Furthermore, an alternative technique - the reverse tap - could have ensured that quantitative easing was much more effective [see Appendix I].

## Keynesians Proved Wrong

The resilience of the economy in 2013 in particular provided confirmation that a tighter fiscal policy need not derail a recovery and might even prove constructive. Following the initial surge in government spending in 2009, fiscal policy became restrictive. Federal government spending began to fall in $ terms during 2010. [See chart 2g] After a brief rise in 2011, it stagnated again in 2012.[31] It began to contract more quickly in 2013, as a stalemate between Democrats and Republicans led to automatic spending cuts alongside higher taxes.[32] During the latter

---

[31] Source: US Treasury. Federal government budget outlays fell 1.8% y/y during fiscal year 2010 [ending in September], rose 4.1% y/y in fiscal year 2011, dropped 1.7% y/y in fiscal year 2012 and shrank by 2.4% y/y in fiscal year 2013.

[32] The 'fiscal cliff' referred to the 'expiration of certain tax policies that will lead to an increase in tax revenue and the automatic spending reductions scheduled to occur under current law [sequestration]'. Source: http://www.cbo.gov/publication/43961 [accessed 6 June 2014]. The tax increases came into effect on 1 January 2013 and the sequestration came into effect on 1 March 2013. The Congressional Budget Office claimed that in the absence of the fiscal tightening, 'economic growth in 2013 would be roughly 1½ points faster than the 1.4 percent real (inflation adjusted) growth that the agency now projects, under current laws, from the fourth quarter of calendar 2012 to the fourth quarter of 2013'. Source: BEA. Despite the tighter fiscal policy, real

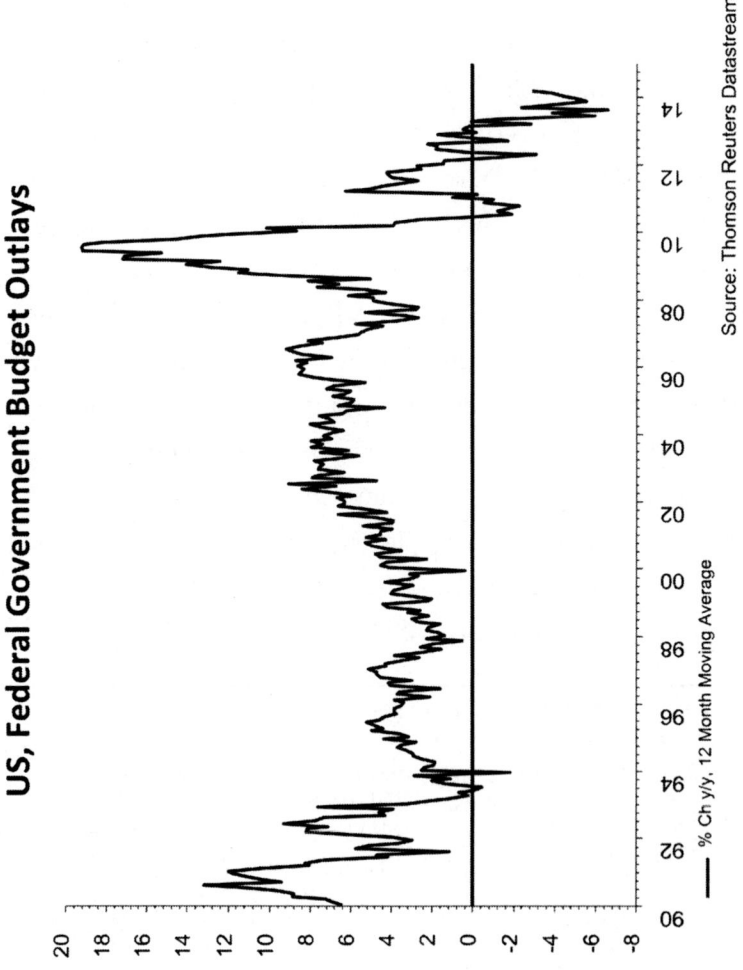

**US, Federal Government Budget Outlays**

% Ch y/y, 12 Month Moving Average

Source: Thomson Reuters Datastream

Chart 2g

months of 2012 and throughout 2013, there were repeated warnings that a tighter fiscal policy would precipitate an economic downturn. However, low bond yields - helped by the falling budget deficit - proved instrumental in driving a recovery in the housing market. Indeed, the Keynesian belief that fiscal policy is the optimal strategy for reflation has been discredited by the trajectory of house prices since the spring of 2009.[33]

The budget deficit was falling quickly too because monetary policy was driving an economic recovery, pushing tax receipts up and reversing some of the losses that had undermined the government finances in the first place.[34] [See chart 2h] On 14 May 2013, the Congressional Budget Office revised its projection for the fiscal year 2012 Federal deficit down more than expected from $845.0billion to $642.0billion, or 4.0% of GDP.[35]

---

GDP rose 2.5% y/y in Q4 2013, 1.1 percentage points faster than the projection of the Congressional Budget Office.

[33] Source: NAR. The median price of existing one-family homes sold did not reach a low until 29 months [July 2011] after the American Recovery and Reinvestment Act of 2009 was passed by Congress [13 February 2009].

[34] Source: US Treasury. The Federal budget deficit fell 37.5% y/y to $680.3billion in fiscal year 2013 [year ending in September 2013]. Part of the increase was due to exceptional dividends from Fannie Mae and Freddie Mac. Excluding these and other Treasury items, the deficit would have fallen 29.2% y/y for fiscal year 2013. Tax receipts were up 13.3% y/y, while spending fell 2.4% y/y [excluding other Treasury expenditure which includes negative outlays in the form of Government-Sponsored Enterprises dividends, spending rose 1.1% y/y].

[35] See *Updated Budget Projections: Fiscal Years 2013 to 2023*, Congressional Budget Office [CBO] Press Release, 14 May 2013. The original CBO estimate for the federal deficit in fiscal year 2013 [year ending in September 2013] was $845.0billion, but this was revised down to $642.0billion. Note the final

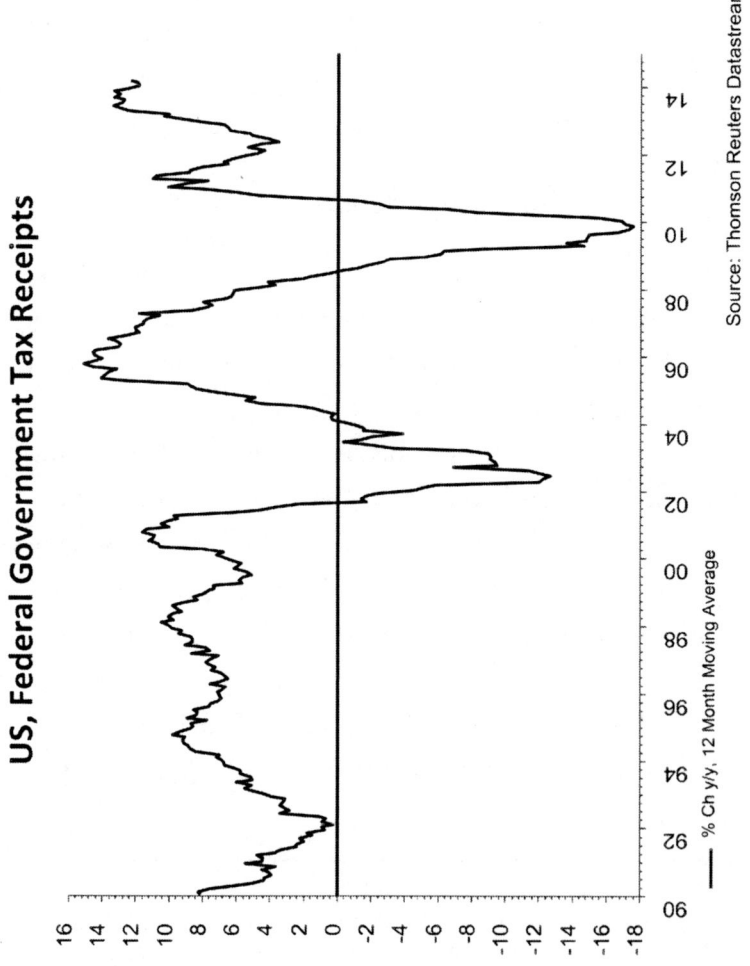

**US, Federal Government Tax Receipts**

% Ch y/y, 12 Month Moving Average

Source: Thomson Reuters Datastream

Chart 2h

[See chart 2i] A correct application of the central bank's monetary tools could underpin an improvement in the fiscal deficit. Furthermore, a tighter fiscal policy could - if the requisite central bank action has been pursued *a priori* - reinforce the economic recovery.

## QE1, QE2 and the Mistakes

Loose fiscal policy in 2009 may have undermined the Federal Reserve's efforts to engineer economic recovery by increasing the liquidity preference of investors and pushing bond yields higher. However, the FOMC's tactics need to be questioned too. The cost of borrowing for homeowners had fallen following the announcement of QE1 on 25 November 2008. The Federal Reserve announced that it would buy $600billion of mortgage bonds.[36] However, soon after the FOMC announced the second instalment of QE1 on 18 March 2009, mortgage rates began to climb again. A further $850billion would be used to buy mortgage bonds and $300billion to buy

---

outcome was higher. See previous footnote.

[36] See *Federal Reserve Press Release*, 25 November 2008. The Federal Reserve announced, 'that it will initiate a program to purchase the direct obligations of housing-related Government-Sponsored Enterprises - Fannie Mae, Freddie Mac, and the Federal Home Loan Banks - and mortgage-backed securities [MBS] backed by Fannie Mae, Freddie Mac, and Ginnie Mae'. It added, 'Purchases of up to $100billion in Government-Sponsored Enterprises direct obligations under the program will be conducted with the Federal Reserve's primary dealers'. In addition, 'Purchases of up to $500billion in MBS will be conducted by asset managers'.

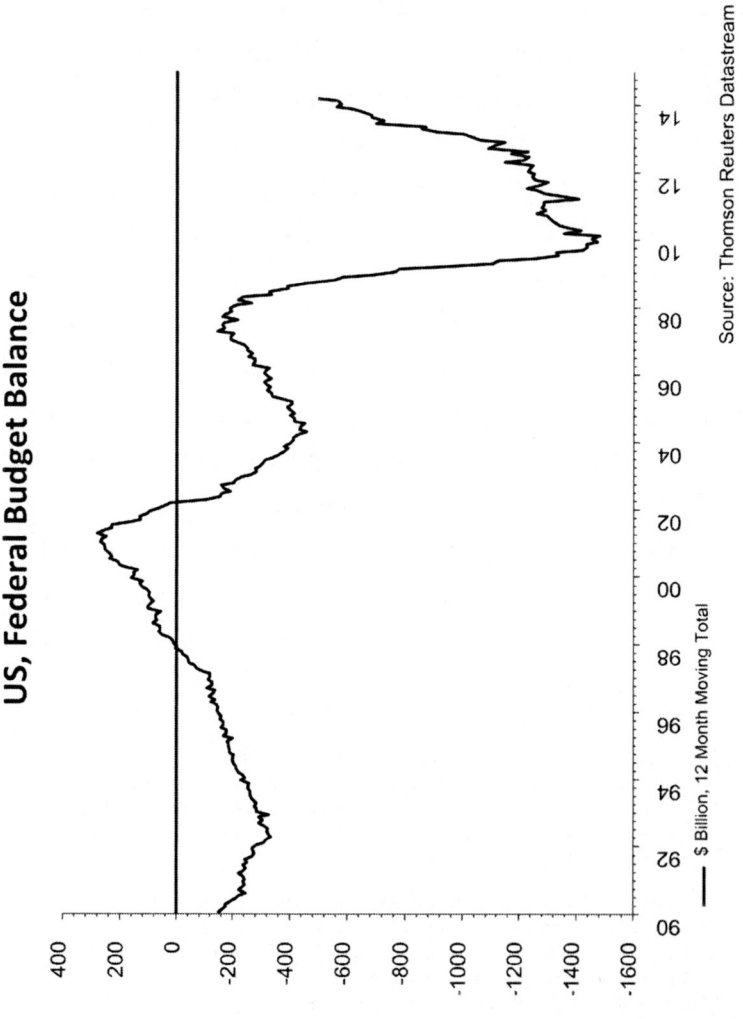

US, Federal Budget Balance

Source: Thomson Reuters Datastream

$ Billion, 12 Month Moving Total

Chart 2i

Treasuries.[37] Despite these purchases, mortgage rates remained far too high in 2009 to arrest the slide in house prices. By early June 2009, mortgage rates had fallen by little more than 1.0% from the highs of 2008.[38] It is instructive to compare this to the much milder *Savings & Loans crisis* of the early 1990s. On this occasion, a more proactive monetary policy - including a bigger fall in short term interest rates - saw mortgage rates fall by 4 per cent between 1990 and 1993.[39] [See charts 2j and 2k]

The surge in government spending during 2009 created a false impression of the economic recovery. Officially, the recession ended in the third quarter of 2009. The US appeared to be enjoying a sustainable recovery. The FOMC chair, Ben Bernanke, was notably upbeat. In August 2009, he said: 'US mortgage rates

---

[37] Ibid. 18 March 2009. The Committee 'decided today to increase the size of the Federal Reserve's balance sheet further by purchasing up to an additional $750billion of agency mortgage-backed securities, bringing its total purchases of these securities to up to $1.25trillion this year, and to increase its purchases of agency debt this year by up to $100billion to a total of up to $200billion. Moreover, to help improve conditions in private credit markets, the Committee decided to purchase up to $300billion of longer-term Treasury securities over the next six months'.

[38] Source: MBA. The Conventional Mortgage Contract Rate, 30-Year, of 5.57% for the second week of June 2009 compares with a peak of 6.59% reached in the fourth week of July 2008. For June 2009, the average of 5.42% compares with an average of 6.41% in July 2008. The average for the second half of 2009 was 5.05%. This compares with an average of 6.09% in the second half of 2008.

[39] Source: MBA. The Conventional Mortgage Contract Rate, 30-Year [monthly] fell from a high of 10.56% in May 1990 to 6.73% in October 1993. The federal funds rate fell from 9.8% [monthly average] in June 1989 to 3.0% in September 1992 [target].

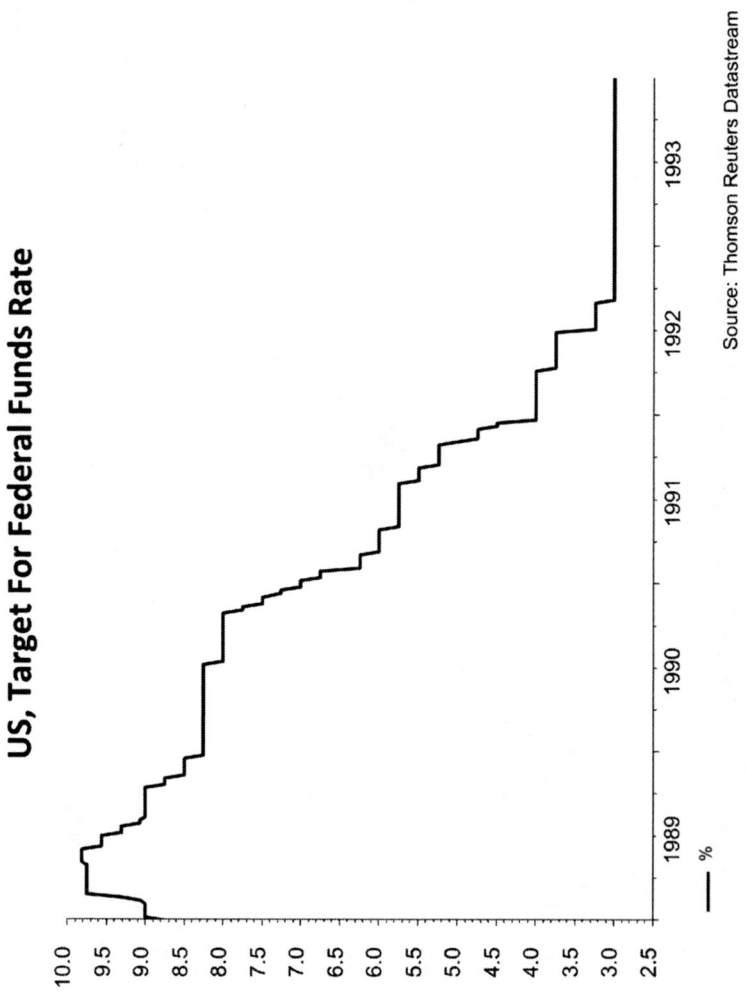

**US, Target For Federal Funds Rate**

— %

Source: Thomson Reuters Datastream

Chart 2j

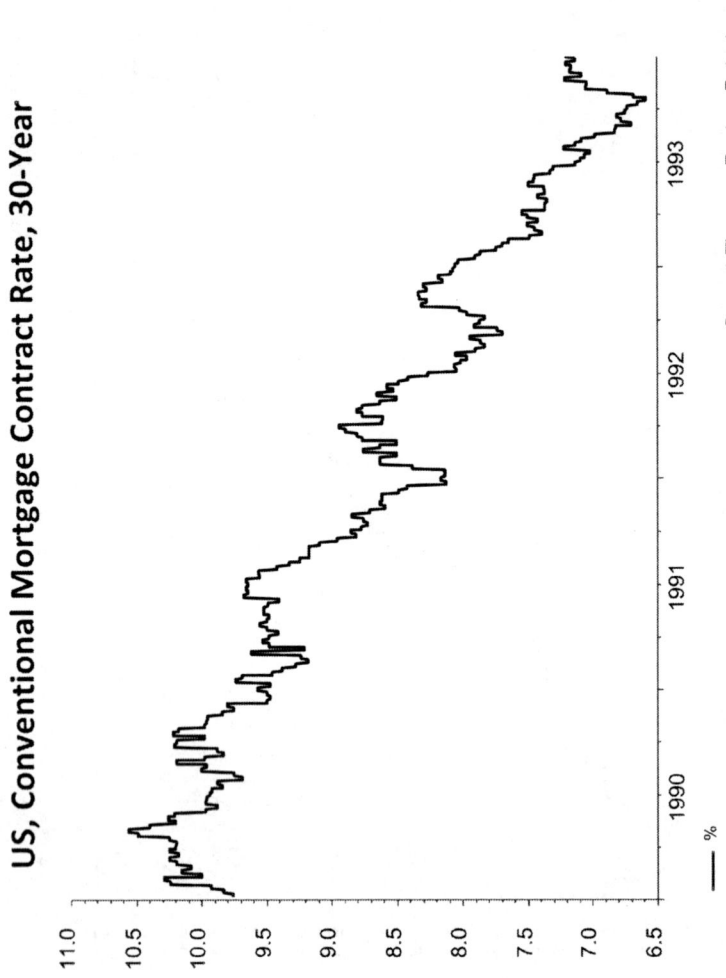

**US, Conventional Mortgage Contract Rate, 30-Year**

Source: Thomson Reuters Datastream

Chart 2k

have declined markedly since the fall [of 2008]'. He concluded: 'After contracting sharply over the past year, economic activity appears to be levelling out, both in the United States and abroad, and the prospects for a return to growth in the near term appear good'.[40]

However, bond yields were rising again when the purpose of quantitative easing should have been to drive them lower. Specifically, the FOMC's explicit desire to exit from quantitative easing was counterproductive. Soon after the Federal Reserve announced its first round of bond purchases, FOMC officials began to publicly discuss policy options for reversing the liquidity side-effects of quantitative easing.[41] The Federal Reserve was

---

[40] See *Reflections on a Year of Crisis*, Ben Bernanke, Federal Reserve Bank of Kansas City's Annual Economic Symposium, Jackson Hole, Wyoming, 21 August 2009.

[41] See *Central Bank Exit Policies*, Donald Kohn, 30 September 2009. See *Federal Reserve Policies to Ease Credit and Their Implications for the Fed's Balance Sheet*, Ben Bernanke, 18 February 2009. Mr Bernanke tried to appease critics of quantitative easing: 'Moreover, other tools are available or can be developed to improve control of the federal funds rate during the exit stage. For example, the Treasury could resume its recent practice of issuing supplementary financing bills and placing the funds with the Federal Reserve; the issuance of these bills effectively drains reserves from the banking system, thereby improving monetary control. As we consider new programs or the expansion of old ones, the Federal Reserve will carefully weigh the implications for the exit strategy. And we will take all necessary actions to ensure that the unwinding of our programs is accomplished smoothly and in a timely way, consistent with meeting our obligation to foster maximum employment and price stability'.
See *Frequently Asked Questions*, Ben Bernanke, 7 December, 2009. Mr Bernanke noted that 'we have been giving careful thought to our exit strategy. We are confident that we have all the tools necessary to withdraw monetary stimulus in a timely and effective way'. Furthermore, 'Operationally, an important tool for adjusting the stance of monetary policy will be the authority, granted to us by the Congress last year, to pay banks interest on

failing to demonstrate the necessary clear commitment to *reflation*. It was an early indication that the *signalling channel* from quantitative easing was being ignored.

## A Tax Credit for Homebuyers

The drop in house prices from late 2005 onwards was ultimately responsible for the punishing bank failures that rocked the US in 2008. Any rebound in the housing market would understandably be seized upon as evidence of a broader turnaround in the economy. After hitting an interim low in April 2009, house prices began to turn higher.[42] However, this was an artefact of the Obama fiscal stimulus, which proved unsustainable. First-time homebuyers were eligible for an $8,000 tax credit for all properties bought between April 2008 [it was retroactively applied] and December that year.[43] The tax

---

balances they hold at the Federal Reserve'. In addition, 'Additional upward pressure on short-term interest rates can be achieved by measures to reduce the supply of funds that banks have available to lend to each other. We have a number of tools to accomplish this. For example, through the use of a short-term funding method known as reverse repurchase agreements, we can act directly to reduce the quantity of reserves held by the banking system'. See also *The Fed's Exit Strategy*, Ben Bernanke, Opinion, Wall Street Journal, 21 July 2009 and *The Federal Reserve's Balance Sheet: An Update*, Ben Bernanke, Federal Reserve Board Conference on Key Developments in Monetary Policy, Washington, 8 October 2009.

[42] Source: NAR. The median price of existing one-family homes sold [seasonally adjusted by Thomson Reuters Datastream] hit a low of $168,665 in April 2009 - a fall of 26.7% since the high of $230,200 in October 2005. It then rose to $174,900 over the following twelve months, an increase of 3.7%, before turning down again.

[43] President Obama signed the First-Time Home Buyer Credit into law in

rebates led to a sharp increase in home buying. Buoyed by this superficial recovery, the US administration extended the tax credit until the end of June 2010 and widened the eligibility.[44] House prices carried on rising in the early months of 2010. However, on 28 August 2010, the National Association of Realtors published its monthly report for existing home sales: this confirmed a sharp downturn in turnover - sales of existing homes had tumbled 29.3% between May and July 2010.[45] [See chart 21] The swift reversal over two months underlined the distortion created by the tax credit. House prices immediately turned down again. The S&P/Case-Shiller index reached a mid-cycle peak in May 2010, coinciding with the top for sales.[46] According to the National

---

13 February 2009. The tax credit allowed first-time buyers to claim 10% of the purchase price of the home [initially up to a maximum of $7,500 but later raised to $8,000]. The initial deadline of 1 December 2009 was subsequently extended on 6 November 2009 to include purchases up to 30 June 2010. See *First-Time Homebuyer Credit Questions and Answers: Basic Information*, Internal Revenue Service (IRS), http://www.irs.gov/uac/First-Time-Homebuyer-Credit-Questions-and-Answers:-Basic-Information [accessed 6 June 2014]. See *About the First-Time Home Buyer Tax Credit*, Elizabeth Weintraub, http://homebuying.about.com/od/buyingahome/a/21808_taxcredit. htm [accessed 6 June 2014].

[44] See *About the First-Time Home Buyer Tax Credit*, Elizabeth Weintraub, http://homebuying.about.com/od/buyingahome/a/21808_taxcredit.htm [accessed 6 June 2014]. President Obama announced the tax credit would be extended until June 2010 for borrowers entering into a contract by 30 April 2010, along with a smaller credit for homeowners who had lived in their properties for 5 of the previous 8 years.

[45] Source: NAR. Existing home sales, single family and condominiums fell from 4.880million [annualised] in May 2010 to 3.450million [annualised] in July 2010.

[46] Source: S&P/Case-Shiller, Home Price Index, 20-City Composite

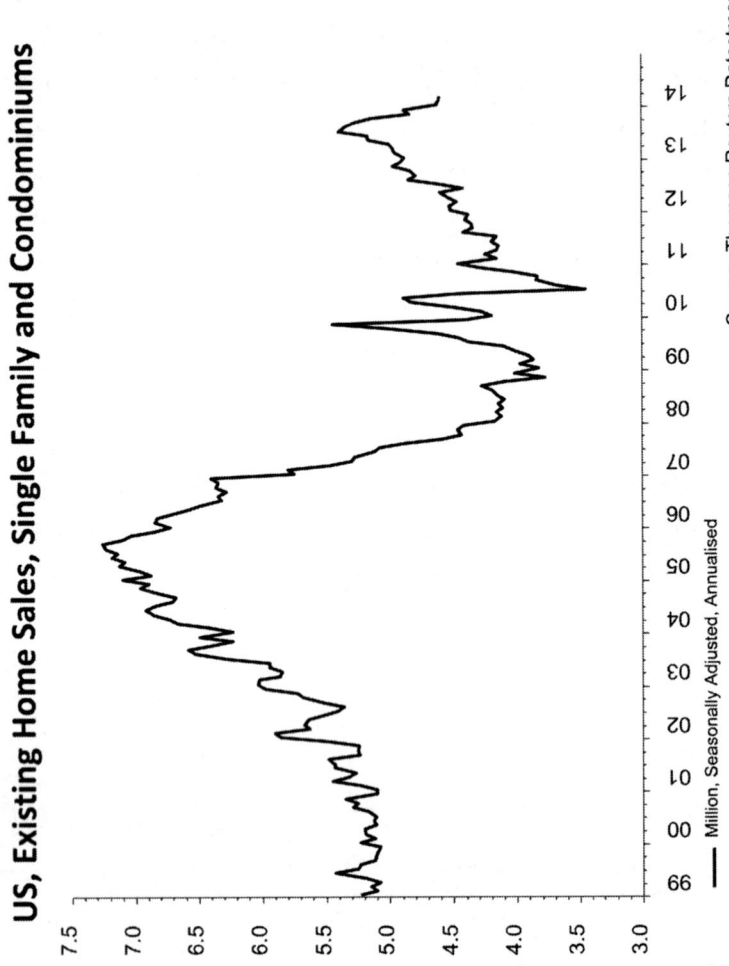

**US, Existing Home Sales, Single Family and Condominiums**

Source: Thomson Reuters Datastream

— Million, Seasonally Adjusted, Annualised

Chart 2l

Association of Realtors, house prices peaked a month earlier.[47]

The US administration's attempt to reflate the housing market with fiscal policy was gaining little traction. The economy stumbled over the summer of 2010. The Federal Reserve was forced to act: on 3 November 2010, the FOMC announced that it would buy a further $600billion of longer-term Treasury securities by the end of the second quarter in 2011, equivalent to $75billion per month [QE2].[48] Mortgage rates fell in anticipation of QE2. However, the drop in borrowing costs again proved short-lived: mortgage rates started to climb soon after the Federal Reserve announcement. By early 2011, 30-year mortgage rates had risen back above 5.0%.[49] The number of homeowners in arrears was still more than double the level witnessed in early 2008, when Bear Stearns failed.[50]

---

[seasonally adjusted]. The S&P/Case-Shiller index rose 4.6% between May 2009 and May 2010 and started to fall again in June 2010, dropping 0.1% m/m. It then fell for another 20 consecutive months.

[47] Source: NAR. The median price of existing one-family homes sold [seasonally adjusted by Thomson Reuters Datastream] rose from $168,700 in April 2009 to a peak of $174,900 in April 2010. It fell 2.6% m/m in May 2010.

[48] See *Federal Reserve Press Release*, 3 November 2010. The Committee announced that it 'intends to purchase a further $600billion of longer-term Treasury securities by the end of the second quarter of 2011, a pace of about $75billion per month'.

[49] Source: MBA. The Conventional Mortgage Contract Rate, 30-Year, rose to 5.13% in the first week of February 2011, up from 4.21% in the second week of October 2010.

[50] Source: MBA. The Residential Mortgage Loans, 90+ Days Delinquent, was 3.62% of all borrowers in Q1 2011, compared with 1.63% in Q1 2008.

House prices carried on dropping, falling below the April 2009 'trough' reached in the immediate aftermath of the Lehman Brothers failure.[51]

## Rate Targeting: Putting the Recovery on Track

After the mistakes with QE1 and QE2, the FOMC realised that it had to change tactics. Too much emphasis had been placed on the supply channel from bond purchases and too little on the signalling channel. The bulk of the Federal Reserve's academic research at the time emphasised the supply channel.[52] However, the decline in bond yields in anticipation of QE1 and QE2, and the subsequent rise after both programmes were implemented, showed that the signalling channel was more important. More recent Federal Reserve research has supported this assessment.[53] In August 2011, the FOMC shifted its policy stance to one that was more aligned with the monetary policy tools advocated by

---

[51] Source: NAR, The median price of existing one-family homes sold [seasonally adjusted by Thomson Reuters Datastream]. The median price fell from $174,900 in April 2010 to $167,700 in February 2011 and carried on sliding for another 16 months.

[52] See for example A *Preferred-Habitat Model of the Term Structure of Interest Rates*, Vayanos & Vila, November, National Bureau of Economic Research, Working Paper 15487, November 2009 and Bond Supply and Excess Bond Returns, Vayanos & Greenwood, January 2010.

[53] See for example *The Signalling Channel for Federal Reserve Bond Purchases*, Michael D. Bauer, Glenn D. Rudebusch, Federal Reserve Bank of San Francisco, Working Paper series, April 2013.

Keynes. By targeting short-term interest rate expectations - instead of focusing on the supply channel from bond purchases - the FOMC began to affect greater control on the economy.

The FOMC shifted to an alternative and more effective strategy - *forward rate guidance* or *rate targeting*. This was an attempt to influence borrowing costs by leaning on market expectations to tackle liquidity preference. On 9 August 2011, the FOMC declared its intention to keep the federal funds target at 0.0% - 0.25% through until 'mid-2013'.[54] It was the first time that the FOMC had specified the duration of low short-term interest rate. In previous statements, the FOMC had stated that it would keep the federal funds target at 0.0% -0.25% 'for an extended period'.[55]

This *calendar guidance* would provide additional assurance for financial markets. The FOMC was attempting to reduce the uncertainty or ambiguity over its commitment to low interest rates. The FOMC could change its mind at any time if the economy improved

---

[54] See *Federal Reserve Press Release*, 9 August 2011. The FOMC announced that the 'economic conditions - including low rates of resource utilization and a subdued outlook for inflation over the medium run - are likely to warrant exceptionally low levels for the federal funds rate at least through mid-2013'.

[55] Ibid. 18 March 2009. The FOMC decided that it 'will maintain the target range for the federal funds rate at 0 to 1/4 percent and anticipates that economic conditions are likely to warrant exceptionally low levels of the federal funds rate for an extended period'. The FOMC used the phrase 'extended period' in all press releases between 18 March 2009 and 22 June 2011.

and inflation rose too quickly. The statement merely expressed the FOMC's expectation of where the federal funds rate target would be by the middle of 2013 based on its economic projections. Nevertheless, the policy shift had an immediate impact. The implied interest rate for the 3-month Eurodollar contract, June 2013, fell 25 basis points [0.25%] in just one day.[56] [See chart 2m]

Even though the federal funds target rate had been held at 0.0% - 0.25% since 16 December 2008, financial markets had repeatedly considered the possibility that interest rates would rise before too long. The tendency of financial markets to 'bet' on a rise in short-term interest rates had been a major problem, slowing the economic recovery. Inflated expectations for short-term rates would also filter through to higher Treasury yields and, of course, dearer mortgages.

The failure to control interest rate expectations lies at the heart of the *Liquidity Preference Theory*, one of Keynes's most important insights. However, during the first two rounds of quantitative easing [QE1] and [QE2], the FOMC did not recognise the significance of guiding interest rate expectations. FOMC officials failed to comprehend the importance of liquidity preference.

---

[56] Source: Thomson Reuters Datastream. The implied interest rate for the 3-month Eurodollar contract, June 2013, fell from 0.84% on 8 August 2011 to 0.59% on 9 August 2011 in response to the Federal Reserve Press Release on 9 August 2011.

# US, Implied Interest Rate for the 3-month Eurodollar Contract

**June 2013**

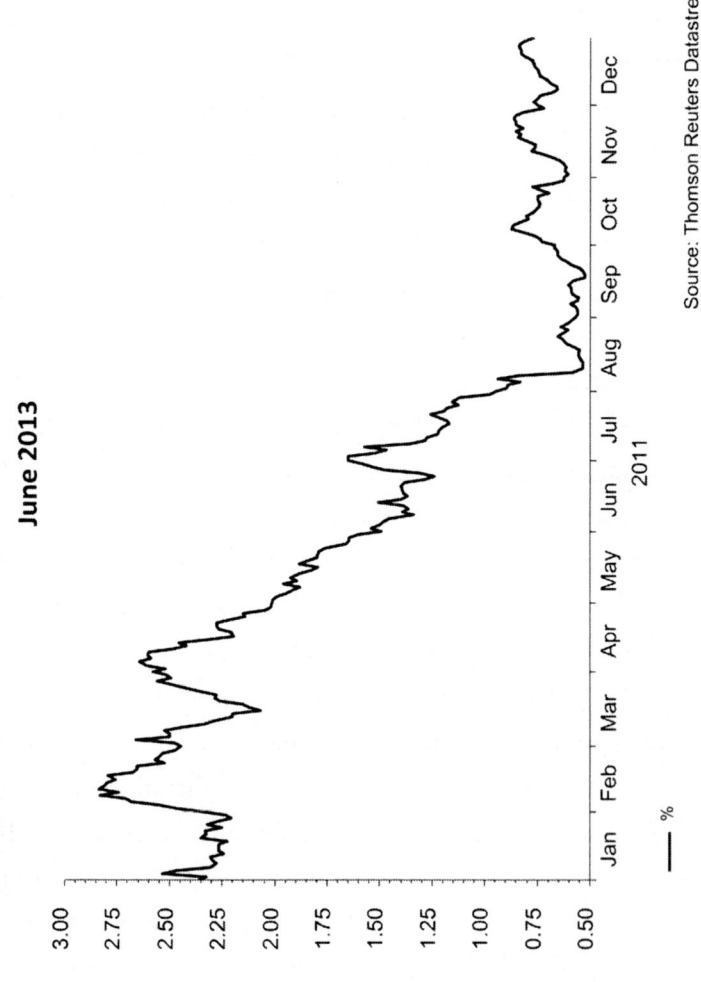

Source: Thomson Reuters Datastream

Chart 2m

103

Treasury yields rose despite the bond purchases. The critical signalling effects were at best mixed, more often than not contradictory. As a result, house prices resumed their slide once the tax credit for home buyers had expired, pushing more homeowners into negative equity.

The precise reasons for the FOMC's shift to rate targeting are intriguing. The Federal Reserve had come under fierce political pressure for pursuing quantitative easing.[57] A number of critics cited the increase in the Federal Reserve's balance sheet. They warned that the US central bank could incur significant capital losses should Treasury yields rise. Other sceptics of quantitative easing fretted over the risks that 'printing money' would lead to higher inflation. The FOMC was also fuelling an undesirable increase in risk-taking through its purchases of Treasuries, claimed others. Furthermore, quantitative easing made it too easy for the US administration to fund its budget deficit. The Federal Reserve was interfering with an important market mechanism, which in the past had been an effective discipline for controlling profligate governments. This might precipitate a crisis in the bond market, tipping the economy back into recession. In summary: quantitative easing would fail to deliver a

---

[57] See Rick Perry: 'quantitative easing akin to treason', The Guardian, 16 August 2011. Rick Perry, the former Republican presidential nominee for the 2012 election, declared that 'Printing more money to play politics at this particular time is almost treacherous, or treasonous, in my opinion'.

sustainable economic recovery. As we shall see, much of the criticism was misguided.

## Operation Twist

The shift to forward rate guidance was followed by *Operation Twist* [*maturity extension programme*], another policy specifically geared to the control of interest rate expectations.[58] Operation Twist was not a new policy weapon. It had been actively promoted by Keynes and used to considerable effect in 1934 [see Chapter 4]. This 'bond switch' was another way of sending a strong signal to financial markets. In one respect, it showed that the FOMC was unbowed by critics. Selling shorter-dated Treasuries and buying bonds with longer maturities potentially increased the risks to the Federal Reserve's balance sheet. If yields did rise by an equal amount across all maturities, the possible losses could now be greater.[59]

---

[58] See *Federal Reserve Press Release*, 21 September 2011. The FOMC announced that it would 'extend the average maturity of its holdings of securities. The Committee intends to purchase, by the end of June 2012, $400billion of Treasury securities with remaining maturities of 6 years to 30 years and to sell an equal amount of Treasury securities with remaining maturities of 3 years or less. This program should put downward pressure on longer-term interest rates and help make broader financial conditions more accommodative'.

[59] These potential losses would only be realised if the Federal Reserve sold its securities [at a loss]. The Federal Reserve Bank does not have to mark to market such instruments as with the case of broker dealers. Indeed, 'Under Federal Reserve accounting rules, a Federal Reserve Bank realises gains or losses on a security only when the security is sold'. See *The Federal Reserve's Balance Sheet and Earnings: A primer and projections*, Seth B. Carpenter et al, Finance and Economics Discussion Series, Divisions of Research & Statistics

If longer term bond yields rose more quickly - or the yield curve steepened - the losses for the Federal Reserve could multiply.

In truth, Operation Twist underpinned the shift to forward rate guidance announced six weeks earlier. The Federal Reserve was demonstrating its commitment to low interest rates. Any perceived threat to its balance sheet was insignificant when set against the Federal Reserve's greater determination to secure economic recovery. Interest rates and hence Treasury yields were unlikely to rise for some time. When they did, the increase might be slow. Furthermore, there was no assumption that the Federal Reserve would be obliged to sell the bonds. Indeed, the FOMC would eventually announce that it had no intention of selling any of its mortgage-backed securities or Treasuries.[60]

There might not be any losses if one took into account the running yield on these bonds or the coupon payments.[61] The Federal Reserve funded its purchase

---

and Monetary Affairs, Federal Reserve Board, Washington, D.C., January 2013, p. 14.

[60] See *Federal Reserve Press Release*, 21 September 2011. The Committee announced, 'To help support conditions in mortgage markets, the Committee will now reinvest principal payments from its holdings of agency debt and agency mortgage-backed securities in agency mortgage-backed securities. In addition, the Committee will maintain its existing policy of rolling over maturing Treasury securities at auction'. For Treasury securities, the Committee decided to reinvest principal payments at the 12 December 2012 meeting.

[61] See *Transcript of Chairman Bernanke's Press Conference*, 18 December

of Treasuries and mortgage-backed securities by the creation of cheap reserves. Buying longer-dated bonds through Operation Twist increased the more immediate profitability of holding these assets on the Federal Reserve balance sheet.

Ultimately, Operation Twist and forward rate guidance were exercises in cajoling market expectations and tackling the critical problem of liquidity preference. The policies worked. Interest rate expectations had already fallen during the spring and summer of 2011 in response to the latest economic stall, and the renewed slide in property and equity prices.[62] However, following the shift to rate targeting and the adoption of Operation Twist, there was no sudden reversal in bond yields, a marked contrast to the experience of QE1 and QE2. During the final weeks of 2011, mortgage rates fell to new lows, with the 30-year benchmark eventually dipping below 4.0% in May 2012.[63] [See chart 2n]

Rate targeting should have been implemented much earlier: but it might also have been redundant, had the

2013. Mr Bernanke noted, 'We've already put $350billion of profits back to the Treasury since 2009, which is about as much as we delivered to the Treasury between 1990 and 2007 combined'.

[62] Source: Thomson Reuters Datastream. The implied interest rate for the 3-month Eurodollar contract, June 2013, fell from a 2011 high of 2.84% [10 February 2011] to 0.84% on 8 August 2011, the day before the introduction of forward rate guidance.

[63] Source: MBA. The Conventional Mortgage Contract Rate, 30-Year fell from 4.37% in the second week of August 2011 [prior to the introduction of forward rate guidance] to 3.96% in the second week of May 2012.

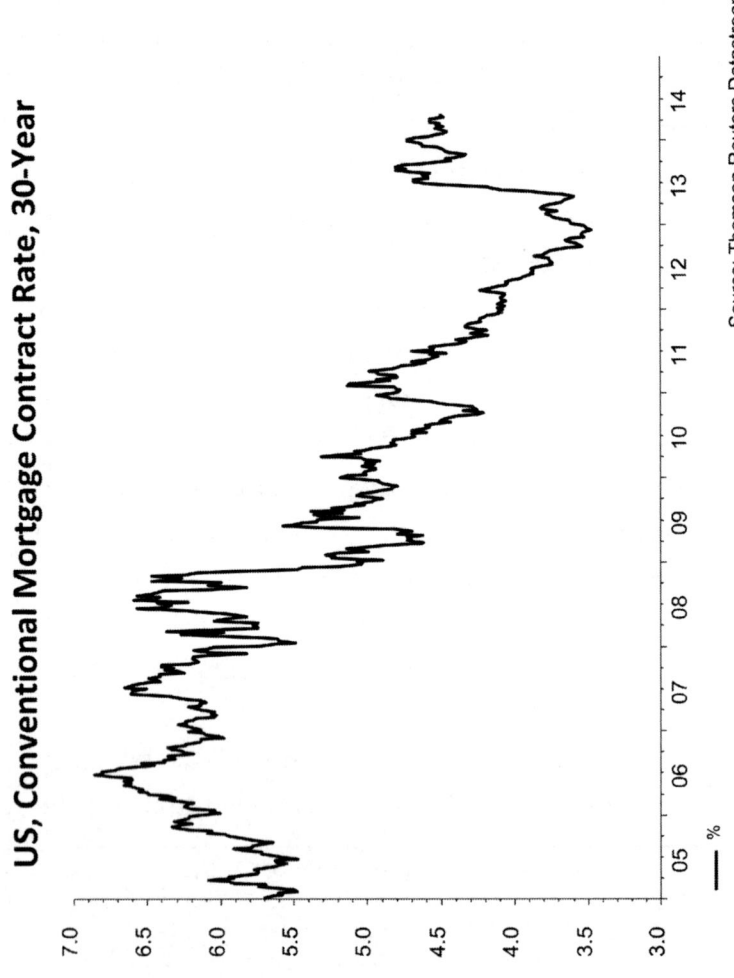

**US, Conventional Mortgage Contract Rate, 30-Year**

Source: Thomson Reuters Datastream

Chart 2n

FOMC pursued a reverse tap. For sure, rate targeting should have been tried before fiscal policy was used so aggressively. Nevertheless, the FOMC was finally sending a consistent, unequivocal message to financial markets: zero interest rates were not a temporary phenomenon. Investors were being given a strong signal not to expect an early reversal in the policy of cheap money.

The only way investors and savers could earn higher rates of return would be to shift into riskier assets. This *portfolio balance effect* became an important transmission mechanism of monetary policy. However, the portfolio balance effect was not being driven by the so-called supply channel. It was not the direct impact of bond purchases that triggered the turnaround. It was the signalling impact of monetary policy that underpinned the portfolio balance effect.

## The Housing Recovery

The impact of the shift to forward rate guidance was swift. The sharp fall in house prices had pushed rental yields up well above bank deposit rates, which had tumbled towards zero in line with the drop in the federal funds target.[64] The more alert and yield hungry investors had already been testing the water prior to the shift to rate

---

[64] See *10 best cities to buy a rental property*, CNNMoney, 12 July 2011 and *How to Find the Best Market for Rental Real Estate Investing*, Money Morning, 13 July 2011.

targeting: prices had tumbled 29.9% between October 2005 and July 2011.[65] However, during the fall of 2011, the housing market finally turned a corner. The recovery was far from hesitant. Within a year, house prices had risen 9.9%.[66] Prices were rising quickly in a number of cities that had suffered disproportionately during the sub-prime crisis. Investors were taking advantage of severely discounted markets, pushing property valuations higher.[67] [See chart 2o]

The FOMC was not being complacent. Stung by the failures of QE1 and QE2, Federal Reserve officials finally realised they had the power to influence bond markets and secure a lasting economic recovery. Indeed, encouraged by the initial success of the new policy, the FOMC announced on 25 January 2012 that interest rates would stay on hold for even longer. The target for the federal funds rate would remain 0.0% - 0.25% until 'at least through late 2014'.[68] Forward rate guidance was

---

[65] Source: NAR. The median price of existing one-family homes sold [seasonally adjusted by Thomson Reuters Datastream] fell from $230,200 in October 2005 to $161,400 in July 2011.

[66] Source: NAR. The median price of existing one-family homes sold [seasonally adjusted by Thomson Reuters Datastream] rose from $161,400 in July 2011 to $177,400 in July 2012.

[67] Source: S&P/Case-Shiller, Home Price Index, 20-City Composite. The 20-city composite index fell 33.7% between April 2006 and January 2012. It dropped by a 3-month annualised rate of 5.4% in December 2011. By contrast, the S&P/Case-Shiller index for Phoenix fell 56.5% between May 2006 and August 2011. It rose by a 3-month annualised rate of 8.6% in December 2011.

[68] See *Federal Reserve Press Release*, 25 January 2012. The FOMC announced

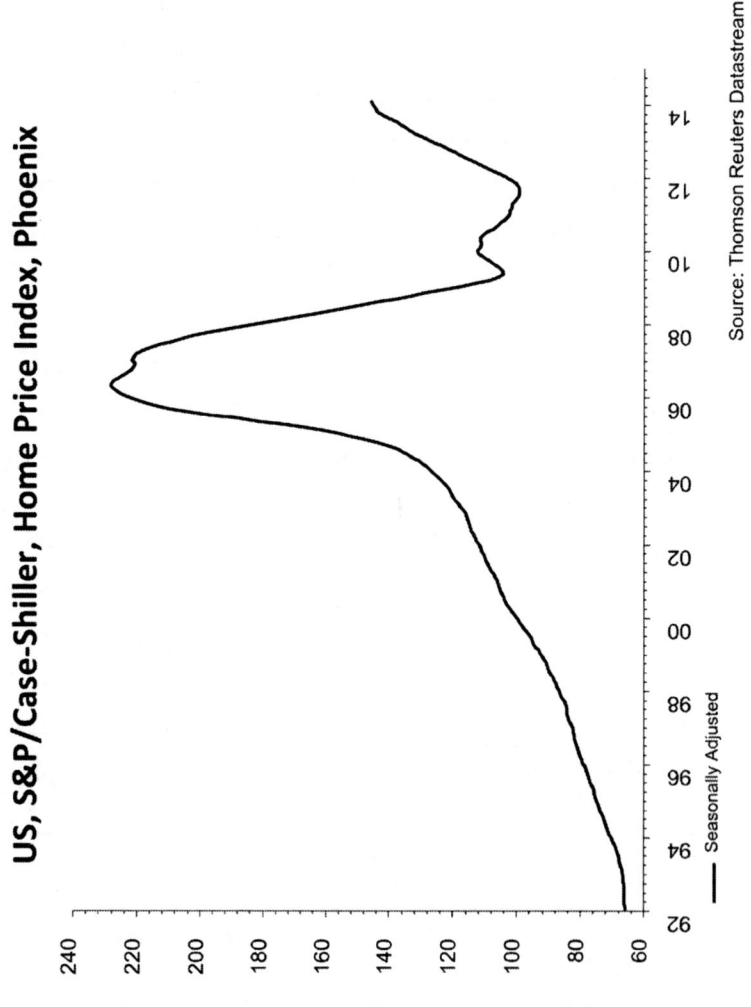

**US, S&P/Case-Shiller, Home Price Index, Phoenix**

Source: Thomson Reuters Datastream

— Seasonally Adjusted

Chart 2o

being used to drive mortgage rates even lower.

The new policy was put to the test in the spring of 2012. The stock market had rallied strongly in the first few weeks of the year, buoyed by the rebound in house prices and stronger economic data. Investors began to sell Treasuries. The 10-year yield climbed quickly from 1.80% on the last day of January 2012 to 2.38% on 6 March.[69] Mortgage rates began to rise again.[70] However, the turnaround in the housing market was still in its infancy. A significant reversal in borrowing costs could short-circuit the recovery. Forward rate guidance needed reinforcing. FOMC officials had to articulate the economic arguments for low interest rates to underpin rate targeting. This was critical to counter the innate tendency of investors and financial markets to sell Treasuries too early during an economic recovery. This recurring problem of liquidity preference showed that central banks had a decisive role to play in shaping and driving market expectations. Policy makers would have to

---

it would 'keep the target range for the federal funds rate at 0.0% - 0.25% and currently anticipates that economic conditions - including low rates of resource utilization and a subdued outlook for inflation over the medium run - are likely to warrant exceptionally low levels for the federal funds rate at least through late 2014'.

[69] Source: Thomson Reuters Datastream, US Treasury Benchmark Bond 10-Year Yield.

[70] Source: MBA. The Conventional Mortgage Contract Rate, 30-Year, climbed from 4.06% in the second week of March 2012 to 4.23% in the third week of March 2012, 14 basis points [0.14%] below the level witnessed prior to the introduction of forward rate guidance on 9 August 2011.

demonstrate their unequivocal determination to persist with low interest rates, to keep interest rate expectations under control. Federal Reserve officials, including the chair Ben Bernanke, had repeatedly discussed *exit strategies* following the announcements of QE1 and QE2.[71] They had created the impression that the FOMC was not committed to the policy of low interest rates, sowing doubts in the minds of investors.[72] Investors were unlikely to hold on to their Treasuries if the FOMC was simultaneously discussing the alternatives for unwinding quantitative easing. Bond purchases could not work if central banks did not provide the requisite assurance to investors.

---

[71] See footnote 42.

[72] See *The Federal Reserve's Asset Purchase Program*, Janet Yellen, 8 January 2011. Ms Yellen described how, 'Given the very high level of reserve balances, changes in the interest rate on reserves might not be fully reflected in the federal funds rate and other short-term market rates. In that event, the Federal Reserve can use tools it has developed and tested to drain or immobilize bank reserves, thereby enhancing our control over the federal funds rate. To build the capability to drain large quantities of reserves, the Federal Reserve has expanded the range of its counterparties for reverse repurchase operations beyond the primary dealers and has developed the infrastructure necessary to use agency MBS as collateral in such transactions. The Federal Reserve has also put in place a Term Deposit Facility through which it can offer deposits to member institutions that are roughly analogous to the certificates of deposit that these institutions offer to their customers. We have tested both of these tools by conducting several small-scale operations and have the ability to initiate them quickly if needed. The use of reverse repurchase operations and the Term Deposit Facility would allow the Federal Reserve to drain hundreds of billions of dollars of reserves from the banking system should conditions necessitate'.

## The FOMC's Social Agenda

The point was acknowledged on 26 March 2012 as Ben Bernanke laid out a strong, clear case for keeping interest rates low. The FOMC chair focussed on long-term unemployment, warning 'millions of families continue to suffer the day-to-day hardships associated with not being able to find suitable employment'.[73] Endemic long-term unemployment was elevated to a major policy goal in a bid to remind investors why there would be no early reversal in monetary policy. Despite the nascent economic recovery, the FOMC was not going to take any risks. Long-term unemployment remained well above the levels witnessed in any previous recession during the post-1945 era. [See chart 2p] There was a moral imperative for the ultra-loose monetary policy. Highlighting the blight of long-term unemployment underlined the FOMC's commitment to low interest rates.

The long-term jobless rate had fallen from its peak of April 2010.[74] Nevertheless, the decline had been slow: more than 40% of the unemployed had been out of work for over six months since December 2009.[75] Mr

---

[73] See *Recent Developments in the Labor Market*, Ben Bernanke, 26 March 2012, p. 8.

[74] Source: BLS. Unemployment, 27 weeks & over, as percent of the civilian labour force, reached a high of 4.4% in April 2010. It had dropped to 3.5% by February 2012. However, this was above the cyclical peak of 2.6% reached in June 1983, the previous post-1945 high.

[75] Source: BLS. Unemployment, 27 weeks & over, as a share of total

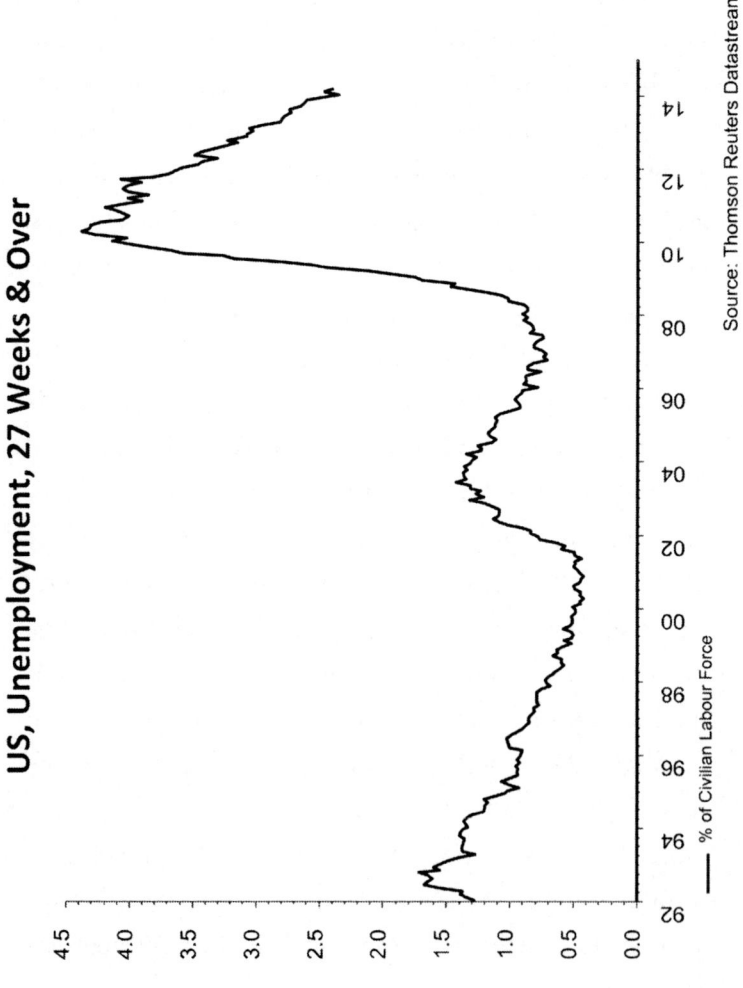

US, Unemployment, 27 Weeks & Over

—— % of Civilian Labour Force

Source: Thomson Reuters Datastream

Chart 2p

115

Bernanke warned, 'By way of comparison, the share of unemployment that was long term in nature never exceeded 25% or so in the severe 1981-82 recession'. Furthermore, studies suggested, 'that unemployed people suffer from a higher incidence of stress-related health problems such as depression, stroke, and heart disease, and they may have a lower life expectancy. The children of the unemployed achieve less in school and appear to have reduced long-term earnings prospects'.[76]

The Federal Reserve had a clear social agenda. Mr Bernanke's speech was a direct challenge to the hawks on the FOMC and the Federal Reserve's political opponents. The FOMC had two targets - price stability and full employment. The more sympathetic members of the FOMC [i.e. doves] intended to fulfil the Federal Reserve's dual mandate and would not be deterred. The message was driven home by the current FOMC chair [and at the time deputy chair], Janet Yellen. Ms Yellen highlighted that an 'exceptionally large fraction of those now unemployed' had been out of work for six months or more. There was a danger that 'individuals with such long term unemployment spells could become less employable as their skills deteriorate and they lose their connections

unemployment, peaked at 45.3% in April 2010. This had dropped to 41.8% in February 2012. However, this was above the cyclical peak of 26.0% reached in June 1983, the previous post-1945 high.

[76] See *Recent Developments in the Labor Market*, Ben Bernanke, 26 March 2012, p. 9-10.

to the labour market'.[77] As a result, the FOMC had to be more proactive. Delays in securing a strong recovery would prove costly.

Ms Yellen was careful not to provide ammunition for sceptics of quantitative easing. The persistence of long-term unemployment was not - at this juncture - structural, she argued. If it were, the policy hawks might claim that the natural rate of unemployment consistent with price stability had risen. It would be harder to justify low interest rates. Instead, Ms Yellen turned the argument on its head: there was indeed a risk that the natural rate of unemployment would climb if the Federal Reserve did not act decisively.

The policy challenge facing the FOMC became even more apparent when the Bureau of Labor Statistics reported that the US had generated an average of just 73,000 jobs in May and June 2012. By contrast, employment had risen by a monthly average of 226,000 in the first three months of the year.[78] Speaking at the Boston Economic Club, Ms Yellen was quick to admit that the Federal Reserve did not have time on its side, if it wanted to avoid turning 'what was initially cyclical

---

[77] See *The Economic Outlook and Monetary Policy*, Janet Yellen, 11 April 2012, p. 6.

[78] Source: BLS, Total employment for non-farm industries. These numbers were available from The Employment Situation, released on 1 June 2012. They were subsequently revised to show an average monthly increase of 99.0k for May and June 2012, and an average monthly gain of 276.0k for Q1 2012.

into structural unemployment'.[79] Ms Yellen declared 'I am convinced that scope remains for the FOMC to provide further policy accommodation either through its forward rate guidance or through additional balance-sheet actions'.[80] It was a rallying call from the FOMC's most determined interventionist.

At the April 2012 meeting, the FOMC had already announced that it would 'regularly review the size and composition of its securities holdings'. It was 'prepared to adjust those holdings as appropriate to promote a stronger economic recovery in a context of price stability'.[81] At the June 19-20th FOMC meeting, Operation Twist was extended to the end of 2012.

## Nailing Down the Recovery

On 13 September 2012 the FOMC went a step further and announced another round of quantitative easing [QE3] with a difference: there would be no time limit to the asset purchases. The Federal Reserve would buy $40billion of mortgage-backed securities a month

---

[79] See *The Economic Outlook and Monetary Policy*, Janet Yellen, 6 June 2012, p. 9. The FOMC deputy chair reiterated that the bulk of the rise in unemployment during the Great Recession had been, 'cyclical, not structural in nature', p. 3. Nevertheless, the persistence of 'high unemployment could wreak long-term damage', p. 8.

[80] Ibid. p. 17.

[81] See *Federal Reserve Press Release*, 25 April 2012.

*indefinitely*.[82] At the same time, the anticipated date for the first hike in the target for the federal funds rate was pushed back a further six months to mid-2015.[83] For many investors this extension to forward rate guidance was overshadowed by the re-introduction of quantitative easing. Nevertheless, unlimited quantitative easing was undoubtedly more powerful than QE1 and QE2. Furthermore, the FOMC had concluded that the open-ended nature of quantitative easing would reinforce its rate targeting, sending a strong message that it was determined to keep interest rates on hold to underpin a stronger economic recovery.

Opponents of the Federal Reserve decried the latest intervention as *QE infinity*, another reckless gamble by the US central bank that would simply inflate its balance sheet with limited benefits. According to the critics, the costs of unwinding this policy would grow alongside the ultimate risks for financial markets. They warned that any boost to equity markets, driven by the liquidity impact of the bond purchases, would be short-lived and do nothing to resolve the underlying problems that led to the sub-prime crisis. The FOMC was undeterred: on

---

[82] Ibid. 13 September 2012. The Committee agreed 'to increase policy accommodation by purchasing additional agency mortgage-backed securities at a pace of $40billion per month'. The Committee did not set a time limit to these purchases.

[83] Ibid. The FOMC announced that 'exceptionally low levels for the federal funds rate are likely to be warranted at least through mid-2015'.

12 December 2012, QE3 was more than doubled, as the FOMC announced it would purchase $45billion of longer term Treasury securities per month.[84]

For some QE3 was a sign of desperation. Previous attempts to secure a strong economic recovery had failed. A federal funds target of 0.0% - 0.25%, two rounds of quantitative easing, forward rate guidance and Operation Twist had not delivered a sustainable recovery. There was little point in another round of bond purchases. It was clear that there were 'diminishing marginal returns' from the Federal Reserve's policy actions.

For a short while, it appeared as if some of these criticisms were valid. In contrast to the previous announcements on quantitative easing, the S&P 500 initially failed to make significant headway.[85] However, the policy was working, but not in a way that was immediately obvious. In the months prior to the adoption of QE3, the rise in house prices had shown signs of a stall. Specifically, the existing home sales report published by the National Association of Realtors had pointed to a

---

[84] Ibid. 12 December 2012. The Committee announced that it 'will purchase longer-term Treasury securities after its program to extend the average maturity of its holdings of Treasury securities is completed at the end of the year, initially at a pace of $45billion per month'.

[85] Source: Thomson Reuters Datastream. The S&P 500 composite index closed at 1460.0 on 13 September 2012, up from 1436.6 on 12 September. However, for the remainder of 2012, it largely trended sideways, slipping to 1426.2 on 31 December 2012. Thereafter, the stock market started to rise more quickly, with the S&P 500 composite index closing above 1500 on 25 January 2013 [1503.0] for the first time since 10 December 2007.

deceleration in the monthly gains for the median house price. The extension of forward rate guidance to June 2015 and the introduction of QE3 on 12 September 2012 were timely. Mortgage rates dropped to new lows in the fall of 2012 and the monthly change for the median house price rebounded.[86] Mortgage arrears fell quickly and the number of 'foreclosures started' by lenders tumbled.[87] [See chart 2q] Investor buying of foreclosed properties had been a key driver of the initial turnaround in house prices. The drop in 'foreclosures started' would lead to a fall in repossessions, reducing the supply of discounted houses for investors. The rise in prices would accelerate pulling more homeowners out of negative equity.[88]

The FOMC, it appeared, had finally taken into account *some* of the lessons from Keynes and liquidity

---

[86] Source: NAR. The median price of existing one-family homes sold [seasonally adjusted by Thomson Reuters Datastream] rose 12.1% over the next ten months [October 2012 - July 2013].

[87] Source: MBA. Residential Mortgage Loans, All Foreclosures Started, fell from 1.03% of all loans in Q2 2012 to 0.70% in Q4 2012. Residential Mortgage Loans, Total Delinquent, dropped from 7.58% of all loans to 7.09% over the comparable period. Residential Mortgage Loans, 90+ Days Delinquent, dropped from 3.19% of all borrowers to 2.89% over the comparable period. The median price of existing one-family homes sold rose 2.8% [seasonally adjusted by Thomson Reuters Datastream] in the final three months of 2012, and then leapt 9.9% during the first eight months of 2013.

[88] Source: Zillow Negative Equity Report, March 2012. According to Zillow, at the peak [Q1 2012], 31.4% of US homeowners with a mortgage were in negative equity. To calculate negative equity, the estimated value of a home is matched to all outstanding mortgage debt and lines of credit associated with the home, including home equity lines of credit and home equity loans. By Q3 2013, negative equity had dropped to 21.0%.

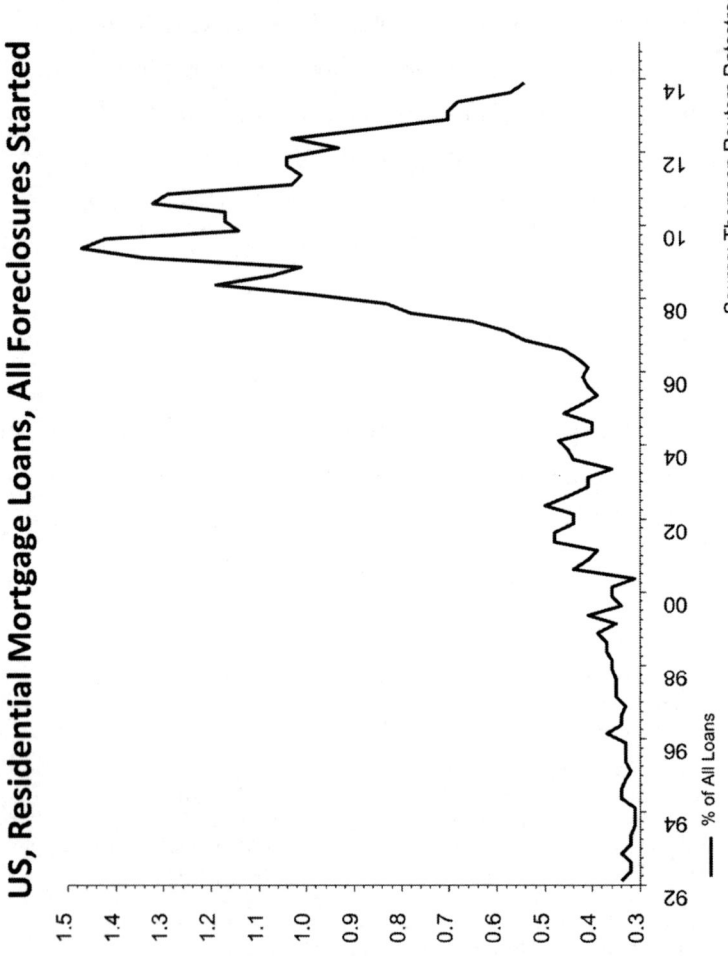

**US, Residential Mortgage Loans, All Foreclosures Started**

% of All Loans

Source: Thomson Reuters Datastream

Chart 2q

preference of investors. By choosing not to specify a size or withdrawal date for QE3, the FOMC was reinforcing its commitment to keeping interest rates low, already demonstrated by the more important extension of forward rate guidance.

## Quantitative Targets

However, in its final meeting of 2012, the FOMC replaced its calendar-based guidance with a focus on economic 'goals'. The FOMC announced that the 'exceptionally low range for the federal funds rate' would be appropriate 'at least as long as the unemployment rate remains above 6.5% percent, inflation between one and two years ahead is projected to be no more than half a percentage point above the committee's 2 percent longer-run goal, and longer-term inflation expectations continue to be well anchored'.[89] These *quantitative targets* showed that the FOMC had not fully grasped the importance of liquidity preference.

For most critics of quantitative easing, the tolerance of higher inflation was proof that the Federal Reserve was prepared to take risks with price stability in a bid to reverse the damage inflicted by the Great Recession. For

---

[89] See *Federal Reserve Press Release*, 12 December 2012. The FOMC also announced that the ultra-low interest rate would 'remain appropriate for a considerable time after the asset purchase program [QE3] ends'. Furthermore, this more accommodative monetary policy would remain in place for a considerable time after the 'economy strengthens'.

others, the 6.5% unemployment threshold implied that the natural jobless rate, or the *non-accelerating inflation rate of unemployment* (*NAIRU*), had risen since the last economic cycle. There was a risk that the FOMC would - based on this threshold, or these quantitative targets - be obliged to raise interest rates sooner than indicated by the June 2015 target.

In truth, these targets should have been secondary to calendar-based guidance, if the Federal Reserve wanted to embrace a policy of cheap, but tight money. The essence of liquidity preference is time: the innate tendency of investors to sell longer-dated bonds early in an economic recovery, pushing yields higher, is a direct function of their maturity. Bonds with a long maturity will require a longer commitment, specified in calendar terms, for investors to be reassured, otherwise they will sell.

The confusion sown by this new policy forced Federal Reserve officials to clarify the new framework. On 11 February 2013, Ms Yellen declared that the quantitative targets were 'thresholds for possible action, not triggers that will necessarily prompt an immediate increase in the FOMC's target rate'. She reiterated: 'when one of these thresholds is crossed, action is possible but not assured'.[90]

The move to quantitative goals was not the end of the

---

[90] See *A Painfully Slow Recovery for America's Workers: Causes, Implications, and the Federal Reserve's Response*, Janet Yellen, 13 February 2013, p. 17.

interest rate forecasts that had underpinned the calendar-based approach to forward rate guidance and had proved so effective in driving the recovery in house prices. The FOMC continued to publish the interest rate forecasts of officials. When the Committee introduced calendar-based forward rate guidance in August 2011, officials would agree by majority vote on the minimum time the federal funds target rate was likely to remain at 0.0% - 0.25%. From January 2012 onwards, the Federal Reserve published the interest rate forecasts for all members of the FOMC, including those who did not have a vote.[91] These projections provided a detailed insight that went beyond the FOMC statement. There was a persistent downward revision of interest rate forecasts for most FOMC members, particularly from June 2012 onwards [see tables on pages 126 and 127]. In particular, a number of the more hawkish officials were forced to revise down their projections for the target for the federal funds rate substantively.[92] However, the formal end of calendar-based guidance implied that these revisions received

---

[91] The projections for the appropriate target for the federal funds rate made by individual FOMC members were published after the FOMC meetings held in January, April, June, September, December 2012 and March, June, September and December 2013 . These projections were made anonymously.

[92] See *Federal Reserve Accessible Materials*. On 20 June 2012, six FOMC members projected a federal funds rate of above 0.0% - 0.25% for year-end 2013. Four of these predicted a rate between 1.0% and 2.0%. By December, 2012, only two members maintained that the rate would be higher than 0.0% - 0.25%. No members forecast a rate of above 1%. The projections for the federal funds rate for year-end 2014 show a similar story. In June 2012, eight members predicted a rate higher than 1.0%, but this fell to four by December.

**Year End 2013**

|       | Jan 2012 | Apr 2012 | Jun 2012 | Sep 2012 | Dec 2012 | Mar 2013 | Jun 2013 | Sep 2013 | Dec 2013 |
|-------|------|------|------|------|------|------|------|------|------|
| 0.25  | 11 | 11 | 13 | 15 | 17 | 18 | 18 | 17 | 17 |
| 0.50  | 1 |   | 1 | 2 | 1 |   | 1 |   |   |
| 0.75  | 2 | 1 | 1 | 1 | 1 | 1 |   |   |   |
| 1.00  | 1 | 2 | 1 |   |   |   |   |   |   |
| 1.25  |   | 1 | 2 |   |   |   |   |   |   |
| 1.50  |   |   |   |   |   |   |   |   |   |
| 1.75  | 1 | 2 | 1 | 1 |   |   |   |   |   |
| 2.00  | 1 |   |   |   |   |   |   |   |   |
| 2.25  |   |   |   |   |   |   |   |   |   |
| 2.50  |   |   |   |   |   |   |   |   |   |
| 2.75  |   |   |   |   |   |   |   |   |   |
| 3.00  |   |   |   |   |   |   |   |   |   |
| 3.25  |   |   |   |   |   |   |   |   |   |
| 3.50  |   |   |   |   |   |   |   |   |   |
| 3.75  |   |   |   |   |   |   |   |   |   |
| 4.00  |   |   |   |   |   |   |   |   |   |
| 4.25  |   |   |   |   |   |   |   |   |   |
| 4.50  |   |   |   |   |   |   |   |   |   |
| **Total** | 17 | 17 | 19 | 19 | 19 | 19 | 19 | 17 | 17 |
| **Mean**  | 0.56 | 0.60 | 0.51 | 0.38 | 0.30 | 0.29 | 0.26 | 0.25 | 0.25 |

**Year End 2014**

|       | Jan 2012 | Apr 2012 | Jun 2012 | Sep 2012 | Dec 2012 | Mar 2013 | Jun 2013 | Sep 2013 | Dec 2013 | Mar 2014 |
|-------|------|------|------|------|------|------|------|------|------|------|
| 0.25  | 6 | 4 | 6 | 13 | 14 | 14 | 15 | 14 | 15 | 15 |
| 0.50  | 2 | 3 | 4 |   | 1 | 1 |   |   |   |   |
| 0.75  | 1 | 1 | 1 |   |   |   |   | 2 | 1 |   |
| 1.00  | 2 | 2 |   | 2 | 2 | 2 | 3 |   |   | 1 |
| 1.25  |   |   |   | 2 | 1 |   |   |   | 1 |   |
| 1.50  | 1 | 1 | 2 |   |   |   | 1 |   |   |   |
| 1.75  |   |   | 2 |   |   | 1 |   | 1 |   |   |
| 2.00  | 1 | 2 | 1 | 1 |   |   |   |   |   |   |
| 2.25  |   |   |   |   |   |   |   |   |   |   |
| 2.50  | 3 | 3 | 1 |   | 1 |   |   |   |   |   |
| 2.75  | 1 |   | 1 | 1 |   | 1 |   |   |   |   |
| 3.00  |   | 1 | 1 |   |   |   |   |   |   |   |
| 3.25  |   |   |   |   |   |   |   |   |   |   |
| 3.50  |   |   |   |   |   |   |   |   |   |   |
| 3.75  |   |   |   |   |   |   |   |   |   |   |
| 4.00  |   |   |   |   |   |   |   |   |   |   |
| 4.25  |   |   |   |   |   |   |   |   |   |   |
| 4.50  |   |   |   |   |   |   |   |   |   |   |
| **Total** | 17 | 17 | 19 | 19 | 19 | 19 | 19 | 17 | 17 | 16 |
| **Mean**  | 1.12 | 1.32 | 1.11 | 0.80 | 0.61 | 0.55 | 0.43 | 0.40 | 0.34 | 0.30 |

Table 2a (*this page and following page*)
Projections for the Appropriate Target for the Federal
Funds Rate made by Individual FOMC Members

| | Year End 2015 | | | | | | | Year End 2016 | | | Long Run | | | | | | | | | |
|---|---|---|---|---|---|---|---|---|---|---|---|---|---|---|---|---|---|---|---|---|
| | Sep 2012 | Dec 2012 | Mar 2013 | Jun 2013 | Sep 2013 | Dec 2013 | Mar 2014 | Sep 2013 | Dec 2013 | Mar 2014 | Jan 2012 | Apr 2012 | Jun 2012 | Sep 2012 | Dec 2012 | Mar 2013 | Jun 2013 | Sep 2013 | Dec 2013 | Mar 2014 |
| 0.25 | 1 | 1 | 1 | 1 | 2 | 3 | 2 | 1 | | | | | | | | | | | | |
| 0.50 | 2 | 5 | 7 | 1 | 1 | 3 | 2 | | 1 | | | | | | | | | | | |
| 0.75 | 3 | 3 | 1 | 2 | 5 | 4 | 2 | | | 1 | | | | | | | | | | |
| 1.00 | 4 | 3 | 2 | 3 | 3 | 2 | 5 | 1 | 1 | | | | | | | | | | | |
| 1.25 | | 2 | 4 | 4 | 1 | 1 | 1 | | 2 | 1 | | | | | | | | | | |
| 1.50 | 3 | | | 2 | 2 | 1 | 1 | 1 | 4 | | | | | | | | | | | |
| 1.75 | | | | 3 | | | | 5 | 1 | 2 | | | | | | | | | | |
| 2.00 | | 1 | 1 | | | 1 | 1 | 2 | | 3 | | | | | | | | | | |
| 2.25 | | | | | | | 1 | | 2 | 2 | | | | | | | | | | |
| 2.50 | 2 | 1 | | 1 | | | | 2 | 1 | 1 | | | | | | | | | | |
| 2.75 | | | | | | | | 2 | 1 | 2 | | | | | | | | | | |
| 3.00 | | | 1 | 3 | | | | | 1 | 1 | | | | | 1 | | | | | |
| 3.25 | | | | | 2 | 1 | 1 | | | 1 | | | 1 | 1 | | | | | | |
| 3.50 | 1 | 1 | | | 1 | | | | | | 1 | 1 | 1 | 1 | 1 | 1 | 1 | 1 | | |
| 3.75 | 1 | 1 | 1 | | | | | | | 1 | 7 | 1 | 1 | 2 | 3 | 2 | 2 | 2 | 4 | 4 |
| 4.00 | | | | | | | | | | | 3 | 6 | 6 | 6 | 5 | 1 | 1 | 2 | 2 | 2 |
| 4.25 | 1 | 1 | | | | | | | | | 6 | 2 | 5 | 5 | 6 | 9 | 9 | 10 | 9 | 8 |
| 4.50 | | | 1 | | | | | | | 1 | | 7 | 5 | 4 | 3 | 3 | 3 | 3 | 2 | 2 |
| **Total** | 19 | 19 | 19 | 19 | 17 | 17 | 16 | 17 | 17 | 16 | 17 | 17 | 19 | 19 | 19 | 19 | 19 | 17 | 17 | 16 |
| **Mean** | 1.72 | 1.41 | 1.30 | 1.34 | 1.25 | 1.06 | 1.13 | 2.26 | 2.18 | 2.42 | 4.21 | 4.19 | 4.11 | 4.07 | 4.04 | 4.01 | 4.01 | 3.93 | 3.88 | 3.88 |

Projections for the Appropriate Target for the Federal Funds Rate made by Individual FOMC Members

little coverage.

Indeed, these rate forecasts were largely overlooked by bond investors. At the 18 December 2013 meeting the FOMC's median projection for the federal funds rate was reduced from 0.40% to 0.34% for the year-ending 2014 and from 1.25% to 1.06% for the year-ending 2015. Despite the downward revisions, the implied interest rate for the three-month Eurodollar contract, December 2014, rose from 0.36% to 0.45% over the subsequent four trading days. For December 2015, it climbed from 0.89% to 1.17%.[93] The calendar-based interest rate forecasts had been downgraded by the FOMC, but they were revealing: even though house prices were rising and the unemployment rate was falling, FOMC officials were still lowering their expectations of interest rates at various dates in the future.[94] The drop in the interest rate forecasts was most pronounced when the economy hit a soft patch. However, it continued even when the economy was improving. Inflation was subdued - and lower than many critics of quantitative easing had predicted. This

---

[93] Source: Thomson Reuters Datastream.

[94] See *Federal Reserve Accessible Materials*. The FOMC's forecast for the appropriate target for the federal funds rate were being lowered in 2012 and 2013. For 2012, see footnote 93 for more information. Between December 2012 and June 2013, the FOMC revised down its forecast for the federal funds rate for the year-end 2014. Four members predicted a rate of above 1.0% in December compared to just one member in June, while the mean forecast was reduced from 0.61% to 0.43%. Similarly, the average forecast for the appropriate target for the federal funds rate for the year-end 2015 was revised down from 1.41% to 1.34%.

would, in theory, provide the latitude for the FOMC to combat liquidity preference more aggressively.

The downward revision to these interest rate forecasts reflected the growing realisation - particularly among the hawks - that the risks of a rise in inflation had been overstated. In one notable case, the president of the Minneapolis Fed, Narayana Kocherlakota, substantively altered his view on the likelihood of a pick-up in *core inflation* in 2012.[95] More broadly, the collective inflation forecast of FOMC officials was pushed downwards over the course of 2012 and into 2013. Significantly, this occurred alongside a fall in projections for the unemployment rate.[96] The inference was clear - the trade-off between inflation and unemployment or NAIRU was improving. However, this merely cast doubt on the wisdom of the 6.5% unemployment threshold introduced by the FOMC on 12 December 2012.[97]

---

[95] See *Planning for Liftoff*, Narayana Kocherlakota, 20 September 2012, p. 3. Mr Kocherlakota suggested that the federal funds rate should be kept 'extraordinarily low until the unemployment rate has fallen below 5.5%'. Mr Kocherlakota had previously been described as one of the more hawkish members of the FOMC.

[96] See *Federal Reserve Accessible Materials*. On 13 September 2012, the central tendency of the projections for the price index for personal consumption expenditures, excluding food and energy [core consumption deflator] was 1.7% - 2.0% y/y for Q4 2013. This was lowered to 1.2% - 1.3% y/y on 19 June 2013. The projections for the [civilian] unemployment rate continued to fall too. On 13 September 2012, the central tendency of the projections for the unemployment rate was 7.6% - 7.9% in Q4 2013. This was lowered to 7.2% - 7.3% on 19 June 2013. Note, projections are from the fourth quarter of the previous year to the fourth quarter of the year indicated.

[97] To compound the confusion from dropping calendar-based guidance, Ms

The shift to quantitative targets was ostensibly designed to improve the transparency of the Federal Reserve's monetary policy and provide greater clarity to financial markets. Investors would not have to rely upon the FOMC's forecasts: they could judge for themselves when interest rates would have to rise. The transition from the emergency monetary policy to a normalised federal funds target should, as a result, proceed more smoothly. The FOMC believed that by discounting a tighter monetary stance over a longer time frame, the adjustment in interest rate expectations would be

Yellen emphasised that FOMC participants 'continue to estimate that the longer-run normal unemployment lies in a range of 5.2 to 6 percent'. *See Federal Reserve Press Release*, 12 December 2012. The FOMC admitted that it would 'consider other information, including additional measures of labour market conditions'. The unemployment rate was an imperfect measure of labour market slack. Significant numbers had left the labour force, pushing down the labour market participation rate. It appeared that the decline in the labour force was largely due to a weaker labour market. This was true in the immediate aftermath of the 2008 financial crisis. The 'not in the labour force, want a job' total rose from a 2007 low of 4.352million [October 2007] to a peak of 6.979million in August 2012. However, it has been falling subsequently and dropped to 6.060million in February 2014. By contrast, the 'not in the labour force, does not want a job' total has risen sharply over the comparable period - from 75.180million in October 2007 to 85.301million by February 2014. Since January 2008, the labour market participation rate has dropped from 66.231% to 63.024% in February 2014, a decline of 3.21 percentage points. The total for 'not in the labour force, wants a job' has risen from 2.083% to 2.453%, a rise of 0.37 percentage points. Thus, over this period, 88.5% of the dip in the participation rate is due to the rise in 'not in the labour force, does not want a job'. The FOMC has persistently failed to recognise this point. It was only in January 2014, that they belatedly made reference to this shift: 'Much of the downward trend in the labour force participation rate since the start of the recession was seen as the result of shifts in the demographic composition of the workforce and the retirement of older workers; the extent of the cyclical portion of the decline was viewed by some as difficult to gauge at present'. Source [for labour market data]: BLS and see *Minutes of the Federal Open Market Committee*, 28-29 January 2014, p. 14.

less disruptive for financial markets. Nevertheless, the basic premise of quantitative targets remained. Indeed, according to some FOMC members, calendar-based guidance could prove quite disruptive when it came to reversing the policy. Markets would have less time to adjust to a tighter monetary policy.[98] FOMC officials were concerned that the 'challenge of *normalizing* [author's italics] the current stance of monetary policy' could result in 'an abrupt tightening of financial conditions'.[99]

Speaking in New York on 25 March 2013, New York Federal Reserve President William Dudley reviewed the experiences of 1994 and 2004, when 'economic recoveries got underway in earnest after sustained periods of unusually low short-term rates'. Bond yields had risen sharply and markets had 're-priced suddenly' as new information 'led investors to significantly revise their view of the outlook or the Fed's reaction function'.[100] Ms Yellen had also emphasised the benefits of quantitative guidance before the new framework was adopted on 12 December 2012. The FOMC deputy chair supported the new approach 'because it would enable the public

---

[98] See *Minutes of the Federal Open Market Committee*, 23-24 October 2012, p. 2. The FOMC first discussed this desire for greater transparency at the October 2012 meeting. The subsequent minutes detailed that a staff presentation had 'focused on the potential effects of using specific threshold values of inflation and the unemployment rate to provide forward guidance'.

[99] See *The Economic Outlook and the Role of Monetary Policy*, William C. Dudley, 25 March 2013.

[100] Ibid.

to immediately adjust its expectations concerning the timing of lift-off in response to new information affecting the economic outlook'. As a result, 'this market response would serve as a kind of automatic stabiliser'.[101] However, the introduction of 'this automatic stabiliser' showed the FOMC was reluctant to affect a true policy of cheap, but tight money. Indeed, in response to the introduction of quantitative targets, interest rate expectations had risen.[102]

## The Significance of Low Inflation

By shifting to quantitative goals, the anchor provided by calendar-based guidance was diluted. The FOMC was unwittingly underestimating the importance of liquidity preference. In mitigation, Ms Yellen's desire to secure full employment was underlined by her willingness to go beyond the FOMC's stated intention of keeping interest rates on hold until mid-2015. The then deputy chair of the FOMC claimed that the optimal policy involved

---

[101] See *Revolution and Evolution in Central Bank Communications*, Janet Yellen, 13 November 2012, p. 22. Ms Yellen admitted that this new framework need not specifically be designed as a tool to smooth the transition to a tighter monetary policy. It could be employed in the opposite direction. Indeed, 'information suggesting a weaker outlook would automatically induce market participants to push out the anticipated date of tightening and vice versa'.

[102] Source: Thomson Reuters Datastream. The implied interest rate for the 3-month Eurodollar contract, December 2015 was 0.80% on 11 December 2012, the day before the quantitative guidance was introduced. It rose in response to the Federal Reserve Press Release on 12 December 2012, climbing to 1.11% on 30 January 2013.

'keeping the federal funds rate close to zero until early 2016'. She also suggested that interest rates could well rise more slowly through to 2018.[103] Specifically, the federal funds rate could climb by less than the median of forecasts from a survey of the Federal Reserve's primary dealers. It was widely assumed that the federal funds target would gradually rise to 4% beyond 2015, 'the long-run value expected by most dealers as well as most FOMC participants'.[104] Ms Yellen was casting doubt on this presumption.

By delaying lift-off and suppressing the normalisation of interest rates, the Federal Reserve could, according to Ms Yellen, generate a 'faster reduction in unemployment' although inflation would 'slightly' overshoot the [then] 2% objective.[105] Of course, this rested on the assumption that financial markets would not be unnerved by the tolerance of higher inflation. It was important that long-term inflation expectations remain 'firmly anchored'. The target for the federal funds rate could then be set on a path that would 'balance the benefits from a faster reduction of the unemployment rate against the losses

---

[103] See *Revolution and Evolution in Central Bank Communications*, Janet Yellen, 13 November 2012, p. 16. 'The optimal policy to implement this 'balance approach' to minimizing deviations from the inflation and unemployment goals involves…keeping the federal funds rate below the baseline path through 2018'.

[104] Ibid. p. 15.

[105] Ibid. p. 16.

from a temporary and modest increase of inflation above 2 percent'.[106]

In truth, this caveat was superfluous. Inflation fell more quickly than many financial market participants or FOMC officials expected. By the late spring of 2013, the Federal Reserve's favourite measure of inflation had fallen to just 1.15%.[107] This was comfortably less than half the new, higher threshold of 2.5% and well below the original 2.0% target. The higher objective set at the December 2012 meeting had been unnecessary, perhaps counterproductive. The FOMC could have introduced a much lower target for unemployment and retained the previous inflation objective of 2%. This would have mitigated concerns that the FOMC was taking risks with price stability. It would have sent a clearer message to the bond market: the FOMC wanted to bring unemployment down more quickly and it could do so because inflation was not a risk.

Indeed, the FOMC was more powerful than perhaps it even realised. Growth in China was slowing[108] and import

---

[106] Ibid. p. 17.

[107] Source: BEA. The price index for personal consumption expenditure, less food & energy [core consumption deflator] was up 1.16% y/y in May 2013. This was down from a high of 2.45% y/y in February 2007 and a post-2008 'peak' of 2.04% y/y in March 2012.

[108] The Chinese government had cut its target for economic growth to 7.5% for 2012. See *Wen issues China growth warning*, Financial Times, 5 March 2013.

prices were falling as a result.[109] By pushing inflation in the US higher, the rapid expansion of the Chinese economy following the collapse of Lehman Brothers had previously complicated, possibly even undermined, the Federal Reserve's attempts to engineer a stronger US recovery. The jobless rate was already approaching the FOMC's projection for the end of 2013 as it fell to 7.5% in March 2013.[110] An average of 210,000 jobs had been created in the previous six months.[111]

An important contributor to liquidity preference was the fear that an ultra-loose monetary policy necessarily increased the threat of higher inflation. However, with inflation falling so quickly, the anticipated date for the first rate hike could be left unchanged [mid-2015] even as the economic recovery gathered momentum. Monetary policy could become more potent. The Federal Reserve might discover that its array of policy tools was proving more effective than before.

The argument was recognised by Sarah Bloom Raskin, a member of the FOMC and a governor at the Federal Reserve. Ms Bloom Raskin suggested: 'it is possible that accommodative monetary policy could be increasingly

---

[109] Source: BLS, Import Price Index, all commodities. Import prices started to turn down again in May 2012 and had dropped by 2.7% within a year [April 2013].

[110] Source: BLS, Total unemployment as percent of the civilian labour force (official unemployment rate).

[111] Source: BLS, Total employment for non-farm industries.

potent' because of the potential impact in reflating the housing market.[112] Higher house prices would ensure 'more and more households have enough home equity to gain renewed access to mortgage credit and the ability to refinance their homes at lower rates'.[113] There may come a point where keeping mortgage rates constant could increase the reflationary impact of monetary policy. Critics had assailed the policy of quantitative easing for providing 'diminishing returns', but the opposite could be true. An inflexion point might occur, where quantitative easing delivered 'increasing returns'.

Large numbers of borrowers had been unable to refinance their fixed rate mortgages during the early years of the sub-prime crisis. If the value of their homes fell below the outstanding mortgage balance, lenders refused to refinance: homeowners with negative equity were trapped. However, this destructive dynamic during the downturn could now be turned on its head.

At first, the rally in share prices from early 2013 onwards seemed to be little more than a typical New Year flourish.[114] Indeed, when the minutes of the 29-30 January FOMC meeting were released, the S&P 500

---

[112] See *Aspects of Inequality in the Recent Business Cycle*, Sarah Bloom Raskin, 18 April 2013, p. 15.

[113] Ibid. p. 15-16.

[114] Source: S&P/Thomson Reuters Datastream. The S&P 500 Composite Price Index rose from 1426.2 on 31 December 2012 to 1530.9 on 19 February 2013.

fell.[115] A small number of Federal Reserve officials had questioned the wisdom of continuing QE3, but the equity market soon regained its poise because corporate profits were strong and house prices were rising. The recovery in house prices was being driven by a combination of low mortgage rates and strong investor demand. Low short-term and deposit rates underpinned investor demand. Low mortgage rates in turn reinforced the impact of investor demand on prices, by reducing delinquencies and the supply of foreclosed properties on to the housing market.

It was far from clear whether the Federal Reserve's asset purchases were the main driving force behind either of these dynamics. Targeting of interest rate expectations could well be more important. Indeed, the response of the housing market to the August 2011 shift to forward rate guidance suggested that the signalling channel and its impact on bond yields had been more significant.

Indeed, FOMC officials had continued to revise their forecasts for interest rates down again and would carry on pushing them lower through 2013.[116] Although this

---

[115] Source: S&P/Thomson Reuters Datastream. The minutes for the 29 - 30 January 2013 FOMC meeting were released on 20 February 2013. The S&P 500 Composite Price Index fell from 1530.9 on 19 February 2013 to 1487.8 on 25 February. According to the minutes, 'A number of participants stated that an ongoing evaluation of the efficacy, costs, and risks of asset purchases might well lead the Committee to taper or end its purchases before it judged that a substantial improvement in the outlook for the labour market had occurred'.

[116] See *Federal Reserve Accessible Materials, 17 - 18 December 2012.* The

was not conveyed explicitly to investors, the reality of an interest rate hike was receding even as the recovery in the housing market broadened out across much of the US. Unemployment remained too high and inflation was too low. The turnaround in property prices had initially been concentrated in the cities and states most affected by the sub-prime crisis. It had subsequently spread to other cities, such as Boston and New York.[117]

The stock market raced ahead despite some investors worrying that the Federal Reserve was fuelling another bull market at the cost of financial stability. FOMC officials, for the most part, argued that monetary policy was a blunt instrument for dealing with the potential side-effects from asset prices rising too quickly. Prior to the sub-prime crisis, financial stability, in the words of Janet Yellen, had been a 'junior partner' in monetary policy.[118] Stung by the severity of the Great Recession,

---

FOMC's forecast for the appropriate target for the federal funds rate for the year-end 2013 fell from 0.38% to 0.30%. For the year-end 2014, it dropped from 0.80% to 0.61%. For the year-end 2015, it tumbled from 1.72% to 1.41%. The continued decline in the FOMC's forecast for the appropriate target for the federal funds rate through 2013 can be seen in the table on page 127.

[117] Source: S&P/Case-Shiller, Home Price Index, 20-City Composite [seasonally adjusted]. The annual growth rate for house prices in New York turned positive in January 2013 [0.4%] and rose to 6.3% in December 2013. The annual rate for Boston turned positive in July 2012 [0.9%] and accelerated to 9.6% in December 2013. The y/y rate turned positive in Phoenix in January 2012 [1.3%] and was 15.3% in December 2013. As previously indicated, prices in Phoenix had fallen heavily in the subprime crisis. See footnote 68.

[118] See *Panel Discussion on 'Monetary Policy: Many Targets, Many Instruments. Where Do We Stand?'* Janet Yellen, 16 April 2013, p. 4.

there was now a 'strong preference' among FOMC officials 'to rely on micro- and macro prudential supervision and regulation as the main line of defence'.[119] Speaking in Chicago on 10 May 2013, Mr Bernanke suggested the Federal Reserve's monitoring of the financial system was an important policy tool too, even though it received less attention than the writing and implementation of new rules.[120] Since the Great Recession, the US regulatory framework had evolved from a more fragmented approach to one with the Federal Reserve now responsible for macro-prudential stability. The establishment of the Financial Stability Oversight Council reflected this important shift.

Nevertheless, at this early stage of the economic recovery the FOMC was careful not to stand in the way of a broad reflation in asset prices. On 22 April 2013, the National Association of Realtors revealed another rise in house prices.[121] A day later, the S&P 500 finally closed above its previous all-time high reached in October 2007. On 3 May 2013, the Bureau of Labor Statistics reported a

---

[119] Ibid. p. 5.

[120] See *Monitoring the Financial System*, Ben Bernanke, 10 May 2013, p. 4. Mr Bernanke suggested that 'Probably our best defense against complacency during extended periods of calm is careful monitoring for signs of emerging vulnerabilities and, where appropriate, the development of macro-prudential and other policy tools that can be used to address them'.

[121] Source: NAR. The median price of existing one-family homes sold jumped 1.9% m/m [seasonally adjusted by Thomson Reuters Datastream] and 11.8% y/y in March 2013. This was the biggest y/y increase since November 2005.

larger rise in non-farm employment than expected and a further drop in unemployment.[122] The S&P 500 climbed above 1,600 for the first time as investors concluded that the Federal Reserve was on track to reverse the damage inflicted by the sub-prime crisis.[123] It might take two or three years or perhaps longer to restore full employment. It might take another year or two before house prices had risen back to the levels reached in late 2005. Nonetheless, monetary - not fiscal - policy was proving a powerful weapon for reflation.

## The Recovery: Monetary Versus Fiscal Policy

Indeed, the reality of how far government spending cuts and tax increases would undermine the economic recovery had been overhyped. A more restrictive fiscal policy would ensure [Treasury] bond yields remained low at a critical point during the recovery of the housing market. The extension of forward rate guidance in September 2012 and the introduction of QE3 had injected renewed momentum into the rise in house

---

[122] Source: BLS. Total employment for non-farm industries rose 165,000 in April 2013 according to the first [preliminary] estimate, up 120,000 in March 2013. The April increase was subsequently revised [7 February 2014] to 203,000, while the March increase was revised to 141,000. The average increase for the first four months of 2013 was a healthy 205,000.

[123] Source: Thomson Reuters Datastream. The S&P composite price index rose from 1597.6 on 2 May 2013 to 1614.4 on 3 May 2013.

prices. Ironically, the *fiscal cliff* provided the impetus for an even swifter acceleration in property prices. This was a classic example of *crowding-in*: a restrictive fiscal stance reinforcing the potency of a loose monetary policy via lower bond yields.

Consumer confidence was rising because personal finances were improving. The recovery in house prices was proving remarkably effective at repairing household balance sheets. The proportion of households in negative equity was falling quickly. This was facilitating a further drop in mortgage arrears, making it easier for banks to cut their foreclosure inventory.[124] The diminishing supply of repossessed or foreclosed homes was reinforcing the appreciation in property prices. The 'discount' on the sale of *foreclosed homes* and for *short sales* was falling quickly.[125]

Inflation was remarkably low and the FOMC had considerable latitude to hold interest rate expectations down. The decision of the Chinese government to aim for lower economic growth and prioritise financial stability

---

[124] Source: University of Michigan. The University of Michigan current personal finance index had climbed from a low of 58.0 in August 2009 to a peak of 107.0 in May 2013 before dropping to 99.0 in February 2014. Source: MBA. Residential mortgage loans, 30 days delinquent rate fell sharply during 2013, from 3.21% in Q1 2013 to 2.89% in Q4.

[125] Source: NAR. The mean price discount of foreclosed property sales fell from 22% in December 2011 to 14% in October 2013, the lowest since April 2009, before rising to 16% in January 2014. Distressed sales [foreclosed and short sales] as a % of total sales fell from 32% to 15% between December 2011 and January 2013.

to quell runaway house prices provided a big window of opportunity for the Federal Reserve. The FOMC had revised down its projections for core inflation at the 11 -12 December 2012 meeting and this was lowered again in March 2013.[126] Indeed, core inflation had already fallen sharply in the early months of 2013, partly reflecting the sizeable drop in commodity prices and slower growth in China. On 31 May 2013, core inflation for April fell further to a new low of just 1.05% y/y.[127]

The slide in inflation pressures implied that forward rate guidance could become even more potent. The FOMC did not expect short-term interest rates to rise until mid-2015. There was a real opportunity for the Federal Reserve to counter any fallout from a withdrawal of bond purchases. Any indication from the FOMC that it was ready to scale back on QE3 could lead to a rise in interest rate expectations. Investors might conclude that the end of QE3 would soon be followed by the first rate hike even though Federal Reserves officials had repeatedly stressed that the two policy decisions were separate. Indeed, the initial shift to rate targeting in

---

[126] See *Federal Reserve Accessible Materials.* The central tendency for the projection for the price index for personal consumption expenditures, excluding food and energy [core consumption deflator] - the FOMC's preferred measure of inflation - was revised down from 1.6 % -1.9% to 1.5% - 1.6% on 20 March 2013.

[127] Source: BEA. This was subsequently revised up to 1.21% y/y following the BEA's benchmark revisions on 2 August 2013.

August 2011 had not been accompanied by quantitative easing. Equally, the drop in the federal funds target in late 2008 had preceded any bond purchases.

Nevertheless, there was a danger that investors would conflate the two policy weapons. Indeed, as previously mentioned, more recent Federal Reserve research had shown that the signalling impact of bond purchases had been sizeable. Early estimates of the drop in Treasury yields and mortgage rates attributable to Federal Reserve bond purchases had wrongly concluded that the policy operated largely via the *supply channel*.

Many of the earlier papers leant heavily on the work of Dimitri Vayanos and Jean-Luc Vila, who provided a model for the term structure of interest rates based on the 'interaction between investor maturity clienteles and risk-averse arbitrageurs'.[128] Their model emphasised the portfolio balance effect of central bank asset purchases from the supply channel and downplayed the signalling channel, which follows directly from Keynes's Liquidity Preference Theory. This focus on the portfolio balance effect - specifically via the 'scarcity' or duration channels - had significant ramifications for the FOMC's choice of policy weapons, with Federal Reserve officials still [in the summer of 2013] underestimating the importance of

---

[128] See A *Preferred-Habitat Model of the Term Structure of Interest Rates*, Dimitri Vayanos and Jean-Luc Vila, National Bureau of Economics Research, November 2009.

providing unambiguous guidance on short-term rates.

In reality, there was an important 'announcement' effect too. Quantitative easing sent a strong signal to investors that central banks were committed to an ultra-loose monetary policy, including zero rates. Furthermore, on some estimates, the signalling channel was just as important, if not more important, than the supply channel impact of quantitative easing.[129] For this reason, the FOMC needed to tread carefully. The S&P 500 had hit a fresh high of 1669.2 on 21 May 2013.[130] Nevertheless, speculation over when the FOMC might start running down its bond purchases was beginning to cause significant gyrations in US equities by the end of May.[131]

## Mismanaging Liquidity Preference

The Federal Reserve had come under sustained criticism since November 2008 for allowing quantitative easing to inflate its balance sheet to support the US economic recovery. The FOMC meeting of 19-20 June 2013 thus provided the ideal opportunity should it want to announce

---

[129] See *The Signalling Channel for Federal Reserve Bond Purchases*, Michael D. Bauer, Glenn D. Rudebusch, Federal Reserve Bank of San Francisco, Working Paper series, 3 April 2013.

[130] Source: Thomson Reuters Datastream.

[131] Source: Thomson Reuters Datastream. The S&P composite price index fell from 1669.2 on 21 May 2013 to 1608.9 on 5 June 2013.

an orderly withdrawal of QE3. The unemployment rate had fallen to 7.6%: it had declined more quickly than the Federal Reserve had expected.[132] Nevertheless, if the Federal Reserve wanted to withdraw from QE3, there was plenty of scope for the FOMC to emphasise interest rates would not have to rise. Low inflation and particularly subdued wage gains implied the Federal Reserve had the latitude to demonstrate to markets that stopping bond purchases was not the end of low interest rates.[133] In any case, the historically high profit margins enjoyed by US companies implied that any pick-up in wage costs would have a limited impact on inflation. Ironically, the former FOMC chair Ben Bernanke had articulated the point in June 2004.[134] Nevertheless, short-term interest rate

---

[132] Source: BLS. Total unemployment as percent of the civilian labour force [official unemployment rate] fell to 7.6% in May 2013, although this was subsequently revised to 7.5%. At the FOMC meeting on 19 - 20 March 2013, the projection for the unemployment rate had been lowered to 7.3% - 7.5%. In December, it had been 7.4% - 7.7%. The forecast was revised down again to 7.2% - 7.3%.

[133] Source: BLS. Average hourly earnings [of production and non-supervisory employees, non-farm industries] had risen from the low of 1.3% y/y in October 2012 to 1.9% y/y by May 2013. However, this was well down from the rates of increase seen prior to the 2008 financial crisis. Average hourly earnings peaked at 4.2% y/y in December 2006.

[134] See *Monetary Policy and the Economic Outlook: 2004*, Ben Bernanke, 4 January 2004. Mr Bernanke noted 'The high level of [profit] markups is an important and perhaps insufficiently recognized feature of the current economic situation. To the extent that firms can maintain these markups, profits will continue to be high, supporting investment and equity values. To the extent that product-market competition erodes these markups, as is likely to occur over time, downward pressure will be exerted on the inflation rate, even if, as is likely, the recent declines in unit labor cost do not persist'.

expectations had started to rise ahead of the 19-20 June 2013 meeting.[135] This was a warning: if the FOMC had wanted to scale back bond purchases, they had to send a coherent message to markets that it intended to pursue a policy of *cheap* money.

Instead, the press conference following the release of the FOMC statement triggered a sharp rise in interest rate expectations, a jump in Treasury bond yields and a 4.8% drop in the S&P 500.[136] The FOMC statement was unremarkable. However, in the subsequent press conference, Ben Bernanke revealed that the FOMC expected that asset purchases would come to an end when the jobless rate was 'in the vicinity of 7 percent'.[137] This was only 0.6% above the rate prevailing at the meeting - just 0.5% according to the revised data.[138] Indeed, the unemployment forecast was cut sharply to reflect the improvement in the labour market. However, projections for inflation were lowered too.[139]

---

[135] Source: Thomson Reuters Datastream. The US Treasury Benchmark Bond 10-Year Yield climbed from 1.64% on 1 May 2013 to 2.18% on 18 June 2013, while the implied interest rate for the 3-month Eurodollar contract, June 2015, rose from 0.55% to 0.80% over the same period.

[136] Source: Thomson Reuters Datastream. In the four trading days following the press conference, the S&P 500 composite price index fell from 1651.8 [19 June 2013] to 1573.1 [23 June 2013, a drop of 4.8%] while the US Treasury Benchmark Bond 10-Year Yield jumped from 2.18% to 2.55%.

[137] See *Transcript of Chairman Bernanke's Press Conference*, 19 June 2013, p. 5.

[138] Source: BLS, Total unemployment as percent of the civilian labour force (official unemployment rate).

[139] See *Federal Reserve Accessible Materials, 18 - 19 June 2013*. The central

This should have allowed the FOMC to convince markets that a withdrawal of bond purchases would not be followed by an early rate hike. The distinction between the asset purchase programme and forward rate guidance was discussed by Ben Bernanke at his press conference after the FOMC meeting on 19 June 2013 and in the subsequent minutes. However, few investors were listening. Instead, the liquidity preference of investors was amplified by some unguarded comments from the FOMC chair. In response to a journalist from Reuters, who questioned the wisdom of allowing bond yields and mortgage rates to rise again, Mr Bernanke replied: 'if interest rates go up for the right reasons - that is, both optimism about the economy and an accurate assessment of monetary policy - that's a good thing. That's not a bad thing'.[140] The adverse reaction of financial markets to Mr Bernanke's comments perplexed FOMC officials. Over the subsequent weeks, there was a series of strong rebuttals from Committee members claiming that markets had overreacted.[141]

---

tendency of the projections for the price index for personal consumption expenditures, excluding food and energy [core consumption deflator] for Q4 2013 was revised from 1.5% y/y - 1.6% y/y on 19 - 20 March 2013 to 1.2% y/y - 1.3% y/y on 18 - 19 June 2013. For Q4 2014, it was revised from 1.7% y/y - 2.0% y/y on 19 - 20 March 2013 to 1.5% y/y - 1.8% y/y on 18 - 19 June 2013.

[140] See *Transcript of Chairman Bernanke's Press Conference*, 19 June 2013, p. 9.

[141] See *3 more Fed officials chastise 'feral hogs'*, The Wall Street Journal, 27 June 2013. Several FOMC members, including William Dudley, Jerome Powell and Dennis Lockhart, were all critical of the market reaction following the FOMC statement on 19 June 2013.

In truth, Mr Bernanke and other FOMC officials had underestimated the important signalling channel of its available policy weapons. It had again overplayed the supply channel. Mr Bernanke had repeatedly argued that long-term rates were affected by the stock of assets that the Federal Reserve holds on its balance sheet. One Financial Times journalist challenged Mr Bernanke at the press conference, highlighting the 'very sharp rise in real interest rates that we've seen in recent weeks,' which seemed to contradict the FOMC chair's interpretation.[142] His response was revealing: 'Well, we were a little puzzled by that. It was bigger than it could be explained by changes to the ultimate stock of asset purchases within reasonable ranges. So I think we have to conclude that there are other factors at work as well including again, some optimism about the economy, maybe some *uncertainty* arising'.[143]

With the last phrase the FOMC chair had unwittingly highlighted the liquidity preference that can make the control of long-term interest rates more difficult at abnormally low yields. As the economic recovery became more secure, the pressure for an increase in the federal funds rate would inevitably rise. It was incumbent upon the FOMC - particularly the chair - to underline publicly

---

[142] See *Transcript of Chairman Bernanke's Press Conference*, 19 June 2013, p. 9-10.

[143] Ibid. p. 10.

and vocally its commitment to keeping interest rates on hold, leaning against the innate tendency of markets to discount higher interest rates. The FOMC chair failed this test at the press conference.

## Rowing Back

Over subsequent days and weeks, FOMC officials were obliged to undo the damage inflicted by Mr Bernanke's press conference. There was a relentless campaign to draw attention to the difference between asset purchases and forward rate guidance. There could still be a significant delay between the end of QE3 and the first rate hike, FOMC officials claimed. The markets were not convinced. Interest rate expectations fell, but the decline was concentrated in shorter-dated contracts. The implied interest rate for the 3-month Eurodollar contract, June 2015 - when the FOMC expected the first rate hike - had risen 35 basis points in the four trading days following Mr Bernanke's press conference.[144] It fell back to new lows before the end of the year. By contrast, the implied interest rate for the 3-month Eurodollar contract, December 2016, rose 66 basis points: the subsequent

---

[144] Source: Thomson Reuters Datastream. The implied interest rate for the 3-month Eurodollar contract, June 2015, rose from 0.80% on 18 June 2013 to 1.15% on 22 June 2013. It subsequently fell back to a new low of 0.53% on 18 December 2013.

pullback was modest.[145] By the end of 2013, markets were still discounting a series of interest rate hikes from mid-2015 onwards.[146]

That did not stop equity markets hitting new highs, with the S&P 500 breaking decisively through 1700 on 16 October 2013 and then 1800 on 22 November 2013.[147] A government shutdown, as Republicans and Democrats locked horns over the Federal debt ceiling, did little to damp the bull market either. Despite the strong hints at Ben Bernanke's press conference on 19 June, the FOMC wrong-footed investors and decided not to announce a withdrawal of QE3 at its 17 - 18 September 2013 meeting. The FOMC argued the economy was not strong enough to withstand a withdrawal of the stimulus. In truth, the FOMC misread the data, which, with subsequent revisions showing the economy was recovering well.[148]

---

[145] Source: Thomson Reuters Datastream. The implied interest rate for the 3-month Eurodollar contract, December 2016, climbed from 1.99% on 18 June 2013 to 2.65% on 22 June 2013. It subsequently dropped to 1.85% on November 2013.

[146] Source: Thomson Reuters Datastream. The implied interest rate for the 3-month Eurodollar contract, June 2015, was 0.68% compared to 1.13% for December 2015, 2.36% for December 2016 and 3.39% for December 2017. For the June 2015 3-month Eurodollar contract, the implied interest rate on 31 December 2013 was 0.14% above the low of 2 May 2013 [0.54%]. For December 2016, it was 1.09% above the low of 2 May 2013 [1.27%], while for December 2017 it had climbed 1.47% from the low of 1 May 2013 [1.92%].

[147] Source: Thomson Reuters Datastream.

[148] Source: BLS. Total employment for non-farm industries rose 169,000 in August 2013 according to the BLS on 6 September 2013. For July 2013, total employment for non-farm industries climbed 104,000. These increases were subsequently revised [7 February 2014] to 149,000 [July 2012] and 202,000

However, the press conference following the September FOMC meeting was remarkable in one other respect. Mr Bernanke belatedly acknowledged that forward rate guidance was a more effective policy weapon than bond purchases.[149] He conceded, 'We have asset purchases, and we have rate policy and guidance about rates. It's our view that the latter, the rate policy, is actually the stronger, the more reliable tool'. The unrelenting focus on QE3 had diminished the profile of forward rate guidance. The FOMC was now trying to shift the focus of investors back to a policy weapon that had been very potent from the summer of 2011 onwards.

The FOMC was partly responsible for the misplaced emphasis on bond purchases. From the early months of the crisis, quantitative easing had been the first line of attack. The Federal Reserve had belatedly shifted to forward rate guidance over two-and-a-half years later. In the eyes of many commentators, bond purchases were the dominant policy tool. It was perhaps unsurprising

---

[August 2012] respectively.

[149] See *Transcript of Chairman Bernanke's Press Conference*, September 2013, p. 20 - 21. 'Again, you know, and I think people don't fully appreciate that we have two tools: We have asset purchases, and we have rate policy and guidance about rates. It's our view that the latter, the rate policy, is actually the stronger, more reliable tool. And when we get to the point where we can, you know, where we are close enough to full employment that rate policy will be sufficient, I think that we still be able to provide - even if asset purchases are reduced - we will still be able to provide a highly accommodative monetary background that will allow the economy to continue to grow and move towards full employment'.

that the introduction of QE3 in September 2012 had overshadowed the simultaneous decision to extend forward rate guidance to mid-June 2015. The Federal Reserve has at times appeared decidedly unsure of its optimal strategy. It had applied its non-conventional policies, without always fully understanding the importance of Keynes's Liquidity Preference Theory.

Nevertheless, the focus on short rate expectations or forward rate guidance is an incomplete weapon for tackling liquidity preference close to the *Zero Lower Bound*. As Mr Bernanke also noted, in his press conference after the 17 - 18 December 2013 meeting, there are limits to forward rate guidance 'because, beyond a certain point, markets may not accept - you know, may not view the long distance, way-ahead guidance as being credible'.[150]

The Federal Reserve is winding down one of the three subsequent tools - QE3 - but it is not entirely clear whether the FOMC will be able to deliver the low long term interest rates required to sustain an investment driven economic recovery. The focus will [as of March 2014] remain on forward rate guidance. In its own right, this may well prove to be a more effective weapon than bond purchases.

---

[150] See *Transcript of Chairman Bernanke's Press Conference*, 18 December 2013, p. 12.

# Appendix I

# Reverse Taps

Chapter 3 discusses the work of John Maynard Keynes and its relevance to the conduct of monetary policy when a country is embedded in a deep recession. His arguments were - and still are - pertinent when central banks have cut short-term interest rates to their lowest possible levels [Zero Lower Bound] and a recovery has failed to materialise, or remains inadequate. Keynes's policy prescriptions should have been embraced by the Federal Reserve from 2008 onwards in response to the financial crisis in the US. Instead, many of his arguments were overlooked. Ignoring Keynes's monetary analysis has proved costly. The monetary policy response to the collapse of the US housing market could and should have been much more effective. This would have materially reduced the long delays that will have occurred before full employment is eventually restored in the US. Taking the analysis of Keynes one step further, it will be argued in this section that a *reverse tap* could have mitigated some of the economic contraction witnessed in the aftermath of 2008 and brought about a swifter recovery.

A reverse tap is essentially quantitative easing, but with one unique feature: The central bank has an implicit or explicit target for long-term rates, and it stands ready to buy any amount of bonds to secure this objective. Critics will fret over the potential risks of exiting a reverse tap, but this should be seen as a secular policy, one that would buttress a shift to a cheap, but tight monetary policy. By targeting long-term interest rates more effectively, this policy will put the onus on financial stability, to ensure investment in the real economy becomes the driver of an economic recovery. In other words, a secular policy implies that central banks should consider a permanent target for long-term interest rates. In addition, it can be seen that smaller government debt burdens would facilitate this policy and render discussions of exit strategies obsolete.[1] In this sense, *cheap, but tight money* could be effectively underpinned by budget surpluses, aimed at bringing outstanding government debt down to manageable levels, allowing a central bank more latitude to control long-term interest rates. Specifically, it would help central banks backstop their target for long-term interest rates, with less potential risk to their balance

---

[1] Source: Federal Reserve [Securities Held Outright], BEA [GDP, Current Prices], Organisation for Economic Cooperation and Development [OECD, General Government Gross Financial Liabilities]. Securities Held Outright by the Federal Reserve rose to $3.950trillion by 20 March 2014. This was equivalent to 23.1% of Q4 2013 GDP [annualised]. The Government gross financial liabilities as a share of GDP was 102.1% in 2012.

sheet.

In Chapter 15 of *The General Theory of Employment, Interest and Money*, Keynes outlined the *monetary policy tools* that followed logically from his *Liquidity Preference Theory*.[2] This theory is also discussed in more detail in Chapter 3. Keynes argued that if a central bank was prepared to 'deal *both ways* [author's italics] on specified debts of all maturities', this would widen the central bank's control over all rates of interest [short- and long-term].[3] In other words, if a central bank extends the range of securities that it is willing to buy and sell, it can influence the shape of the yield curve. He added, 'In Great Britain, the field of deliberate control appears to be widening' in response to monetary policies he had articulated.[4]

The impact of *The General Theory* in the UK was evident in the 1945 National Debt Enquiry report, which adopted much of Keynes's analysis as the intellectual foundation for a more radical post-war monetary policy.[5] Among other tasks, the National Debt Enquiry was charged with the responsibility of outlining the rate

[2] See *The Theory of Employment, Interest and Money*, John Maynard Keynes, University Press Cambridge, 1973.

[3] Ibid. p. 205.

[4] Ibid. p. 206.

[5] See *Keynes's General Theory, The Rate of Interest and 'Keynesian' Economics*, Geoff Tily, p. 84.

of interest policy that should prevail after the war. Keynes believed it was incumbent upon central banks to challenge the prevailing 'wisdom' or the status quo to ensure borrowing costs remained low enough to facilitate an economic recovery. He argued at the National Debt Enquiry that 'if individuals had received a high reward rate of interest in the past they would continue to expect a high reward into the future'.[6]

A reverse tap involves a central bank setting the price of any particular government bond and standing ready to buy any quantity needed to ensure an implicit target for yields is fulfilled. A central bank has the ability to set the price for bonds of a certain maturity. It could also offer to buy bonds across a range of maturities. In effect, the central bank has the ability to influence the shape of the entire *yield curve*. The essential point of a reverse tap is setting the price of a bond above the prevailing market level, to push yields lower. The central bank would be effectively fixing the rate of interest not just at the short end of the maturity spectrum [the policy rate], but at the long end of the yield curve too. If, for example, the prevailing yield of a 10-year bond was 3.25%, but the central bank wanted this to fall to 3.0%, it could simply offer to buy the amount required [theoretically unlimited] at the new [higher] price consistent with this

---

[6] Ibid. p. 199.

lower yield.

Keynes argued that the success of any large-scale asset purchases depended upon the conviction of the central bank. A reverse tap would eliminate any doubts in the minds of investors *vis-à-vis* the central bank's determination and crucially, its ability to control borrowing costs. Nevertheless, critics might argue that a reverse tap runs the risk of a central bank being forced to buy more bonds than it perhaps wanted to ensure this target for [lower] yields was hit. A central bank would have no control over the size of its balance sheet.

This argument misses the point. If a central bank is clear about the rate it is targeting for bonds of a particular maturity, the market price would adjust rapidly to reflect this particular yield. Furthermore, if the central bank was committed to a secular policy of lower interest rates under a cheap, but tight monetary policy framework, this would reduce the fears of investors of a sudden and sharp rise in rates in the future.

As a result, the increase in the central bank's balance sheet might be relatively modest. Indeed, it is not inconceivable that the Federal Reserve would have been obliged to buy fewer bonds under a reverse tap compared with QE1, QE2 and QE3. In response to these three policies, the Federal Reserve's balance sheet has risen more than eightfold since 2008 without the FOMC being in control of long-term interest rates.[7]

If a central bank announced a reverse tap and then immediately discussed possible exit strategies, investors might well be minded to sell most if not all of their bonds to a central bank. Any discussion of exit strategies [as seen repeatedly in 2009 and 2010] would feed into the potential mistrust of the central bank's actions: a reverse tap would inevitably be controversial given criticisms of the Federal Reserve since the introduction of QE1 in November 2008.

By contrast, a reverse tap would be more effective if the policy was seen as secular and part of a broader shift that included effective constraints on credit growth. Investors might then understand that the low long-term interest rate was not an aberration: other policy tools will be applied to control the economy during an upswing to prevent any build-up in inflation pressures and preserve financial stability. This dual policy of cheap, but tight money is also discussed further in Chapter 3.

The application of tight money is crucial to the ability of a central bank to ensure a reverse tap is successful. Investors would come to understand that the interest rates - and by extension bond yields - are not, under this new policy paradigm, the primary tool to control the economic cycle once the recovery has begun. Effective

---

[7] Source: Federal Reserve. Securities Held Outright, rose from $479.6billion on 2 September 2008 to $3.95trillion in 19 March 2014.

financial regulation and control of credit growth would become equally, if not more important policy tools. That will in turn reduce the potential rise in a central bank's balance sheet in response to a reverse tap.

A reverse tap would also be effective if it was combined with greater control of the government debt burden. The persistent budget deficits run by governments in recent decades have undermined the ability of central banks to control the long-term interest rate. If the Federal debt burden was much lower - it reached 75.6% of GDP at the end of fiscal year 2012 - the potential risks to the Federal Reserve's balance sheet from a reverse tap would be commensurately reduced.[8] The maximum amount a central bank can be forced in a reverse tap will be determined by the size of the government debt outstanding.

## A Reverse Tap in 2008?

The Federal Reserve and the Bank of England flouted the principle of a reverse tap when they embarked upon quantitative easing in response to the crisis of 2008. Both central banks set nominal targets for their asset purchases, ignoring the liquidity preference of investors. From their perspective, the relationship between money and demand was deemed to be exogenous and not

---

[8] Source: BEA, US Treasury.

endogenous, as suggested by Keynes. As a result, they had far less control over long-term interest rates and the speed of the recovery than they might have imagined.

The subsequent shift to forward rate guidance in the summer of 2011 needs to be seen in the context of these mistakes. If the Federal Reserve had taken a very different approach to QE1 and QE2 - framing this around a reverse tap and establishing a clear target for long-term interest rates - the FOMC may well not have needed to use forward guidance, both in its own right initially and later alongside bond purchases. By pushing long-term interest rates and mortgage costs down more quickly from 2009 onwards, the recovery may have taken hold earlier and might have been much more robust.

The ineffectiveness of QE1 and QE2 was not just due to tactical mistakes with the implementation of these policies. The failure to take into account liquidity preference extended to fiscal policy. Because the Federal budget deficit was so large, critics fretted that bond purchases were facilitating an excessive rise in the Federal government's debt burden. Quantitative easing was seen by some investors as unsustainable and tantamount to 'deficit financing' with potentially adverse consequences for inflation. This concern would possibly have been even greater with a reverse tap. If the US administration was seen to be taking risks with the Federal government's finances, the Federal Reserve's balance sheet might have risen much more quickly. The FOMC might have then come under even heavier pressure from hawks and critics to abandon a reverse tap. Investors would have been more amenable to attempts to fix long-term interest rates if they believed that the Federal Reserve was not underwriting fiscal profligacy. Therefore, it would certainly have been helpful if the US administration had not tried to invoke an incorrect interpretation of Keynes's work to justify its economic policies.

For the Federal Reserve, the fixed targets for bond purchases that accompanied QE1 and QE2 failed to provide the same certainty for investors that could have been provided by a reverse tap. This error was compounded by the rush to reassure investors that the FOMC had contingency plans for unwinding QE1 and QE2. By the summer of 2011, the FOMC had accepted some of the principles that lay behind a reverse tap when it adopted forward rate guidance and Operation Twist. There was a focus on expectations with the implicit aim of controlling the long-term interest rate. Similarly, with its commitment to buy mortgage backed securities and Treasuries on an unlimited basis, QE3 was designed to provide a degree of certainty that was lacking with QE1 and QE2.

The three policy weapons [*forward rate guidance*, *Operation Twist* and *QE3*] pursued since the summer of 2011 were more effective than QE1 and QE2. However, they have been substitutes for reverse taps - a more robust and emphatic tool that was totally ignored from 2008 onwards.

# Appendix II

# US Monetary Policy Diary

## Summary

| | |
|---|---|
| 25 November 2008 | QE1 announced [$600billion in asset purchases] |
| 16 December 2008 | Forward rate guidance begins |
| 18 March 2009 | QE1 increased from $900billion to $1.75trillion |
| 16 March 2010 | QE1 comes to an end |
| 3 November 2010 | QE2 announced |
| 22 June 2011 | QE2 comes to an end |
| 9 August 2011 | Calendar-based forward rate guidance - through to mid-2013 |
| 21 September 2011 | Operation Twist and reinvest principal payments of MBS |
| 25 January 2012 | Forward rate guidance extended to late-2014 |
| 20 June 2012 | Operation Twist extended by a further six months [end-2012] |
| 13 September 2012 | QE3 announced - $45billion in asset purchases per month Forward rate guidance extended to mid-2015 |
| 12 December 2012 | QE3 increased [to include |

| | purchases of Treasuries] - total asset purchases now $85 per month<br>Calendar-based forward rate guidance replaced by quantitative forward rate guidance. |
|---|---|
| 18 December 2013 | **Tapering begins as asset purchases reduced from $85billion to $75billion per month** |

## 2007

**31 January 2007**
Federal funds target rate left unchanged at 5.25%

**21 March 2007**
Federal funds target rate left unchanged at 5.25%

**9 May 2007**
Federal funds target rate left unchanged at 5.25%

**28 June 2007**
Federal funds target rate left unchanged at 5.25%

**7 August 2007**
Federal funds target rate left unchanged at 5.25%

**10 August 2007**
Unscheduled meeting due to financial market worries.

The Federal Reserve announced that it would provide 'liquidity to facilitate the orderly functioning of financial markets'. It would also 'provide reserves as necessary through open market operations to promote trading in the federal funds market at rates close to the Federal Open Market Committee's target rate of 5.25%'.

## 17 August 2007

Unscheduled meeting due to financial market worries.

The FOMC announced its willingness to 'act as needed to mitigate the adverse effects on the economy' from the increasing disruption to financial markets.

## 18 September 2007

Federal funds target rate lowered 50 basis points to 4.75%

## 31 October 2007

Federal funds target rate lowered 25 basis points to 4.50%

## 6 December 2007

Unscheduled meeting due to liquidity situation in certain markets.

A swap arrangement with the ECB was established 'in an amount not to exceed $20billion'.

## 11 December 2007

Federal funds target rate lowered 25 basis points to 4.25%

## 12 December 2007

The Bank of Canada, the Bank of England, the European Central Bank, the Federal Reserve and the Swiss National Bank announced measures to address the elevated pressures in short-term funding markets. Actions taken include the establishment of a temporary Term Auction Facility and the establishment of foreign exchange swap lines with the European Central Bank and the Swiss National Bank.

## 21 December 2007

The Federal Reserve announced that it intends to conduct bi-weekly auctions for the Term Auction Facility for as long as necessary to address elevated pressures in short-term funding markets.

# 2008

## 9 January 2008

Unscheduled meeting to discuss rate cut

## 22 January 2008

Unscheduled meeting to lower interest rates.

Federal funds target rate lowered 75 basis points to 3.50%

## 30 January 2008

Federal funds target rate lowered 50 basis points to 3.00%

## 7 March 2008

The Federal Reserve announced 'two initiatives to address heightened liquidity pressures in term funding markets. First, the amounts outstanding in the Term Auction Facility will be increased to $100billion. Second, the Federal Reserve will initiate a series of term repurchase transactions that are expected to cumulate to $100billion'.

## 11 March 2008

Unscheduled meeting.

The Federal Reserve announced the expansion of its securities lending. Under the Term Securities Lending Facility, the Federal Reserve is to 'lend up to $200billion of Treasury securities to primary dealers secured for a term of 28 days [rather than overnight, as in the existing program] by a pledge of other securities, including federal agency debt, federal agency residential-mortgage-backed securities [MBS], and non-agency AAA/Aaa-rated private-label residential MBS'. In addition, 'Securities will be made available through an auction process', which will be held weekly beginning 27 March 2008.

Furthermore, the Committee authorised an increase in the temporary reciprocal currency arrangements with the European Central Bank by $10billion [up to $30billion] and the Swiss National Bank by $2billion [up to $6billion]. The term of this arrangement was extended until 30 September 2008.

Finally, the size of the Term Auction Facility was boosted to $100billion and the Federal Reserve committed to 'undertake a series of term repurchase transactions that will cumulate to $100billion'.

## 18 March 2008

Federal funds target rate lowered 75 basis points to 2.25%

## 30 April 2008

Federal funds target rate lowered 25 basis points to 2.0%

**25 June 2008**

Federal funds target rate left unchanged at 2.0%

**24 July 2008**

Unscheduled meeting to discuss Term Auction Facility, Primary Dealer Credit Facility and Term Securities Lending Facility

**30 July 2008**

The Federal Reserve announced several steps to enhance the effectiveness of its existing liquidity facilities, including the introduction of longer terms to maturity in its Term Auction Facility.

It also announced:

- the extension of the Primary Dealer Credit Facility and the Term Securities Lending Facility through to January 30, 2009;
- the introduction of auctions of options on $50billion of draws on the Term Securities Lending Facility;
- the introduction of 84-day Term Auction Facility loans as a complement to 28-day Term Auction Facility loans;
- an increase in the Federal Reserve's swap line with the European Central Bank to $55billion from $50billion.

**5 August 2008**

Federal funds target rate left unchanged at 2.0%

**14 September 2008**

The Federal Reserve Board announced 'several initiatives to provide additional support to financial markets, including enhancements to its existing liquidity facilities'.

## 16 September 2008

Federal funds target rate left unchanged at 2.0%

## 18 September 2008

The Bank of Canada, the Bank of England, the European Central Bank [ECB], the Federal Reserve, the Bank of Japan, and the Swiss National Bank announced 'coordinated measures designed to address the continued elevated pressures in US Dollar short-term funding markets'.

## 24 September 2008

Swap lines were established with Central Banks of Australia, Denmark, Norway, and Sweden to address 'elevated pressures in US Dollar short-term funding markets'.

## 29 September 2008

Unscheduled meeting to discuss swap lines.

The Federal Reserve announced 'further coordinated actions to expand significantly the capacity to provide US Dollar liquidity'. This was 'in response to continued strains in short-term funding markets'.

Furthermore, the committee decided to increase the size of the 84-day maturity Term Action Facility from $25billion to $75billion per auction. Additional short-dated Term Auction Facility would take place in November for a total amount of $150billion. In addition, authorisation of swap lines with other Central Banks was raised from a combined $290billion to $620billion.

## 7 October 2008

The Federal Reserve Board announced 'the creation

of the Commercial Paper Funding Facility [CPFF], a facility that will complement the Federal Reserve's existing credit facilities to help provide liquidity to term funding markets. The CPFF will provide a liquidity backstop to US issuers of commercial paper through a special purpose vehicle that will purchase three-month unsecured and asset-backed commercial paper directly from eligible issuers'.

### 8 October 2008

Unscheduled meeting to lower interest rates.

Federal funds target rate lowered 50 basis points to 1.50%. The Committee took this action 'in light of evidence pointing to a weakening of economic activity and a reduction in inflationary pressures'.

### 13 October 2008

The FOMC statement revealed that 'In order to provide broad access to liquidity and funding to financial institutions, the Bank of England [BoE], the European Central Bank [ECB], the Federal Reserve, the Bank of Japan, and the Swiss National Bank [SNB] are jointly announcing further measures to improve liquidity in short-term US Dollar funding markets'.

### 14 October 2008

The FOMC authorised an increase in the size of 'its temporary reciprocal currency arrangement [swap line] with the Bank of Japan, so that the Bank of Japan can provide US Dollar funding in quantities sufficient to meet demand'.

In addition, the Treasury announced a voluntary capital purchase programme. A broad array of financial institutions would be eligible to participate in this programme by selling preferred shares to the US government.

Furthermore, 'After receiving a recommendation from the boards of the Federal Deposit Insurance Corporation [FDIC] and the Federal Reserve, and consulting with the President, Secretary Paulson signed the systemic risk exception to the FDIC Act, enabling the FDIC to temporarily guarantee the senior debt of all FDIC-insured institutions and their holding companies, as well as deposits in non-interest bearing deposit transaction accounts'.

Finally the FOMC announced further details of its Commercial Paper Funding Facility [CPFF] programme, which provided a broad backstop for the commercial paper market. This was in order to 'further increase access to funding for businesses' in all sectors of the economy. The CPFF would 'fund purchases of commercial paper of 3 month maturity from high-quality issuers'.

### 21 October 2008

The Federal Reserve Board announced 'the creation of the Money Market Investor Funding Facility [MMIFF], which will support a private-sector initiative designed to provide liquidity to US money market investors'.

### 29 October 2008

Federal funds target rate lowered 50 basis points to 1.0%

### 25 November 2008
**Unscheduled meeting - QE1 announced**

**[$600billion in asset purchases].**

The Federal Reserve announced a programme to purchase up to $100billion in direct obligations of housing-related government-sponsored entities [GSE direct obligations] as well as purchases of up to $500billion in mortgage-backed securities [MBS]. The purchase of GSE direct obligations will begin the following week and the purchase of MBS will begin before year-end.

The Committee also introduced the Term Asset-Backed Securities Loan Facility [TALF], 'a facility that will help market participants meet the credit needs of households and small businesses by supporting the issuance of asset-backed securities collateralised by student loans, auto loans, credit card loans, and loans guaranteed by the Small Business Administration. Under the TALF, the Federal Reserve Bank of New York will lend up to $200billion on a non-recourse basis to holders of certain AAA-rated ABS backed by newly and recently originated consumer and small business loans'.

## 8 December 2008

The Federal Reserve announced the extension through to 30 April 2009 of three liquidity facilities: Primary Dealer Credit Facility, the Asset-Backed Commercial Paper Money Market Fund Liquidity Facility, and Term Securities Lending Facility. These facilities had previously been authorised through January 30, 2009.

## 16 December 2008
**Forward rate guidance begins.**

The committee announced the establishment of a target range of 0% - 0.25% for the federal funds rate.

Furthermore, the FOMC also announced that 'The Committee continues to anticipate that economic conditions are likely to warrant exceptionally low levels of the federal funds rate for some time'.

# 2009

### 16 January 2009

Unscheduled meeting.

The committee met by conference call 'to discuss issues associated with establishing an explicit objective for inflation. The Committee made no decisions on whether to establish such an objective'. [Details disclosed in the minutes of the 28 January 2009 meeting].

### 28 January 2009

Federal funds target rate range left unchanged at 0% - 0.25%.

The committee announced 'The Federal Reserve continues to purchase large quantities of agency debt and mortgage-backed securities to provide support to the mortgage and housing markets, and it stands ready to expand the quantity of such purchases and the duration of the purchase program as conditions warrant. The Committee also is prepared to purchase longer-term Treasury securities if evolving circumstances indicate that such transactions would be particularly effective in improving conditions in private credit markets'.

### 7 February 2009
Unscheduled meeting.

The Committee met by conference call in a joint session with the Board of Governors 'to discuss the potential role of the Federal Reserve in the Treasury's forthcoming financial stabilisation plan. After hearing an overview of the version of the plan envisioned at the time of the meeting, meeting participants discussed in principal elements and shared a range of perspectives on its implications for financial markets and institutions. The Federal Reserve's primary direct role in the plan would be through an expansion of the previously announced Term Auction Lending Facility, which would be supported by additional funds from the Troubled Asset Relief Program'.

### 18 March 2009
**QE1 increased from $900billion to $1.75trillion.**

**Forward rate guidance language changed [to include extended period].**

Federal funds target rate range left unchanged at 0% - 0.25%. However, the FOMC changed its language stating that it 'will maintain the target range for the federal funds rate at 0 to 1/4 percent and anticipates that economic conditions are likely to warrant exceptionally low levels of the federal funds rate for an *extended period*'.

In addition, the FOMC announced that 'To provide greater support to mortgage lending and housing markets, the Committee decided to increase the size of the Federal Reserve's balance sheet further by purchasing up to an additional $750billion of agency mortgage-backed securities, bringing its total purchase of these securities to up to $1.25trillion this year, and to increase purchases of agency debt up to $100billion to a total of up to $200billion'.

Moreover, the Federal reserve decided to purchase up to $300billion of longer-term Treasury securities over the next six months 'to help improve conditions in private credit markets'. The Federal Reserve has launched the Term Asset-Backed Securities Loan Facility to facilitate the extension of credit to households and small businesses and anticipates that the range of eligible collateral for this facility is likely to be expanded to include other financial assets'. The Committee stated its preparedness to 'employ all available tools to promote economic recovery and to promote price stability'.

## 29 April 2009

Federal funds target rate range left unchanged at 0% - 0.25%

## 3 June 2009

Unscheduled meeting.

The Committee convened by conference call in a joint session with the Board of Governors 'to review recent economic and financial developments, including changes in the Federal Reserve's balance sheet'. [Details disclosed in the minutes of the 24 June 2009 meeting]

### 24 June 2009

Federal funds target rate range left unchanged at 0% - 0.25%.

The Committee stated that the Federal Reserve will 'make adjustments to its credit and liquidity programs as warranted'.

### 12 August 2009

Federal funds target rate range left unchanged at 0% - 0.25%.

The Federal Reserve decided that the purchase of $300billion longer-term securities would be complete by the end of October. The statement stipulated that 'To promote a smooth transition in markets as these purchases of Treasury securities are completed, the Committee has decided to gradually slow the pace of these transactions and anticipates that the full amount will be purchased by the end of October'.

### 23 September 2009

Federal funds target rate range left unchanged at 0% - 0.25%.

The Committee decided that the purchase of agency debt and agency mortgage-backed securities would now be complete by the 'end of the first quarter of 2010'.

### 4 November 2009

Federal funds target rate range left unchanged at 0% - 0.25%.

The Committee announced that the purchase of agency debt will now stop at $175billion, rather than $200billion. Nonetheless, the statement stipulated that 'The amount of agency debt purchases, while somewhat less than the previously announced maximum of $200billion, is consistent with the recent path of purchases and reflects the limited availability of agency debt'.

## 16 December 2009

Federal funds target rate range left unchanged at 0% - 0.25%.

The FOMC announced that 'The Committee and the Board of Governors anticipate that most of the Federal Reserve's special liquidity facilities will expire on February 1, 2010'.

# 2010

## 27 January 2010

Federal funds target rate range left unchanged at 0% - 0.25%.

The Committee announced that the 'temporary liquidity swap arrangements between the Federal Reserve and other central banks will expire on February 1 [2010]'.

## 16 March 2010

**QE1 comes to an end.**

Federal funds target rate range left unchanged at 0% - 0.25%

## 28 April 2010

Federal funds target rate range left unchanged at 0% - 0.25%.

The Committee announced that it had 'closed all but one of the special liquidity facilities'. The remaining programme, the 'Term Asset-Backed Securities Loan Facility' is scheduled to close in full by 30 June 2010.

### 9 May 2010

Unscheduled meeting to discuss swap lines with central banks.

The Federal Open Market Committee authorised 'temporary reciprocal currency arrangements [swap lines] with the Bank of Canada, the Bank of England, the European Central Bank and the Swiss National Bank ... to continue until the end of January 2011'.

The Committee also announced that the 're-establishment of its temporary US Dollar liquidity swap arrangement with the Bank of Japan', will continue until the end of January 2011.

### 23 June 2010

Federal funds target rate range left unchanged at 0% - 0.25%.

### 10 August 2010

Federal funds target rate range left unchanged at 0% - 0.25%.

### 21 September 2010

Federal funds target rate range left unchanged at 0% - 0.25%.

The Committee announced that it 'is prepared to provide additional accommodation if needed to support the economic recovery and to return inflation, over time, to levels consistent with its mandate', whereas previously it had been stated that the Committee will 'employ its policy tools as necessary to promote economic recovery and price stability'.

## 15 October 2010
Unscheduled meeting.

The Committee met by videoconference to 'discuss issues associated with its monetary policy framework, including alternative ways to express and communicate the Committee's objectives, possibilities for supplementing the Committee's communication about its policy decisions, the merits of smaller and more frequent adjustments, and the potential costs and benefits of targeting a term interest rate. The agenda did not contemplate any policy decisions and none were taken'.

## 3 November 2010
**QE2 announced.**

Federal funds target rate range was left unchanged at 0% - 0.25%

The Committee announced its intention to purchase a further $600billion of longer-term Treasury securities by the end of June 2011, at a pace of $75billion per month. The FOMC will also maintain its 'existing policy of reinvesting principle payments from its securities holdings'.

## 14 December 2010
Federal funds target rate range left unchanged at 0% - 0.25

# 2011

### 26 January 2011

Federal funds target rate range left unchanged at 0% - 0.25%

### 15 March 2011

Federal funds target rate range left unchanged at 0% - 0.25%

### 27 April 2011

Federal funds target rate range left unchanged at 0% - 0.25%

### 22 June 2011
### QE2 comes to an end

Federal funds target rate range left unchanged at 0% - 0.25%.

The Federal Reserve announced that the purchase of $600billion of longer-term Treasury securities was complete. The statement stipulated that in monitoring the economic outlook, the Committee would 'act as needed to best foster maximum employment and price stability'. This is a shift from stating that the Committee 'will employ its policy tools as necessary'.

### 1 August 2011

Unscheduled meeting.

The FOMC met by videoconference to 'discuss issues associated with contingencies in the event that the Treasury was temporarily unable to meet its obligations because the statutory federal debt limit was not raised or in the event of a downgrade of the US sovereign credit rating'. [Details disclosed in the minutes of the August 9 meeting].

## 9 August 2011

### Calendar-based forward rate guidance - through to *mid-2013*.

Federal funds target rate range left unchanged at 0% - 0.25%.

The FOMC stated its intention to keep the federal funds target rate at this rate 'through mid-2013'. The statement revealed that 'The Committee currently anticipates that economic conditions - including low rates of resource utilization and a subdued outlook for inflation over the medium run - are likely to warrant exceptionally low levels for the federal funds rate at least through mid-2013'. This was the first time that a date was specified. Previously the Committee had said that it would keep the federal funds target rate unchanged 'for an extended period'.

In addition, 'The Committee also discussed the range of policy tools available to promote a stronger economic recovery'.

## 21 September 2011

### Operation Twist and reinvest principal payments of MBS.

Federal funds target rate range was left unchanged at 0% - 0.25%.

The Committee decided to extend the average maturity of its holdings of securities. 'The Committee intends to purchase, by the end of June 2012, $400billion of Treasury securities with remaining maturities of 6 years to 30 years and to sell an equal amount of Treasury securities with remaining maturities of 3 years or less'.

It was also announced that 'the Committee will now reinvest principal payments from its holdings of agency debt and agency mortgage-backed securities in agency mortgage-backed securities'.

## 2 November 2011

Federal funds target rate range left unchanged at 0% - 0.25%

## 28 November 2011

Unscheduled meeting.

The FOMC discussed 'a proposal to amend and augment the Federal Reserve's temporary liquidity swap arrangements with foreign central banks in light of strains in global financial markets'.

## 13 December 2011

Federal funds target rate range left unchanged at 0% - 0.25%.

# 2012

## 25 January 2012

**Forward rate guidance extended to late-2014.**

Federal funds target rate left unchanged at 0% - 0.25%. However, the FOMC announced that it 'anticipates that economic conditions - including low rates of resource utilization and a subdued outlook for inflation over the medium run - are likely to warrant exceptionally low levels for the federal funds rate at least through late 2014'.

### 13 March 2012

Federal funds target rate range left unchanged at
0% - 0.25%

### 25 April 2012

Federal funds target rate range left unchanged at
0% - 0.25%

### 20 June 2012

**Operation Twist extended by a further six months
[*end-2012*].**

Federal funds target rate range left unchanged at
0% - 0.25%.

The Committee decided 'to continue through the
end of the year [previously set to expire in June]
its program to extend the average maturity of its
holdings of securities. Specifically, the Committee
intends to purchase Treasury securities with
remaining maturities of 6 years to 30 years at the
current pace and to sell or redeem an equal amount
of Treasury securities with remaining maturities
of approximately 3 years or less. The continuation
of this program should put downward pressure on
longer-term interest rates and help to make broader
financial conditions more accommodative'.

The Committee also announced that it is 'prepared
to take further action as appropriate to promote
a stronger economic recovery and sustained
improvement in labor market conditions'.

### 1 August 2012

Federal funds target rate left unchanged at 0% -
0.25%

## 13 September 2012

**QE3 announced - $45 billion in asset purchases per month.**

**Forward rate guidance extended to mid-2015.**

Federal funds target rate range left unchanged at 0% - 0.25%.

The Committee agreed to 'increase policy accommodation by purchasing additional agency mortgage-backed securities at a pace of $40 billion per month'. Alongside the current programme to extend the average maturity of its holdings by $45 billion per month, 'these actions ... together will increase the Committee's holdings of longer-term securities by about $85 billion each month through the end of the year'.

The FOMC also broadened its intention for policy accommodation. The statement stipulated that 'If the outlook for the labor market does not improve substantially, the Committee will continue its purchases of agency mortgage-backed securities, undertake additional asset purchases, and employ its other policy tools as appropriate until such improvement is achieved in a context of price stability'. It also stated for the first time that the FOMC would 'take appropriate account of the likely efficacy and costs of such purchases.'

Furthermore, the Committee announced that it 'expects that a highly accommodative stance of monetary policy will remain appropriate for a considerable time after the economy strengthens ...'. The Committee also 'anticipates that exceptionally low levels for the federal funds rate are likely to be warranted at least through mid-2015.'

## 24 October 2012

Federal funds target rate range left unchanged at
0% - 0.25%

## 12 December 2012

**QE3 increased [to include purchases of
Treasuries] - total asset purchases now $85billion
per month.**

**Rolling over of maturing Treasury securities
announced.**

**Calendar-based forward rate guidance replaced by
quantitative forward rate guidance.**

Federal funds target rate range left unchanged at
0% - 0.25%.

The Committee announced that it 'will continue
purchasing additional agency mortgage-backed
securities at a pace of $40billion per month. The
Committee will also purchase longer-term Treasury
securities after its program to extend the average
maturity of its holdings of Treasury securities is
completed at the end of the year, initially at a pace
of $45billion per month ... and, in January, will
resume rolling over maturing Treasury securities at
auction'.

In addition, the accommodative stance of monetary
policy 'will remain appropriate for a considerable
time after the asset purchase program ends' as
well as for a considerable time after the 'economic
recovery strengthens'.

Furthermore, 'The Committee ... currently
anticipates that this exceptionally low range for

the federal funds rate will be appropriate at least as long as the unemployment rate remains above 61/2 percent, inflation between one and two years ahead is projected to be no more than a half percentage point above the Committee's 2 percent longer-run goal, and longer-term inflation expectations continue to be well anchored. The Committee views these thresholds as consistent with its earlier date-based guidance. In determining how long to maintain a highly accommodative stance of monetary policy, the Committee will also consider other information, including additional measures of labor market conditions, indicators of inflation pressures and inflation expectations, and readings on financial developments. When the Committee decides to begin to remove policy accommodation, it will take a balanced approach consistent with its longer-run goals of maximum employment and inflation of 2 percent'.

## 2013

### 20 January 2013
Federal funds target rate range left unchanged at 0% - 0.25%

### 20 March 2013
Federal funds target rate range left unchanged at 0% - 0.25%

### 1 May 2013
Federal funds target rate range left unchanged at 0% - 0.25%.

However, the Committee changed its language stating that it is 'prepared to increase or reduce the pace of its purchases to maintain appropriate policy accommodation as the outlook for the labor market or inflation changes'.

## 19 June 2013

Federal funds target rate range left unchanged at 0% - 0.25%.

However, the language on inflation and outlook was changed.

New language on inflation:

• 'Partly reflecting transitory influences, inflation has been running below the Committee's longer-run objective'.

Old language on inflation: [had been in place for four FOMC meetings]

• 'Inflation has been running somewhat below the Committee's longer-run objective, apart from temporary variations that largely reflect fluctuations in energy prices'.

New language on outlook:

• 'The Committee sees the downside risks to the outlook for the economy and the labor market as having diminished since the fall'.

Old language on outlook:

• 'Labor market conditions have shown some improvement in recent months, on balance, but the unemployment rate remains elevated'.

## 31 July 2013

Federal funds target rate range left unchanged at

0% - 0.25%.

However, the Committee recognised that 'inflation persistently below its 2 percent objective could pose risks to economic performance, but it anticipates that inflation will move back toward its objective over the medium term'.

### 18 September 2013

Federal funds target rate range left unchanged at 0% - 0.25%.

However, the Federal Reserve recognised that 'The housing sector has been strengthening, but mortgage rates have risen further'.

In addition, the FOMC stated that 'The downside risks to the outlook for the economy and the labor market as having diminished, on net, since last fall, but the tightening of financial conditions observed in recent months, if sustained, could slow the pace of improvement in the economy and labor market'. Nonetheless, the statement added that 'Taking into account the extent of federal fiscal retrenchment, the Committee sees the improvement in economic activity and labor market conditions since it began its asset purchase program a year ago as consistent with growing underlying strength in the broader economy. However, the Committee decided to await more evidence that progress will be sustained before adjusting the pace of its purchases'.

### 30 October 2013

Federal funds target rate range left unchanged at 0% - 0.25%.

The Committee announced that it 'await more evidence that progress will be sustained before adjusting the pace of its asset purchases'.

## 18 December 2013
**Tapering begins as asset purchases reduced from $85billion to $75billion per month.**

Federal funds target rate left unchanged at 0% - 0.25%.

However, the Federal Reserve announced that 'In light of the cumulative progress towards maximum employment and the improvement in the outlook for labor market conditions, the Committee decided to modestly reduce the pace of its asset purchases. Beginning in January, the Committee will add to its holdings on agency mortgage-backed securities at a pace of $35billion per month rather than $40billion per month, and will add to its holdings on longer-term Treasury securities at a pace of $40billion per month rather than $45billion per month'.


# 2014

## 29 January 2014
**Asset purchases reduced from $75billion to $65billion per month.**

Federal funds target rate range left unchanged at 0% - 0.25%.

The FOMC announced that 'In light of the cumulative progress towards maximum employment and the improvement in the outlook for labor market conditions, the Committee decided to make a further reduction in the pace of its asset purchases. Beginning in February, the Committee will add to its holdings on agency mortgage-backed securities at a pace of $30billion per month rather than $35billion per month, and will add to its holdings on longer-term Treasury securities at a pace of $35billion per month rather than $40billion per month'.

## 19 March 2014

**Asset purchases reduced from $65billion to $55billion per month.**

**Quantitative forward rate guidance dropped.**

The Federal reserve announced that 'The Committee continues to anticipate, based on its assessment of these factors [a wide range of information, including measures of labor market conditions, indicators of inflation pressures and inflation expectations, and readings on financial developments], that it likely will be appropriate to maintain the current target range for the federal funds rate for a considerable time after the asset purchase program ends, especially if inflation continues to run below the Committee's 2 percent longer-run goal, and provided that longer-term inflation expectations remain well anchored'.

# Chapter 3

# Keynes and Liquidity Preference

The primary aim of *quantitative easing* [QE] or *large-scale asset purchases* has been to reduce the 'risk-free' *rate* and thus encourage other borrowing costs to fall, for corporates and households. The very essence of this policy should be the attack on the *rate of interest*, both short- and long-term. A central bank can influence interest rate expectations when it buys government debt. Long-term rates or bond yields are primarily shaped by investors' interest rate expectations over an extended period of time. By influencing expectations, central banks can bring down the long-term interest rate or the government bond yield. They can lower the risk-free or *pure rate* underpinning all credit costs. As Keynes noted in *The General Theory of Employment, Interest and Money* [1936], the *money-rate of interest* [the risk-free or pure rate] is responsible 'for setting the pace for all the other commodity-rates of interest'.[1]

Nevertheless, the purpose of quantitative easing has

---

[1] See *The General Theory of Employment, Interest and Money*, John Maynard Keynes, 1936, p. 235.

frequently been misunderstood since late-2008. The policy is effective when it is used to guide interest rate expectations. It is not enough for central banks to buy assets and assume that monetary policy has become more accommodating. The signalling effects of quantitative easing are more important than the buying of assets *per se*. Indeed, quantitative easing is only one part of a wider policy framework required when central banks operate close to the *Zero Lower Bound*. As we saw in Chapter 2, large-scale asset purchases can be ineffective and even counterproductive when central banks lose sight of interest rate expectations and particularly *liquidity preference*. *The General Theory* makes important inferences for the conduct of monetary policy that were ignored in the aftermath of the 2008 financial crisis. The significance of rate targeting and not letting interest rate expectations rise prematurely, as occurred following the Federal Reserve's implementation of quantitative easing from November 2008 and November 2010 onwards [*QE1* and *QE2* - see glossary], can be understood through the prism of *The General Theory*.

## The Importance of *The General Theory*

Bond yields cannot always be relied upon to fall enough during an economic downturn. Keynes warned that if all borrowing costs are not brought down quickly, there might not be a recovery or it might be too slow to restore full employment. Once the recovery begins, it is liable to stall. The smallest hint of change in monetary policy may trigger a sharp, adverse movement in long-term interest rates, as seen in the US in the summer of 2013. This was discussed in Chapter 2. Tentative shifts in bond purchases or quantitative easing may have an exaggerated impact on expectations through the *signalling channel*, even if the monetary authorities have no intention of changing their policy rate.

Quantitative easing is not about flooding financial markets with yet more liquidity. It is meant to be a surgical and nuanced attempt to mitigate the fallout from a devaluation of capital by lowering borrowing costs. If there has been over-accumulation of capital during an economic upswing it will be devalued in a crisis. Nonetheless, in the absence of an appropriate structure of lending rates, the cycle of *debt deflation* can become entrenched. The analysis by Irving Fisher implies that falling [asset] prices will push up the real debt burden. Real debt-servicing costs may rise, not fall, prolonging the adjustment to high levels of debt and sending the economy into a *debt trap*.[2]

It is the potential impact on the risk-free rate that makes quantitative easing effective. The policy does

---

[2] See *Boom & Depressions Some First Principles*, Irving Fisher, Global Financial History Series, 2011, Chapters 2 and 3.

much more than free-up private sector resources to buy riskier assets through the *portfolio balance effect*. It encourages risk averse private sector funds back into the credit market through the control of interest rate expectations. In this sense, it works as a *credit multiplier*, drawing larger sums of private capital back into heavily discounted assets - financial and real.

An important aspect of this policy is the impact on investor *confidence* [for both real and financial investors] from anchoring interest rates. In the aftermath of a deep financial crisis, investors will only return to the fray in sufficient numbers when they are sure that central banks will keep interest rates pegged at ultra-low levels. If investors suspect that central banks are not committed to such a policy, it will not succeed. The importance of the Federal Reserve's shift to *forward rate guidance* in August 2011 was a case in point and was covered in Chapter 2. To recap, this proved critical in securing a turnaround in US house prices in the summer of 2011 and reversing the deflationary impact of foreclosures or repossessions. This important policy shift set the stage for a swifter drop in foreclosures, which was necessary to break the slide into debt deflation.[3]

---

[3] According to the Mortgage Bankers Association of America [MBA], the All Foreclosure Inventory for Residential Mortgage Loans as a share of all borrowers was 4.43% in Q3 2011. This compares with a low of 0.97% in Q3 2005. By Q3 2013, this had fallen to 3.08%. All Foreclosures Started for Residential Mortgage Loans as a share of all borrowers was 1.04%, up from a

Keynes was clear on the significance of *central bank guidance*. He warned, 'a monetary policy which strikes public opinion as being experimental in character or easily liable to change may fail in its objective of greatly reducing the long-term rate of interest, because $M_2$ [money supply] may tend to increase almost without limit in response to a reduction of $r$ [the rate of interest] below a certain figure. The same policy, on the other hand, may prove easily successful if it appeals to public opinion as being reasonable and practicable and in the public interest, rooted in strong conviction, and promoted by an authority unlikely to be superseded'.[4]

If central banks are not minded to keep short-term interest rates low — when they palpably have the very weapons to secure such an objective — investors would not be persuaded to take extra risks in a low inflation or deflationary environment. Risk aversion implies an unwillingness to sell short-term securities and cash and buy into riskier assets including long-term bonds. A debt trap could intensify as investors sought liquidity and safety. This was precisely the point made by Keynes during the early 1930s when he repeatedly argued for policies to drive long-term rates down. He warned early

---

low of 0.39% in Q2 2005. By Q3 2013, this had dropped to 0.57%.

[4] See *The General Theory of Employment, Interest and Money*, Keynes, 1936, p. 203.

in the *Great Depression* that it could prove difficult to secure the same reduction in long-term rates compared to the short rate or the central bank rate. Keynes was also critical of the failure of governments to alter their *debt management* policies during the early 1930s. As we shall see later in this chapter, Keynes believed that it may be necessary to increase issuance of short-term debt to underpin the requisite low long-term interest rates.

## Liquidity Preference Theory

Keeping borrowing costs at the requisite level is not just a question of expectations. Keynes also understood the subtle significance of 'liquidity' in preventing the necessary decline in longer-term rates. Keynes couched his argument for a more proactive monetary policy in terms of *liquidity preference*. The long-term rate of interest, or the bond yield, depends on the future path of short-term interest rates, the *liquidity premium* and any *risk premium* [i.e. risk of default]. Thus, the spread between long- and short-term government assets can partly be seen as reward for illiquidity. It should be emphasised: illiquidity in this context does not refer to a dearth of buyers and sellers *per se*, which is the more conventional definition. When markets are usually described as illiquid, this typically refers to a low level of transactions or turnover. If investors are illiquid, this implies a willingness to invest in longer-dated assets. When investors are liquid, this reflects a desire to remain in cash or buy shorter-dated assets.

The *Liquidity Preference Theory* provides the fundamental rationale for quantitative easing. It offers perhaps the best theoretical framework for understanding how such a monetary policy should operate. Conventionally, the case for quantitative easing is predicated upon the proximity of the Zero Lower Bound. However, the Liquidity Preference Theory offers a more complete rationale for central bank bond purchases and a clear insight into the policies required to secure an economic recovery against the backdrop of very low inflation. While the focus of this book will largely be on the US, the Liquidity Preference Theory can be used to judge the efficacy of the policies adopted at other central banks, including the Bank of England, the European Central Bank and the Bank of Japan.

The failure to understand the Liquidity Preference Theory would lead to policy mistakes in the US from early 2009 onwards, which delayed the return to full employment. Nonetheless, it is also true that the economic recovery has gained significant traction in the US since the summer of 2011 without causing inflation, despite the trenchant criticisms of quantitative easing.[5]

---

[5] Source: Bureau of Labor Statistics. The unemployment rate peaked at 10.0% in the US in October 2009 before falling. It remained essentially flat

In the UK, employment has hit record highs.[6] Indeed, the UK enjoyed a strong economic recovery in 2013, contrary to the claims of *post-war Keynesians*, who criticised the government's tight fiscal policy. With the correct application of monetary policy, the recovery will continue. The major economies of the West can secure full employment again. Nevertheless, this will only happen if central banks [and governments] fully understand the real lessons of *The General Theory* and Keynes's analysis.

## The Importance of Bond Yields

Keynes identified liquidity preference as a major obstacle to securing the necessary drop in market rates. As Geoff Tily argues in his excellent book *Keynes's General Theory, The Rate Of Interest And 'Keynesian' Economics*, this was the 'most important monetary innovation in *General Theory*'.[7] Critically, the relationship between the price and yield on a government bond is not linear. As

---

in the first nine months of 2011 [it fell from 9.1% in January 2011 to 9.0% in September 2011]. It has fallen significantly since then, more than the predictions of the FOMC and most market participants. By January 2014, it had dropped to 6.6%.

[6] Source: Office of National Statistics. According to the Labour Force Survey, employment [aged 16+] fell from 29.572million for March to May 2008 to 28.807million for January to March 2010. It then rebounded, rising to 30.146million in the three months for October to December 2013.

[7] See *Keynes's General Theory, The Rate Of Interest And 'Keynesian' Economics*, Geoff Tily, Palgrave Macmillan, 2007, p. 183.

the yield falls to ultra-low levels, bond prices tend to rise ever more quickly. Approaching the Zero Lower Bound, the safety margin against a possible rise in interest rates diminishes rapidly: investors stand to lose significant capital if the bond yield were to climb suddenly. A low running yield on bonds might be seen as an insufficient cushion against the perceived risk that interest rates could rise.

As Keynes stressed, 'every fall in $r$ reduces the current earnings from illiquidity, which are available as a sort of insurance premium to offset the risk of loss on capital account'.[8] There is a risk associated with being illiquid, that is, owning longer-dated bonds. As a result, it can be hard to persuade investors to hold bonds with a longer maturity without a high degree of assurance from the central bank. Consequently, there is a natural aversion to low borrowing costs among investors. For Keynes, this was 'perhaps the chief obstacle to a fall in the rate of interest to a very low level'.[9]

Rising liquidity preference, or an aversion to lower borrowing costs, could partly be characterised by the

---

[8] As Keynes added, a 4 per cent running yield on bonds would provide adequate compensation up to the point where investors 'feared that the long-term rate of interest may rise faster than by 4 per cent of itself per annum, i.e. by an amount greater than 0.16 per cent per annum'. He went on to add, 'If however, the rate of interest is already as low as 2 per cent, the running yield only offset a rise in it of as little as 0.04 per cent per annum'. See *The General Theory of Employment, Interest and Money*, Keynes, 1936, p. 202.

[9] Ibid.

notion of *money illusion*. When an economy is sliding towards a recession, interest rates may need to fall quickly. However, investors have become so used to high borrowing costs during a boom that they find it difficult to adjust. In truth, liquidity preference is *wider* than the concept of money illusion. This fear of higher inflation might be irrational, but that was only part of the problem. There was an innate bias towards expecting higher inflation precisely because of the sensitivity of bond prices to small changes in yields. This was the critical point. Even if investors acknowledge that inflation has fallen, there may nevertheless be a reluctance to accept lower bond yields.

The concept of liquidity preference might also be viewed through the prism of hoarding. The propensity to hoard is 'substantially the same' as liquidity preference. However, it is incomplete and misleading if hoarding and non-hoarding are seen as simple alternatives. According to Keynes, the decision to hoard 'is not taken without absolutely or without regard to the advantages offered for parting with liquidity'. In other words, the propensity to hoard will depend on the rate of interest. On this particular point, Keynes concluded, 'The habit of overlooking the relation of the rate of interest to hoarding may be a part of the explanation why interest has been usually regarded as the reward of not-spending, whereas in fact it is the reward of not-hoarding'.[10]

Indeed, Keynes argued that the rate of interest is not a reward for parting with savings: crucially, it is a reward for parting with liquidity. Furthermore, liquidity preference is a decision that awaits the saver, 'namely, in what form he [or she] will hold the command over future consumption which he [or she] has reserved'. Keynes added, 'does he [or she] want to hold it in the form of immediate, liquid command [i.e. in money or its equivalent]? Or is he [or she] prepared to part with immediate command for a specified or indefinite period, leaving it to future market conditions to determine on what terms he [or she] can, if necessary, convert deferred command over specific goods into immediate command over goods in general? In other words, what is the degree of his [or her] *liquidity-preference?*'[11]

In short, liquidity preference is *sequential* to the decision to save. Liquidity preference determines the allocation of savings between liquid and illiquid assets. It also relates to the stock of savings or wealth, not just new savings. In this respect, Keynes's work marked an important break with the *classical school.* Interest rates and particularly longer-term rates were not determined by the supply and demand for savings *per se,* but the

---

[10] Ibid. p. 174.

[11] Ibid. p. 166.

supply and demand for assets. Contrary to the claims of classical economists, Keynes argued that, 'The rate of interest is not the 'price' which brings into equilibrium the demand for resources to invest with the readiness to abstain from present consumption'.[12]

Instead, 'The current rate of interest depends ... not on the strength of the desire to hold wealth, but on the strengths of the desire to hold it in liquid and illiquid forms respectively, coupled with the amount of the supply of wealth in the one form relatively to the supply of it in the other'.[13] In essence, liquidity preference reflects the demand for assets of various degrees of liquidity. As a result, the rate of interest depends on 'both the demand of and supplies for assets across the whole of this spectrum'.[14] As suggested on page 196, this had ramifications for bond issuance or the debt management policies of governments. However, it was also a critical consideration for central banks and their choice of policy tools when faced with a Zero Lower Bound. As we saw in Chapter 2, setting fixed targets for asset purchases, as practised in the early years following the 2008 crisis, proved misguided.

---

[12] See Keynes [CW VII p. 167], referenced in *Keynes's General Theory, The Rate Of Interest And 'Keynesian' Economics*, Tily, 2007, p. 185.

[13] See Keynes [CW VII p. 213], referenced in *Keynes's General Theory, The Rate Of Interest And 'Keynesian' Economics*, Tily, 2007, p. 185.

[14] See *Keynes's General Theory, The Rate Of Interest And 'Keynesian' Economics*, Tily, 2007, p. 185.

# From Monetary Reform [1923] to *The General Theory* [1936]

Keynes set out his vision for an alternative agenda that would challenge the classical theory of interest rates with the publication of A *Tract on Monetary Reform* on 11 December 1923. He advocated a proactive monetary policy arguing that, 'the control [of credit], if they [central banks and governments] choose to exercise it, is mainly in their own hands'.[15] Keynes described how 'The governors of the system would be bank-rate and Treasury bill policy, the objects of government would be stability of trade, prices, and employment and the volume of paper money would be a consequence of the first (just - I repeat - as it is at present) and an instrument of the second, the precise arithmetical level of which *could not and need not be predicted*' [author's italics].[16]

The last phrase implied money supply was an endogenous variable, which had important ramifications for the central bank's choice of policy weapons when fighting recession close to the Zero Lower Bound [see Appendix I, *Reverse Taps*, page 153]. Furthermore, at this early stage, Keynes was hinting at the 'trial and error' approach required by central banks when guiding

---

[15] See Keynes [CW IV, p.144], referenced in *Keynes's General Theory, The Rate Of Interest And 'Keynesian' Economics*, Tily, p. 50.

[16] Ibid.

short rate expectations and influencing or targeting bond yields. The monetary authorities would have to be pragmatic when judging how far to lean against market expectations, carefully assessing the impact of each policy initiative. The point was subsequently reinforced: 'If, however, we are tempted to assert that money is the drink which stimulates the system to activity, we must remind ourselves that there may be several slips between the cup and the lip'.[17]

At this juncture 'Keynes saw the [business] cycle as inevitable, albeit driven by credit, to be at best mitigated by an appropriate monetary policy. The theoretical substance [for his policy proposals] constituted mainly a re-statement of the quantity theory in the light of credit creation'.[18] The key points of his argument were also set out more formally in response to criticisms from the London School of Economics economist Edwin Cannan [1924].

---

[17] See *The General Theory of Employment, Interest and Money*, Keynes, p. 173.

[18] See *Keynes's General Theory, The Rate Of Interest And 'Keynesian' Economics*, Tily, p. 53.

'Let me repeat the quantity equation in the form in which I stated it in A Tract on Monetary Reform:

$$n=p(k+rk')$$

Where:

$n$ = number of units of 'cash' in circulation.[19]

$p$ = price of each 'consumption unit', or in other words the index number of prices.

$k$ = number of consumption units, the monetary equivalent of which the public find it convenient to keep in 'cash'.

$k'$ = ditto which the public find it convenient to keep in bank balances available against cheques.

$r$ = the proportion of their potential liabilities ($k'$) to the public which the banks keep in 'cash'.

Now, the old-fashioned doctrine [classical school] used to be that if $n$ could be kept reasonably steady, all would be well. My object was to point out that if $k$ and $k'$ were capable of violent fluctuation, steadiness of $n$ might be positively harmful and must be reflected in an extreme unsteadiness of $p$ - this being, in fact, what has generally happened in booms and depressions of trade'.[20]

The policy proposals set out in A Tract on Monetary Reform were developed extensively in A Treatise on Money [1930]. Nevertheless, the Treatise was 'more important

---

[19] As being, in the case of Great Britain, 'note circulation plus private deposits at the Bank of England'. See Keynes [CW IV, P.67], referenced in Keynes's General Theory, The Rate Of Interest And 'Keynesian' Economics, Tily, p. 53.

[20] See Keynes [CW XI, p. 416], referenced in Keynes's General Theory, The Rate Of Interest And 'Keynesian' Economics, Tily, p. 53-54.

as the start of his [Keynes's] substantial theoretical analysis'.[21] Keynes recognised 'that his policy initiatives lacked theoretical justification'.[22] In the *Tract*, the credit cycle was treated as 'given or commonly known' in line with the classical school. In the *Treatise*, Keynes argued that classical economics was 'relevant only to a commodity money economy; a new theory was necessary for a credit economy'.[23] Furthermore, the theoretical objective of Keynes was to construct a framework of a credit economy. This would in turn be used to support a more radical and effective monetary policy to mitigate economic slumps. Keynes argued, 'The most striking change in the investment factors of the post-war world compared with the pre-war world is to be found in the high level of the market-rate of interest'.[24] However, the immediate focus was on the Great Depression. Economic activity 'depended on the long-term rate of interest, over which the authorities had a degree of control'. Central bank intervention was needed 'because a divergence could open up between market and classical *natural rates of interest*; under such conditions policymakers could and

---

[21] See *Keynes's General Theory, The Rate Of Interest And 'Keynesian' Economics*, Tily, p. 52.

[22] Ibid. p. 52.

[23] Ibid. p. 54.

[24] See Keynes [CW VI, p. 377], referenced in *Keynes's General Theory, The Rate Of Interest And 'Keynesian' Economics*, Tily, p. 56.

should act to bring the market rate back into line'.[25]

Keynes was also making the case for a greater control of credit during the upswing or boom. However, he was advocating alternative policy tools, rather than simply resorting to a rapid rise in interest rates. The *Treatise* put forward the rate of interest [short- and long-term] 'both as cause and as solution to the problems facing Britain and the world'.[26] Indeed, 'high long-term interest rates coupled with excessive shifts of the *marginal efficiency of capital*' [27] were 'the conditions for extreme movements in the business cycle'.[28] To prevent such a scenario, the authorities would have to buttress a policy of low rates with effective constraints on credit growth.

## The Gold Standard 'Constraint'

The gold standard had, of course, compromised monetary policy early in the Great Depression. Keynes had been a vociferous critic, calling gold a 'barbarous relic' and citing

---

[25] Ibid.

[26] See Keynes's *General Theory, The Rate Of Interest And 'Keynesian' Economics*, Tily, p. 56.

[27] Ibid. p. 298. The marginal efficiency of capital was defined as 'that rate of discount which would make the present value of the series of annuities given by the returns expected from the capital-asset during its life just equal to its supply price'. This provided the marginal efficiencies of 'particular types of capital-assets'. See *The General Theory of Employment, Interest and Money*, Keynes, 1936, p. 135.

[28] See Keynes's *General Theory, The Rate Of Interest And 'Keynesian' Economics*, Tily, p. 298.

its 'evil consequences'.[29] He had opposed the decision of Winston Churchill as Chancellor to take Britain back on to the gold standard on April 28 1925. As he warned, preserving an uncompetitive, fixed exchange rate to gold necessitated higher borrowing costs to stem the loss of gold reserves, which led to endemic unemployment for the rest of the decade. The gold standard restricted a central bank's room for manoeuvre. However, it was not the root cause of all economic ills. As we shall argue in Chapter 4, the contribution of the gold standard to the Great Depression has been overstated. In *A Treatise on Money*, the rate of interest was cited as both the primary cause and the solution to the economic problems facing Britain and the world, not the gold standard. Central banks had the policy options to mitigate the constraints imposed by the gold standard. It was not a straightjacket and there were offsetting policy actions that could and should have been pursued.

## Interest Rates Too High

Keynes elaborated upon his policy prescription when he spoke to the UK Committee of Finance and Industry in February 1930. The Chancellor of the Exchequer [Philip Snowden] had appointed the Committee to

---

[29] See Keynes [CW IV, p. 61 and CW IV, p. 137-8], referenced in *Keynes's General Theory, The Rate Of Interest And 'Keynesian' Economics*, Tily, p. 49.

'inquire into banking, finance and credit' and to make recommendations to 'promote the development of trade and commerce and the employment of labour'.[30] Keynes's presentation to the Committee lasted several days. He had already downgraded the significance of the gold standard and its contribution to the Great Depression, shifting the focus to domestic monetary policy. According to Tily, the 'appropriate domestic monetary policy action had now been more accurately identified'.[31] Keynes was arguing 'that long-term rates of interest could be brought down by central bank purchases of securities *à outrance*'.[32]

In a later response [dated 17 April 1931] to comments from one Committee member, Keynes offered perhaps 'his sharpest and most concise analysis of the Economic Problem to date'.[33] He summarised, 'My fundamental explanation is, of course, that the rate of interest is too high - meaning by the 'rate of interest' *the complex of interest rates* for all kinds of borrowing, long and short, safe and risky'.[34] Keynes added, 'Next comes the question

[30] See Keynes [CW XX, p. 17], referenced in *Keynes's General Theory, The Rate Of Interest And 'Keynesian' Economics*, Tily, p. 55.

[31] See *Keynes's General Theory, The Rate Of Interest And 'Keynesian' Economics*, Tily, p. 56.

[32] See Keynes [CW VI, p. 331], referenced in *Keynes's General Theory, The Rate Of Interest And 'Keynesian' Economics*, Tily, p. 56.

[33] See *Keynes's General Theory, The Rate Of Interest And 'Keynesian' Economics*, Tily, p. 56.

[34] See Keynes [CW XX, p. 272-273], referenced in *Keynes's General Theory, The Rate Of Interest And 'Keynesian' Economics*, Tily, p. 57.

of how far central banks can remedy this. In ordinary times the equilibrium rate of interest does not change quickly, so long as slump and boom conditions can be prevented from developing; and I see no insuperable difficulty in central banks controlling the position'. By contrast, he added, 'The drastic reduction of the whole complex of market-rates of interest [short- and long-term] presents central banks with a problem which I do not expect them to solve unless they are prepared to employ drastic and even direct methods of influencing long-term investments'.[35] Central banks had to be prepared to intervene in markets to drive the risk-free or pure rate lower across all maturities. To reiterate, the bulk of Keynes's work during the Great Depression focused on monetary policy. Keynes was a staunch advocate of lower interest rates. Furthermore, while he was influential in bringing down interest rates in the UK and US, he believed more could have been done.

## War Loan Conversion

The UK Government accepted the theoretical analysis and advice of Keynes when it announced the conversion of the war debt from a 5 per cent issue to a 3.5 per

---

[35] See Keynes [CW XX, p. 272-273], referenced in *Keynes's General Theory, The Rate Of Interest And 'Keynesian' Economics*, Tily, p. 57.

cent issue on 30 June 1932.[36] Keynes applauded the announcement, with the authorities conceding the importance of targeting long-term interest rates. 'A reduction of the long-term rate of interest to a low level is probably the most necessary of all measures if we are to escape from the slump and secure a lasting revival of enterprise. The successful conversion of the War Loan to a 3.5 per cent basis is, therefore, a constructive measure of the very first rate importance; for it represents a direct attack upon the long-term rate, much more effective in present circumstances than the indirect attack of cheap short-term money, useful and necessary though the latter is'.[37]

## Keynes's International Influence

However, the arguments for a more radical monetary policy extended beyond the UK. Keynes travelled to Germany, speaking against deflationary policies and articulating the case for *cheap money* [low short- and long-term interest rates], while advocating a break with the gold standard. A series of cuts had taken the discount rate in Germany down to 4% by February 1933. However,

---

[36] To fund the cost of World War I, the UK government issued a bond in 1917, the Five Percent War Loan. It was scheduled for repayment in 1947, although it could be repaid on three months' notice any time after June 1st 1929.

[37] See Keynes [CW XXI, p. 114], referenced in *Keynes's General Theory, The Rate Of Interest And 'Keynesian' Economics*, Tily, p. 61.

Hitler came to power in April 1933. According to Tily, 'Germany seemingly disengaged itself from the agenda of global monetary reform just as it [lower interest rates] was about to receive its greatest impetus'.[38]

President Roosevelt proved more receptive to Keynes's work following his election victory, setting out a bold agenda for monetary reflation in March 1933. In an open letter to President Roosevelt published in the *New York Times*, Keynes concluded that, 'The turn of the tide in Great Britain is largely attributable to the reduction in the long-term rate of interest which ensued on the success of the conversion of the War Loan... I see no reason why you should not reduce the rate of interest on your long-term government bonds to 2.5 per cent or less, with favourable repercussions on the whole bond market, if only the Federal Reserve System would replace its present holdings of short-dated Treasury issues by purchasing long-dated issues in exchange'.[39]

The impact and influence of Keynes's call for monetary reform in the US was underlined by a letter from US journalist Walter Lippmann. He wrote, 'I don't know whether you realise how great an effect that letter had, but I am told that it was chiefly responsible for the

---

[38] See *Keynes's General Theory, The Rate Of Interest And 'Keynesian' Economics*, Tily, p. 63.

[39] See Keynes [CW XXI, p. 289-97], referenced in *Keynes's General Theory, The Rate Of Interest And 'Keynesian' Economics*, Tily, p. 68-69.

policy which the Treasury is now quietly but effectively pursuing of purchasing long-term Government bonds with a view to making a strong bond market and to reducing the long-term rate of interest'.[40]

## The General Theory

The publication of *The General Theory* built upon much of Keynes's case for a radical shift in policy, which had begun with the publication of *A Tract on Monetary Reform* thirteen years earlier. Despite the collapse of the gold standard and the shift to cheap money, there remained significant resistance to Keynes's monetary theory. *The General Theory* went further than the *Treatise* because Keynes was suggesting that cheap money was not only a necessary response to the economic crisis of the 1930s. The ramifications extended beyond the immediate slump. Critically, *cheap, but tight money* should be viewed as a secular policy, one that mitigates the effects of an unstable economic cycle and reduces the risks of boom and bust. Economic prosperity would depend on the combination of low interest rates and effective constraints to prevent a return to *easy money* or loose credit, which would otherwise drive debt levels higher.

In *The General Theory*, interest rates were determined

---

[40] See Keynes [CW XXI, p 305], referenced in *Keynes's General Theory, The Rate Of Interest And 'Keynesian' Economics*, Tily, p. 69.

by the interaction between the liquidity preference schedule and the supply of money. The level of investment in an economy was in turn determined by the marginal efficiency of capital schedule and the rate of interest. In Chapter 11, Keynes elaborated upon the 'fundamental importance' of the marginal efficiency of capital for monetary policy 'because it is mainly through this factor (much more than through the rate of interest) that the expectation of the future influences the present'.[41]

The analysis of the marginal efficiency of capital focused largely on real assets for convenience. However, it could apply equally to financial assets. Either way, according to Keynes it would be a mistake to regard the marginal efficiency of capital 'primarily in terms of the *current* yield'. This would 'be correct only in the static state where there is no changing future to influence the present'.[42] Expectations were now a critical component of Keynes's analysis. It was important to understand the role of 'changes in expectation, because it is chiefly this dependence which renders the marginal efficiency of capital subject to the somewhat violent fluctuations which are the explanation of the trade [or business] cycle'.[43]

---

[41] See *The General Theory of Employment, Interest and Money*, Keynes, 1936, p. 145.

[42] Ibid.

[43] Ibid. p. 143-144.

Keynes delved deeper into the determinants of 'long-term expectations' in Chapter 12 of *The General Theory*. He warned that, 'It would be foolish, in forming our expectations, to attach great weight to matters which are very *uncertain*. It is reasonable, therefore, to be guided to a considerable degree by the facts about which we feel somewhat confident, even though they may be less decisively relevant to the issue than other facts about which our knowledge is vague and scanty. For this reason the facts of the existing situation enter, in a sense disproportionately, into the formation of our long-term expectations; our usual practice being to take the existing situation and to project it into the future, modified only to the extent that we have more or less definite reasons for expecting a change'.[44]

Furthermore, uncertainty was driven by a lack of confidence in monetary policy. Keynes added, 'The state of long-term expectation, upon which our decisions are based, does not solely depend, therefore, on the most probable forecast we can make. It also depends on the *confidence* with which we make this forecast - on how highly we rate the likelihood of our best forecast turning out quite wrong. If we expect large changes but are very uncertain as to what precise form these changes will take,

---

[44] Ibid p. 148.

then our confidence [in monetary policy] will be weak'.[45] The *state of confidence* had not been analysed carefully Keynes argued, and needed particular consideration. It was important to recognise 'the extreme precariousness of the basis of knowledge on which our estimates of prospective yield have to be made'.[46]

The concept of liquidity preference was then introduced as Keynes sought to provide a more robust framework for his unconventional views on monetary policy. Elaborating at length, he noted 'the professional investor is forced to concern himself with the anticipation of impending changes, in the news or in the atmosphere, of the kind by which experience shows that the mass psychology of the market is most influenced'.[47]

The discussion of liquidity preference widens in Chapter 13, with Keynes stressing the importance of '*uncertainty* as to the future of the rate of interest, i.e. as to the complex of rates of interest for varying maturities which will rule at future dates'.[48] He added, 'If the current rate of interest is positive for debts of every maturity, it must always be more advantageous to purchase a debt than to hold cash as a store of wealth'.[49] However, if the

---

[45] Ibid.

[46] Ibid.

[47] Ibid. p. 155.

[48] Ibid. p. 168.

[49] Ibid. p. 169.

future rate of interest is uncertain, 'there is a risk of a loss being incurred in purchasing a long-term debt and subsequently turning it into cash, as compared with holding cash. The actuarial profit or mathematical expectation of gain calculated in accordance with the existing probabilities - if it can be so calculated, which is doubtful - must be sufficient to compensate for the risk of disappointment'.[50]

There were, for Keynes, some 'matters' where 'there is no scientific basis on which to form any calculable probability whatever'. He added, 'The sense in which I am using the term is that in which the prospect of a European war is uncertain, or the price of copper and the rate of interest twenty years hence'.[51] Individuals with [a stock of] savings did not know what the future rate of interest would be. It was uncertain. Furthermore, this uncertainty operates 'through the capital value of assets'. The point refers specifically to government bonds, which will change in value inversely as interest rate expectations shift. Uncertainty underpins the liquidity preference schedule.

This uncertainty was a much bigger consideration for monetary policy at the Zero Lower Bound. Furthermore, Keynes understood that central banks could and should

---

[50] Ibid.

[51] See Keynes [CW XIV p.113-114], referenced in *Keynes's General Theory, The Rate Of Interest And 'Keynesian' Economics*, Tily, p. 142.

not be complacent in response to this uncertainty. They had a role to play in challenging market expectations if these led to an inappropriate structure of borrowing costs. Investors could not be relied upon to set long-term interest rates at levels that were consistent with an economic recovery or full employment. Keynes warned:

'Just as we found that the marginal efficiency of capital is fixed, not by the 'best' opinion, but by the market valuation as determined by mass psychology, so also expectations as to the future of the rate of interest as fixed by mass psychology have their reactions on liquidity-preference; but with this addition that the individual, who believes that future rates of interest will be above the rates assumed by the market, has a reason for keeping actual liquid cash, whilst the individual who differs from the market in the other direction will have a motive for borrowing money for short periods in order to purchase debts of longer-term. The market price will be fixed at the point at which the sales of the 'bears' and the purchases of the 'bulls' are balanced'.[52]

Keynes acknowledged that it was desirable to have a highly efficient market for dealing with debts. For without this, investors would demand a higher level of cash balances to guard against the risk of incurring a capital loss, if they were forced to sell assets before maturity.

---

[52] See *The General Theory of Employment, Interest and Money*, Keynes, 1936, p. 170.

The precautionary motive for holding money would be higher [see Appendix III, The Demand For Money, page 264]. Nonetheless, 'the existence of an organised market gives an opportunity for wide fluctuations in liquidity-preference due to the speculative-motive'.[53] Making it easier for investors to buy and sell quickly [more liquid, using the conventional interpretation] had ramifications that need to be taken into account when setting monetary policy.

## Keynes and Monetary Policy

The practical implications of liquidity preference for monetary policy are addressed in Chapter 15 of *The General Theory*. The speculative demand for money is critical for the transmission of monetary policy to the real economy. Indeed, it is 'by playing on the speculative-motive that monetary management ... is brought to bear on the economic system'.[54] Expectations of the future rate of interest will shape the speculative-motive for holding assets in liquid balances. The distribution of those opinions will in turn determine the shape of the liquidity preference schedule and the yield curve.

Keynes suggested that the distribution of views will be based around a 'safe' rate of interest. 'It follows that

---

[53] Ibid. p. 170-171.

[54] Ibid. p. 196-197.

a given $M_2$ [the quantity of money held to satisfy the speculative motive] will *not* have a definitive quantitative relation to a given rate of interest of $r$; - what matters is not the *absolute* level of $r$ but the degree of its divergence from what is considered a fairly *safe* level of $r$, having regard to those calculations of probability which are being relied on'.[55] Keynes emphasised the role of the current or existing situation as a guide to the future. He observed that 'facts of the existing situation enter, in a sense disproportionately, into the formation of our long-term expectations'.[56] Market rates could be set passively by a 'norm', where past rates of interest dominate expectations. Furthermore, 'It might be more accurate, perhaps, to say that the rate of interest is a highly conventional, rather than a higher psychological, phenomenon. For its actual value is largely governed by the prevailing view as to what its value is expected to be'.[57]

Speculators have an expectation of a normal rate of interest, towards which the actual or market rate of interest tends to return. This in turn may diverge significantly from the policy rate needed to secure full employment. Individual speculators expect capital gains

[55] See Keynes [CW VII, p. 201], referenced in *Keynes's General Theory, The Rate Of Interest And 'Keynesian' Economics*, Tily, p. 189.

[56] See Keynes [CW VII, p. 148], referenced in *Keynes's General Theory, The Rate Of Interest And 'Keynesian' Economics*, Tily, p. 189.

[57] See *The General Theory of Employment, Interest and Money*, Keynes, 1936, p. 203.

or losses and hence hold bonds or money depending on the difference between actual and normal rates of interest. Lower bond yields will lead to higher expected capital losses from holding government bonds.[58] Furthermore, the liquidity preference schedule will be 'derived as a cumulative distribution function of individual speculators' expectations of the rate of interest and the funds they have set aside for speculation'.[59]

Both the safe or normal interest rate were in some way removed from the concept of the natural rate set out in the *Treatise*. In *The General Theory*, Keynes declares that he was 'no longer of the opinion that the concept of a 'natural' rate of interest, which previously seemed to me a most promising idea, has anything very useful or significant to contribute to our analysis'.[60] Setting interest rates at the required level relies upon ensuring a sufficient supply of money to meet the demand of speculators at the optimal policy rate. To reiterate, the level of money supply required is endogenous and cannot be pre-determined.

Following the crisis of 2008, the Bank of England

---

[58] See *Keynes's General Theory, The Rate Of Interest And 'Keynesian' Economics*, Tily, p. 189. 'The higher (lower) the current rate, the more are capital gains (losses) expected'.

[59] See *Keynes's General Theory, The Rate Of Interest And 'Keynesian' Economics*, Tily, p. 189.

[60] See *The General Theory of Employment, Interest and Money*, Keynes, 1936, p. 243.

initially claimed that quantitative easing would work by targeting a rise in broad money supply. The central bank's objective was also framed in terms of nominal GDP, rather than the rate of interest. According to the minutes of the policy meeting in March 2009, the Monetary Policy Committee claimed that the introduction of quantitative easing would allow focusing 'more directly on the quantity of money it supplied in exchange for assets held by the private sector'.[61] An increase in the supply of money would eventually cause nominal spending to rise, suggesting 'the increase in the level of money balances should be of a similar magnitude to the required increase in nominal GDP'.[62] The Bank of England was not alone in its failure at the outset to understand the purpose of quantitative easing and the transmission mechanism. As we saw in Chapter 2, the Federal Reserve placed too much focus on the *supply channel* or the liquidity impact derived from bond purchases, and not enough consideration to the signalling effects or the shaping of market expectations.

Keynes argued that the impact of any shift in policy extended beyond a change in the supply of money. It was wrong, therefore, to focus on money supply or the size of bond purchases as the target of quantitative easing, or

---

[61] See *Minutes of the Monetary Policy Committee Meeting*, 18 March 2009, p. 8.

[62] Ibid. p. 9.

a measure of its success. The decision of central banks [Federal Reserve, Bank of Japan, Bank of England] since 2008 to announce fixed targets for large-scale asset purchases has been misguided. An increase in money supply would not reduce long-term interest rates if expectations change, shifting the liquidity preference schedule upwards:

'In dealing with the speculative-motive it is, however, important to distinguish between the changes in the rate of interest which are due to changes in the supply of money available to satisfy the speculative-motive, without there having been any change in the liquidity [preference] function, and those which are primarily due to changes in expectation affecting the liquidity [preference] function itself. Open-market operations [large scale asset purchases] may, indeed, influence the rate of interest through both channels; since they may not only change the volume of money, but may also give rise to changed expectations concerning the future policy of the central bank or of the government'.[63]

Keynes was much more interested in the impact of a change in monetary policy on bond yields, than on the quantity of money in circulation: 'the new equilibrium rate of interest [after a change in circumstances or expectations] will be associated with a redistribution of

---

[63] See *The General Theory of Employment, Interest and Money*, Keynes, 1936, p. 197-198.

money-holdings. Nevertheless it is the change in the rate of interest, rather than the redistribution of cash, which deserves our main attention'.[64] Keynes reiterates: a policy announcement that makes no change to a central bank's asset purchases can have a significant [and conflicting] impact on the market rate of interest. The obverse is also true. The monetary authorities have to give more consideration to their management of interest rate expectations than the purchase of assets *per se*.

Furthermore, 'a change in the news which causes revision of expectations, will often be discontinuous, and will, therefore, give rise to a corresponding discontinuity of change in the rate of interest'.[65] The point was amply demonstrated by the FOMC announcement on 9 August 2011 that the federal funds target was likely to remain at 0.0-0.25 per cent until mid-2013. This was the start of *extended forward guidance* and it prompted a big decline in short-term interest rate expectations. The implied three-month interest, based on Eurodollar contracts for June 2013, fell 25 basis points in one day, from 0.84 per cent to 0.59 per cent.[66] This also pulled long-term interest rates down sharply.[67]

---

[64] Ibid. p. 199.

[65] Ibid. p. 198.

[66] Source: Thomson Reuters Datastream.

[67] Source: Thomson Reuters Datastream. The 10-year Treasury yield fell from 2.34% to 2.18% on August 9th.

If news [of a change in policy] is interpreted differently by individuals, Keynes also suggested there will potentially be room for 'increased activity of dealing in the bond market' as a result of a policy announcement. However, 'if the change in the news affects the judgement and the requirements of everyone in precisely the same way, the rate of interest [as indicated by the prices of bonds and debts] will be adjusted forthwith to the new situation without any market transactions being necessary'.[68] If, for example, a central bank announces a policy shift effectively targeting lower long-term interest rates and the policy is seen as credible, there may be few sellers [of bonds]. Prices [and yields] will adjust quickly with few transactions.

## Liquidity Preference and Challenging the Consensus

For Keynes, central banks had considerable power to control an economy beyond setting short-term interest rates. He challenged the conventional view at the time, arguing 'the long-term market-rate of interest will depend, not only on the current policy of the monetary authority, but also on market expectations concerning its future policy'.[69] Self-evidently, 'The short-term rate of

---

[68] See *The General Theory of Employment, Interest and Money*, Keynes, 1936, p. 198.

[69] Ibid. p. 202.

interest is easily controlled by the monetary authority'. It is, therefore, 'not difficult to produce a conviction that its policy will not greatly change in the very near future, and also because the possible loss is small compared with the running yield (unless it is approaching vanishing point)'.[70] Nevertheless, 'the long-term rate may be more recalcitrant when once it has fallen to a level which, on the basis of past experience and present expectations of *future* monetary policy, is considered 'unsafe' [i.e. too low] by representative opinion'.[71]

Bond yields can be influenced or shaped by deliberate policy. 'Any level of interest which is accepted with sufficient conviction as *likely* to be durable *will* be durable'.[72] Central banks have the tools to influence rate expectations and they needed to be used deftly to challenge the consensus. Keynes was later confident enough to assert: 'The monetary authorities can have any rate of interest they like'.[73] Central banks had to demonstrate their commitment to low interest rates through the correct application of open market operations [asset purchases].

However, Keynes highlighted the dangers of a shift

---

[70] Ibid. p. 202-203.

[71] Ibid. p. 203.

[72] Ibid.

[73] See Keynes [CWXX VII p. 390], referenced in *Keynes's General Theory, The Rate Of Interest And 'Keynesian' Economics*, Tily, p. 199.

in the liquidity preference schedule. Central bank policy may have unintended consequences if it causes investors to adjust their expectations, as seen in the case of QE1 and QE2. This was a critical point in relation to monetary policy. In particular, 'an increase in the quantity of money may be expected, cet. par., to reduce the rate of interest, this will not happen if the liquidity preferences of the public are increasing more than the quantity of money'.[74] Implicitly, this point applies equally to fiscal policy. As we shall see, changes in government spending or taxation may have consequences for liquidity preference, which in turn undermines the impact of fiscal stimulus.

If expectations about the future path of interest rates remained too high, there was a danger that longer-term interest rates may instead 'fluctuate for decades about a level which is chronically too high for full employment'.[75] The risk of this occurring was particularly high if the 'prevailing opinion' decreed that the 'rate of interest [or bond yield] is self-adjusting'. Central banks cannot rely upon markets to dictate long-term interest rates. The control of the rate of interest needs to extend across all maturities.

With a fickle and highly unstable marginal efficiency

---

[74] See Keynes [CW VII, p. 173], referenced in *Keynes's General Theory, The Rate Of Interest And 'Keynesian' Economics*, Tily, p. 195.

[75] See *The General Theory of Employment, Interest and Money*, Keynes, 1936, p. 204.

of capital, the difficulty of securing full employment should be clear. Nevertheless, because 'the convention is not rooted in secure knowledge', central banks had a critical role to fulfil in shifting market expectations downwards. Furthermore, the conventional view of interest rates 'will not be always unduly resistant to a modest measure of persistence and consistency of purpose by the monetary authority. Public opinion can be fairly rapidly accustomed to a modest fall in the rate of interest and the conventional expectation of the future may be modified accordingly; thus preparing the way for a further movement - up to a point'.[76]

Keynes referred back to the positive experience of the UK. 'The fall in the long-term rate of interest in Great Britain after her departure from the gold standard [in 1931] provides an interesting example of this; - the major movements were effected by a series of discontinuous jumps, as the liquidity function of the public, having become accustomed to each successive reduction, became ready to respond to some new incentive in the news or in the policy of the authorities'.[77]

The argument was accepted by the influential Economic Advisory Council, which was established in January 1930 to advise the UK government on

---

[76] Ibid.

[77] Ibid.

economic policy. In its February 1937 report, the authors acknowledged that 'psychological considerations play an important part in determining the speed with which the rate of interest is adapted to that required by economic considerations'.[78] Indeed, 'As a result of the very rapid fall in the long-term rate of interest between 1932 and 1935 it is probable that the public would not, in the long run, resist very strongly a further fall in these rates from about 3 per cent to, say, 2.5 per cent'.[79]

Nevertheless, there was an important caveat. The monetary authorities could not afford to miscalculate, as investors would be less acquiescent thereafter. The Council warned that 'if, however, there should now be a serious rise in long-term interest rates, the public reaction in a future situation which called for a second substantial fall in interest rates might be entirely different. The memory that on the last occasion interest rates rose again after their fall might give rise to very serious feelings of distrust as to the permanence of any fall that might then be sought; and the adjustment of economic life to the new situation might be greatly delayed'.[80] The economists on the Council clearly understood liquidity preference.

The final paragraph of the 1937 report described how

---

[78] See *The Economic Advisory Council 1930-1939*, Susan Howson & Donald Winch, p. 353.

[79] Ibid.

[80] Ibid.

'a very large part of the Government debt has either no fixed redemption date, or a very distant one. It is therefore very vulnerable to alterations in the market view of the long-term outlook for interest rates'.[81] Again, appropriate debt management policies could secure lower borrowing costs by an alteration [reduction] in the maturity of debt issues.

## Liquidity Traps and Fiscal Policy

Keynes warned that there might be certain limitations on the ability of central banks to push bond yields low enough to secure an economic recovery. There is a possibility that liquidity preference may also become 'virtually absolute'. In this circumstance 'almost everyone prefers cash to holding a debt which yields so low a rate of interest'. As a result, a central bank would lose 'effective control' over bond yields. The economy would be snared in a *liquidity trap*. Nonetheless, Keynes was not convinced that a liquidity trap was necessarily a threat to reflation. Furthermore, Keynes claimed neither the US nor the UK had properly tested the existence of a liquidity trap. Indeed in 1936 he concluded, 'whilst this limiting case [a liquidity trap] might become practically important in the future, I know of no example of it hitherto'.[82] Keynes

---

[81] Ibid.

[82] See *The General Theory of Employment, Interest and Money*, Keynes, 1936,

believed there had been no liquidity trap in the US in 1932. On the contrary, he argued, 'there was a crisis of the opposite kind'.[83] Indeed, as we shall see in Chapter 4, there was considerable scope to bring long-term interest rates down in the summer of 1932. Most central banks had been too timid, unwilling to deal 'boldly' in long-term debts. Consequently, 'there has not been much opportunity for a test' of a liquidity trap.[84]

It should be emphasised: a liquidity trap does not imply a shortage of liquidity, quite the opposite. It referred to risk aversion and the desire to remain liquid with investors fretting over the potential losses should yields rise from abnormally low levels. This was stopping rates from falling: 'We have assumed so far an institutional factor which prevents the rate of interest from being negative, in the shape of money which has negligible carrying costs. In fact, however, institutional and psychological factors are present which set a limit much above zero to the practicable decline in the rate of interest. In particular the costs of bringing borrowers

---

p. 207. Keynes cites two examples of a 'complete breakdown of stability in the rate of interest, due to the liquidity function flattening out in one direction or the other'. In Russia and Central Europe, a currency crisis had developed after the war, 'when no one could be induced to retain holdings either of money or of debts on any terms whatever'. However, this was not a proper liquidity trap.

[83] Ibid. p. 207-208. In the US, 'at certain dates in 1932, there was a crisis of the opposite kind - a financial crisis or crisis of liquidation, when scarcely anyone could be induced to part with holdings of money on any reasonable terms'.

[84] Ibid. p. 207.

and lenders together and uncertainty as to the future of the rate of interest, which we have examined above, set a lower limit, which in present circumstances may perhaps be as high as 2 or 2.5 per cent on long-term'.[85]

Many post-war Keynesians cite the presence of a liquidity trap to justify a looser fiscal policy. However, central banks have the tools to lower long-term interest rates. To be clear, the *federal funds* target may be at the Zero Lower Bound, but that is not tantamount to a liquidity trap. This refers specifically to long-term interest rates.

Prior to *The General Theory*, Keynes had been more assertive, claiming [in February 1934] that 'no one can foretell at what point the rate of interest will reach its equilibrium level until we actually approach it. But it is highly probable that the equilibrium rate is not actually above 2.5 per cent for long-term gilt-edged investments, and may be appreciably less'.[86]

The merits of a proactive fiscal policy - government spending or tax cuts - to drive an economic recovery need to be considered in the context of a liquidity trap. This is arguably the fault line with post-war Keynesians. Keynes acknowledged, 'if - for whatever reason - the rate of interest [i.e. long-term] cannot be relied upon to fall

---

[85] Ibid. p. 218-219.

[86] See *Keynes's Monetary Theory of Interest*, Tily, BIS Paper No 65, 2010, p. 67 [CW XII, p. 206-207].

fast enough as the marginal efficiency of capital', there may be a case for increased government spending or tax cuts.[87] However, with Keynes asserting [in 1936] that no liquidity trap had been reached, he was self-evidently calling for monetary policy action ahead of fiscal policy. This lesson should have been applied more rigorously in response to the 2008 crisis.

Keynes's interest in fiscal policy was entirely *secondary*. According to Tily, the 'vast majority of Keynes's contributions to economic theory were concerned with monetary economics'.[88] *The General Theory* is first and foremost a statement of Keynes's monetary theory. This conclusion is even harder to refute when the 1936 book is evaluated in its historical context. *The General Theory* follows two important books devoted to domestic and international monetary reform [*A Tract on Monetary Reform* and *A Treatise on Money*]. Keynes spent the vast majority of his time before and during the Great Depression preaching the case for an alternative monetary policy to that advocated by the classical economists. The striking point about *The General Theory* is the comparatively small coverage given to fiscal policy. For example, the index to *The General Theory*

---

[87] See *The General Theory of Employment, Interest and Money*, Keynes, p. 219-220.

[88] See *Keynes's General Theory, The Rate Of Interest And 'Keynesian' Economics*, Tily, Palgrave Macmillan, 2007, p. 314.

contains 111 references to interest rates. There are only ten references to the 'state and investment' and just one for fiscal policy.[89]

The conclusion that fiscal policy is subordinate to monetary reflation may seem surprising given the accepted wisdom. Keynesian economics became synonymous with the active implementation of fiscal policy to fine-tune an economy during the post-1945 era. Economists, policymakers and politicians have propagated this interpretation for years, disregarding the key message of Keynes's analysis. *The General Theory* has been re-invented.

The point was underlined by the economist Richard Kahn who argued [in 1978] that, 'Keynes, in his *General Theory*, writes very little about public expenditure as a means of increasing employment. His main concern was that private investment should be adequately stimulated by low rates of interest'.[90] The best approach to increasing employment during an economic downturn is to stimulate private investment through a policy of cheap, but tight money.

However, the new Keynesian economists had started to disregard the critical work on liquidity preference even

---

[89] See *The General Theory of Employment, Interest and Money*, Keynes, 1936, p. 417, 419, 425. There are two references to fiscal policy in the index on p. 417, but one [p. 263] does not discuss fiscal policy.

[90] See Kahn [1978, p. 2], referenced in *Keynes's General Theory, The Rate Of Interest And 'Keynesian' Economics*, Tily, Palgrave Macmillan, 2007, p. 280.

before Keynes's death in 1946. Post-1946, fiscal policy took centre stage in both practical and theoretical terms. The Liquidity Preference Theory was cast aside and the monetary policy framework articulated by Keynes was quickly diluted. Keynesians offered an alternative 'analytical framework which was then primarily used to interpret the effects of fiscal policy'.[91]

To many outside of financial markets it is perhaps difficult to appreciate the significance of long-term interest rates in driving the economic cycle. The concept of liquidity preference and the unwillingness of investors to hold bonds at very low yields seems opaque. Nevertheless, at a time of deep recession and low inflation, liquidity preference becomes a critical challenge for central banks. The difficulty of managing long-term rates may persist during the recovery phase, delaying the return to full employment. Premature increases in short-term interest rate expectations can easily short-circuit nascent economic upswings. The slowdown in the US housing market following the sharp rate in interest rates [including the 30-year mortgage rate] in the second half of 2013 was a warning shot to the FOMC not to ignore liquidity preference.

For Keynes, control of the bond yield was paramount. At no stage during *The General Theory* did he advocate

---

[91] See *Keynes's General Theory, The Rate Of Interest And 'Keynesian' Economics*, Tily, p. 317.

a looser fiscal policy to drive economic recovery unless bond yields had fallen to an absolute low. Even when he did suggest it might be appropriate for governments to spend, he was careful not to overstate the case. Indeed, he warned 'it is not reasonable, however, that a sensible community should be content to remain dependant on such fortuitous and often wasteful mitigations [loose fiscal policy] when once we understand the influences upon which effective demand depends'.[92]

This is a clear inference that it is wrong for governments to undertake spending projects just for the sake of boosting economic growth, when there are alternative, more desirable remedies that should be tried *a priori*. It would be sub-optimal to promote fiscal policy when the targeting of longer-term interest rates could prove more effective in stimulating a recovery in investment. The support for a more expansionary fiscal policy by US economists Lawrence Summers and Paul Krugman in 2009 was based on a false interpretation of Keynes's work.[93] As we argued in Chapter 2, it can be

---

[92] See *The General Theory of Employment, Interest and Money*, Keynes, p. 220.

[93] See *Why America must have a fiscal stimulus*, Financial Times, 6 January 2008. Mr Summers was appointed Director of the National Economic Council in January 2009. See also, *How late is too late?*, Paul Krugman, *New York Times*, 27 January 2009. See also *interview with Paul Krugman*, BBC World News America, 12 February 2009, 'The stimulus plan is a lot better than nothing, but it is not as big as it ought to be, and not as well focussed as it ought to be'. http://news.bbc.co.uk/1/hi/programmes/world_news_america/7885019.stm [accessed 6 June 2014]. See also *Paul Krugman fear for lost decade*, Observer [UK], 14 June 2009. Mr Krugman played down the

counterproductive to use higher government spending to promote an economic recovery.

Intriguingly, Keynes also hinted at the preferred method of finance and it was not through the issuance of marketable government debt of short or longer maturities. Instead, 'if such a situation were to arise, [liquidity trap], it would mean that the public authority [the government] itself could borrow through the banking system on an unlimited scale at a nominal rate of interest'.[94] This might be preferable to borrowing through the bond market to mitigate the problem of liquidity preference close to the Zero Lower Bound.

This point underlines the overriding concern of Keynes that the control of long-term interest rates is paramount. Bond yields had reached a floor 'for whatever reason', but it was inadvisable for governments to issue marketable debt [particularly long-term]. Indeed, the very existence of a possible floor for bond yields implied there was a danger that the liquidity preference schedule would shift up in response to fiscal stimulus. In other words, investors might consequently have a higher preference for liquidity [i.e. cash]. Keynes recognised that 'the government programme may, through its effect on

significance of the rise in bond yields over the spring and summer of 2009, claiming that this merely reflected higher inflation expectations. His failure to recognise the significance of this bond market sell-off exposes a critical lack of understanding in the way Keynes's policies were meant to work.

[94] See *The General Theory of Employment, Interest and Money*, Keynes, p. 207.

'confidence', increase liquidity-preference'. This in turn 'may retard other investments unless measures are taken to offset it'.[95] He acknowledges that markets may react adversely to fiscal stimulus, undermining the efficacy of this policy. This was a risk precisely because of liquidity preference, which made it harder for central banks to control bond yields.

A liquidity trap might imply that bond yields were impervious to policy initiatives that could push borrowing costs lower. However, there was nothing to stop them from rising again. Indeed, in a liquidity trap, there was every reason to believe that investors will be more sensitive to any policy change that leads potentially to higher inflation expectations. Contrary to conventional belief, quantitative easing does not work by raising inflation expectations to reduce the real cost of borrowing, thus incentivising borrowers. It operates by lowering the nominal rate of interest, firstly to reduce the risk of default and subsequently set the stage for an investment-led recovery. Inflation expectations may eventually rise and that will indeed reduce real interest rates. Nevertheless, this will be a by-product of lower nominal rates delivering stronger economic growth *a priori*.

Investors may be incorrect in their assessment of

---

[95] Ibid. p. 120.

these inflation 'risks'. They may well be overstated in the aftermath of a deep recession. Nevertheless, any policy change that increases the potential [in the view of investors] for a rise in inflation could lead to higher bond yields even when liquidity preference had become 'virtually absolute'. A liquidity trap arises because investors are not willing to accept lower long-term interest rates. This is partly because of the non-linear relationship between bond prices and yields. In this case, the fear of inflation, however misplaced, can have a bigger detrimental impact, raising long-term interest rates. A floor for bond yields increases the risk of a premature reversal in long-term rates. As a result, a liquidity trap does not permit a central bank to become complacent. On the contrary, a liquidity trap implies that central banks [and governments] have to work even harder to ensure long-term interest rates remain low.

Ostensibly, the existence of a possible floor to long-term interest rates suggests that government spending or tax cuts have a dominant role to play in driving an economic recovery. In reality, fiscal policy is only going to succeed in reflating the economy if the monetary authorities can simultaneously prevent long-term interest rates from rising. The importance of Keynes's Liquidity Preference Theory in relation to this point cannot be overlooked. The logic of this theory and Keynes's analysis implies that it may even be optimal to run a tight fiscal policy during an economic downturn, if the risk premium on long-term government debt is too high because of concerns over debt sustainability. It has been wrongly assumed by post-war Keynesians that governments should always run large budget deficits during an economic recession. This is not a correct interpretation of Keynes's analysis. As we shall see, in the few instances where Keynes did call for state intervention, it was to act as a 'balancing factor' and to support monetary policy. In no instance did he advocate fiscal policy before the appropriate monetary policy actions had been taken.[96]

Furthermore, in a discussion on the role of the stimulus afforded by increased public works, Keynes warns that there are several offsets that 'we ought to take into account'. It is not safe to assume that the *fiscal multiplier* will remain constant. For example, 'If a government employs 100,000 additional men [and women] on public works, and if the multiplier is 4, it is not safe to assume that aggregate employment will increase by 400,000. For the new policy may have adverse reactions on investment in *other directions*'.[97] [Author's italics]

The method of financing the increase in government investment needs to be taken into account. The [market] rate of interest may rise, 'so retarding investment in other

---

directions, unless the monetary authority takes steps to the contrary'.[98] Keynes was underlining the importance of ensuring fiscal policy does not conflict with the more important task of maintaining a low bond yield.

## State and Investment

In *The General Theory*, Keynes makes just ten references to the role of the 'state and investment'. Some of these reflect his political preference for a greater 'social' control of the economy. Others elaborate upon the specific role of fiscal policy during an economic recovery. Nonetheless, none of these discussions show Keynes advocating higher government spending or tax cuts *ahead* of the requisite monetary action to reduce short-term interest rates and bond yields. For the sake of completeness we list in this section the ten references to 'state and investment' along with a brief comment.

In isolation, some of Keynes's references to fiscal policy do appear to be a strong call for government intervention. However, each needs to be taken within the context. At the time Keynes wrote *The General Theory*, governments had much lower debt burdens and budget deficits than today [see Chapter 4]. Critically, Keynes never advocated fiscal policy in a way that would accentuate the liquidity preference of investors. Unsustainable budget deficits

---

[98] Ibid.

and debt burdens will undermine investor confidence and increase liquidity preference. This was less of a consideration when Keynes wrote *The General Theory*. If a loose monetary policy is seen as a way of financing a government deficit, this will reinforce the liquidity preference of investors and compromise the efficacy of monetary policy. Keynes would not have advocated this.

Indeed, *Post-war Keynesians* have simply discredited or ignored much of Keynes's work, extracting his comments about fiscal policy without recognising the importance of liquidity preference. In many of Keynes's discussions about fiscal policy, he talks about the fall in the marginal efficiency of capital. Specifically, he argues for rates to be kept low enough in response to this decline, stimulating private sector investment as the primary weapon for reflation.

In the first reference of the 'state and investment', Keynes compares public to private investment in Chapter 8 of *The General Theory*. He addresses a common 'objection to schemes for raising employment by investment under the auspices of public authority that it is laying up trouble for the future. 'What will you do,' it is asked, 'when you have built all the houses and roads and town halls and electric grids and water supplies and so forth which the stationary population of the future can be expected to require?"[99] Keynes dismisses this popular argument against public works, claiming that the so-called threat posed by *over-investment* applies equally to the private sector. Later in *The General Theory*, he goes further and suggests that the term over-investment is overused and occurs less often than widely presumed. More often than not, the underlying economic problem is not over-investment, but a higher, unrealistic expectation of the necessary rate of return. This in turn is elevated or inflated by higher rates of interest resulting from inappropriate central bank policies. In this case, the best remedy to over-investment is not a high rate of interest, which may, according to Keynes, 'deter some use investments and might further diminish the propensity to consume'.[100] Instead, he called for low interest rates, buttressed by tight money. Only this policy combination ensures a sustainable economic recovery.

The <u>second reference</u> is more significant in the context of liquidity preference and is at the end of Chapter 12 of *The General Theory*. Keynes outlines the importance of expectations for monetary policy. He concluded, 'For my own part I am now somewhat sceptical of the success of a merely monetary policy directed towards influencing the rate of interest. I expect to see the State, which is in

---

[99] Ibid. p. 106.
[100] Ibid. p. 321.

a position to calculate the marginal efficiency of capital-goods on long views and on the basis of the general social advantage, taking an ever greater responsibility for directly organising investment; since it seems likely that the fluctuations in the market estimation of the marginal efficiency of different types of capital, calculated on the principles I have described above, will be too great to be offset by any practicable changes in the rate of interest'.[101]

This appears to offer a close approximation to the post-war Keynesian view that government investment should be the primary stabilising tool in an economic downturn. However, Keynes is still acknowledging in this quote the importance of using monetary policy *a priori* to try and reverse an economic downturn: 'Only experience, however, can show how far management of the rate of interest is capable of continuously stimulating the appropriate volume of investment'.[102] If a liquidity trap has not been reached, central banks could still employ tools to lower long-term interest rates, before fiscal policy would be recommended by Keynes. The improvement in the housing market and the economic recovery in the US following the 2008 crisis illustrated the point. Monetary policy has proved much more effective than fiscal stimulus [see Chapter 2].

---

[101] Ibid. p. 164.

[102] Ibid.

For the <u>third reference</u> Keynes suggests that, 'In so far as millionaires find their satisfaction in building mighty mansions to contain their bodies when alive and pyramids to shelter them after death, or, repenting of their sins, erect cathedrals and endow monasteries or foreign missions, the day when abundance of capital will interfere with abundance of output may be postponed. 'To dig holes in the ground', paid for out of savings, will increase, not only employment, but the real national dividend of useful goods and services'.[103]

Keynes is being somewhat facetious. Nevertheless, the next paragraph reinforces the primacy of monetary policy: 'Let us assume that steps are taken to ensure that the rate of interest is consistent with the rate of investment which corresponds to full employment. Let us assume, further, that State action enters in as a balancing factor'.[104] Here again, 'State action' is advocated only after interest rates have been cut.

The <u>fourth reference</u> to 'state and investment' occurs in Chapter 22, titled *Notes On The Trade Cycle*. Keynes suggests 'the duty of ordering the current volume of investment cannot safely be left in private hands'. However, this 'endorsement' of fiscal policy is again sequential to this earlier reference on monetary policy:

---

[103] Ibid. p. 220.

[104] Ibid.

'organised and influenced as they are at present, the market estimation of the marginal efficiency of capital *may* suffer such enormously wide fluctuations that it cannot be sufficiently offset by corresponding fluctuations in the rate of interest'.[105] Keynes makes it clear that cheap money is the priority.

Furthermore, while Keynes was acknowledging the case for state investment, it is important to note that this conclusion follows a discussion of what he refers to as a 'sudden collapse in the marginal efficiency of capital', which may occur at the later stages of a boom.[106] The collapse in the marginal efficiency of capital will be particularly evident in 'those types of capital which have been contributing most to the previous phase of heavy new investment'.[107]

Keynes discusses the possibility that liquidity preference may rise in an economic downturn and this would seriously aggravate the fall in investment.[108] This does not happen until *after* the decline in the marginal efficiency of capital. 'It is this indeed [the collapse in the marginal efficiency of capital] which renders the slump so intractable. Later on, a decline in the rate of interest

---

[105] Ibid. p. 320.

[106] Ibid. p. 315.

[107] Ibid. p. 316.

[108] Ibid.

will be a great aid to recovery and, probably, a necessary condition of it. But, for the moment, the collapse in the marginal efficiency of capital may be so complete that no practicable reduction in the rate of interest will be enough. If a reduction in the rate of interest was capable of proving an effective remedy by itself, it might be possible to achieve a recovery without the elapse of any considerable interval of time and by means more or less directly under the control of the monetary authority. But, in fact, this is not usually the case; and it is not so easy to revive the marginal efficiency of capital, determined, as it is, by the uncontrollable and disobedient psychology of the business world. It is the return of confidence, to speak in ordinary language, which is so insusceptible to control in an economy of individualistic capitalism. This is the aspect of the slump which bankers and business men have been right in emphasising, and which the economists who have put their faith in a 'purely monetary' remedy have underestimated'.[109]

Taken at face value this last sentence indicates a preference for alternative remedies over monetary policy. Keynes is highlighting a scenario where a 'catastrophic' decline in the expected return on investments cannot be reversed by a fall in the rate of interest. However, even in this extreme case, Keynes is not arguing for fiscal

---

[109] Ibid. p. 316-317.

intervention ahead of monetary policy. The correct preferred order of policy tools [monetary ahead of fiscal] is again evident in this quote. The Liquidity Preference Theory remains central to the argument.

The fifth reference to the 'state and investment' centres on a debate over the efficacy of government measures to promote consumption, comparing these with policies aimed at a 'socially controlled rate of investment'. Keynes suggests there may be 'much social advantage to be obtained from investment', but concedes there is 'room, therefore, for both policies to operate together'. It is instructive to note that these options are considered in a scenario where the long-term rate of interest 'never falls below a conventional level'.[110] Nevertheless, as already indicated, Keynes doubted whether the US or the UK ever encountered a liquidity trap during the Great Depression. Once long-term rates had fallen in the US in 1932, a recovery began without the necessity of a looser fiscal policy.[111]

The sixth reference to the 'state and investment' occurs in *Notes on Mercantilism* [Chapter 23]. In a somewhat hypothetical scenario Keynes [self-evidently] observes that 'in a society where there is no question of

---

[110] Ibid. p. 325.

[111] The low for US manufacturing production in the Great Depression occurred in July 1932, before the election of President Roosevelt and the New Deal. See Chapter 4, p. 296-297.

direct investment under the aegis of public authority'
then governments will only have domestic interest rates
[and foreign trade] as possible policy weapons.[112] Keynes
returns to fiscal policy later in Chapter 23 in the context
of 'beggar thy neighbour policies'. He argues, 'It is the
policy of an autonomous rate of interest, unimpeded
by international preoccupations, and of a national
investment programme directed to an optimum level
of domestic employment which is twice blessed in the
sense that it helps ourselves and our neighbours at the
same time'.[113] Again, control of the rate of interest comes
*before* 'a national investment programme'.

The next reference to the 'state and investment' is
brief and occurs in the context of usury laws.[114] It is
inconsequential with respect to the use of fiscal policy
in a recession. The penultimate discussion of the 'state
and investment' considers the 'scale and by what means
it is right and reasonable to call on the living generation
to restrict their consumption, so as to establish in course
of time, a state of full investment for their successors'.
This is partly an 'inter-generational' debate over how far
to promote investment at the expense of consumption
when trying to secure an economic recovery and part of

---

[112] See *The General Theory of Employment, Interest and Money*, Keynes, p.
335.

[113] Ibid. p. 349.

[114] Ibid. p. 351.

a broader, ideological discussion over the role of the state. Nevertheless, there is nothing in this quote to suggest that fiscal policy should be prioritised. Keynes suggests that 'It may turn out that the propensity to consume will be so easily strengthened by the effects of a falling rate of interest, that full employment can be reached with a rate of accumulation little greater than at present.' State action, if required, would be needed to 'supplement' other more effective monetary options.[115]

The final reference again reveals Keynes's opposition to the classical school's unwavering commitment to market forces, which left unchecked, can prove destabilising. He warns, 'the enlargement of the functions of government, involved in the task of adjusting to one another the propensity to consume and the inducement to invest, would seem to a nineteenth-century publicist or to a contemporary American financier to be a terrific encroachment on individualism. I defend it, on the contrary, both as the only practicable means of avoiding the destruction of existing economic forms in their entirety and as the condition of the successful functioning of individual initiative'.[116]

Keynes is railing against critics of state intervention on the grounds that the private sector may not be able

---

[115] Ibid. p. 377.

[116] Ibid. p. 380.

to solve endemic unemployment. He is articulating his 'philosophical' preference for greater involvement of government in the economy. This critique reflects a growing preference for some state control of the economy. Nonetheless, there is no indication here that monetary policy should be relegated behind fiscal measures.

Aside from the ten references to the 'state and investment', there is only one other notable mention of fiscal policy in *The General Theory*. It occurs in relation to the principal objective factors that may influence the propensity to consume. He suggests, 'If fiscal policy is used as a deliberate instrument for the more equal distributions of incomes, its effect in increasing the propensity to consume is, of course, all the greater'.[117] It highlights Keynes's preference for tax cuts on lower waged individuals, but again it does not signal the primacy of fiscal over monetary policy.

## Domestic Monetary Reform and Credit Control

From the *Tract* to *The General Theory*, Keynes had a very clear prescription. It was better to restrain lending through credit controls rather than immediately reverse the policy of low interest rates or cheap money. The authorities should aim for a policy of cheap, but tight

[117] Ibid. p. 95.

money. It was precisely the overt use of interest rates to manage the economy in a liberalised era that had precipitated boom and bust. A lack of restraint on the banks had made it impossible to control the economy through interest rates.

More recently, the case for a dual policy was evident during the housing boom prior to the 2008 crisis. Charles Bean, deputy governor and former chief economist of the Bank of England, acknowledged this point when he argued that raising interest rates during the boom prior to 2007 would have been ineffective in quelling runaway house prices: 'I have to say I think people who take the view, well, if interest rates have only been 25 or 50 basis points [0.25 per cent or 0.5 per cent] higher, none of this would have happened, are frankly rather unrealistic'. According to Bean, interest rates would have needed to be 2 or 3 per cent higher to have 'significantly impacted on the build-up of credit and the asset prices, particularly house prices'. That would have caused a recession anyway. There was clearly a need for 'a second instrument', Mr Bean admitted.[118] Over the past five years, the Bank of England and the Federal Reserve have shifted towards the cheap, but tight money advocated by Keynes. Whether they have travelled far enough to prevent a repeat of the 2007/08 crisis remains to be seen.

---

[118] See *Charlie Bean Interview*, Financial Times, 17 December 2008.

For Keynes, cheap money was not just a solution to economic downturns. It was a secular policy: cheap money was, counter-intuitively, a requisite for a long economic expansion too. 'The remedy for the boom is not a higher rate of interest but a lower rate of interest! For that may enable the so-called boom to last. The right remedy for the trade cycle is not to be found in abolishing booms and thus keeping us permanently in a semi-slump; but in abolishing slumps and thus keeping us permanently in a quasi-boom'.[119]

However, there was a critical distinction between cheap money and easy money. The latter reflected a lack of domestic monetary reform, specifically an absence of controls over credit creation. By extension *dear money* does not eliminate the risks posed by easy money. Dear money or higher rates of interest against the backdrop of inadequate credit control increases the volatility of the business cycle: it is likely to provoke rapid, excessive expansions followed by slumps.

Thus, it is wrong to dismiss the case for low rates of interest simply because this may foster easy credit. There needs to be a dual target for domestic monetary policy. Control over the rate of interest [short- and long-term] must be complemented by adequate control over the monetary system. Indeed, the latter was a prerequisite,

---

[119] See *The General Theory of Employment, Interest and Money*, Keynes, p. 322.

reinforcing the ability of a central bank to implement an appropriate structure of borrowing costs, which *could* in turn deliver full employment and ensure a more stable economic cycle. Cheap, but tight money would reduce the risk of an economic upswing turning into deep recession partly because the cost of servicing any associated debt would be reduced. By contrast, over reliance upon the rate of interest to control the economic cycle - alongside easy money - would increase the likelihood that companies or households will be subsumed by bad debts.

The risks posed by easy money were articulated by Keynes: 'It is of the nature of organised investment markets, under the influence of purchasers largely ignorant of what they are buying and of speculators who are more concerned with forecasting the next shift of market sentiment than with a reasonable estimate of the future yield of capital-assets, that, when disillusion falls upon an over-optimistic and over-bought market, it should fall with sudden and even catastrophic force'.[120] This warning is even more relevant in view of the dotcom downturn [2000 - 2001] and the recent subprime crisis in the US.

Keynes identified two driving forces that can become mutually reinforcing following a period of easy money. Firstly, the marginal efficiency of capital will drop as

---

[120] Ibid. p. 315-316.

firms realise that 'their revenues from investments made during the expansion phase are failing to meet expectations that led them to borrow in the first place'. Secondly, the subsequent loss of confidence in financial markets 'will cause liquidity preference and risk premia to increase, leading to a sharp rise in the rate of interest'.[121] Investment demand, output and employment will all fall sharply, absent the necessary, pre-emptive shift in monetary policy. A regulatory and policy framework that discourages excessive credit growth from developing is thus critical to sustainable economic growth.

Cheap money may eventually increase the *probability* of inflation. The final paragraph [41] of the 1945 National Debt Enquiry's report conceded that 'If the prevailing long-term tap rate becomes chronically too low, in the sense that it encourages new capital formation on a scale tending to inflation, the rate should, in general, be raised'.[122] However, the warning was placed at the end of the National Debt Enquiry's report, which was deliberate. The emphasis of the report was on monetary controls, both domestic and external. A policy of cheap, but tight money would reduce the risks of inflation. Reversing the policy of low interest rates would be a last resort. Furthermore, the likelihood or risk of inflation returning

---

[121] See Keynes's *General Theory, The Rate Of Interest And 'Keynesian' Economics*, Tily, p. 243.

[122] Ibid. p. 89.

would not simply be determined by employment. The question of whether this was higher than the so-called equilibrium or natural rate of interest was only one part of the policy consideration. It would also depend on supply or capacity constraints.

In any case, these risks need to be set against the potential benefits of securing full employment. In addition, there may be preferable alternatives to dear money for taming inflation - namely 'a degree of control over the supply of money in a climate of low interest rates'.[123] A policy of cheap, but tight money would have the advantage of shifting the focus of investment away from financial to real assets. It would, Keynes argued, accelerate the 'euthanasia of the *rentier*'. In the early stages of an economic recovery, the rentier or the investor in financial assets will benefit perhaps disproportionately, as asset prices recover. However, this will be a 'transitional phase which will disappear when it has done its work. And with the disappearance of its rentier aspect, much else in it besides will suffer a sea-change'.[124] The maintenance of low long-term interest rates combined with tight money will in short encourage a shift towards investment in productive capacity. Cheap, but tight money would underpin the ability of the authorities to

---

[123] Ibid. p. 245.

[124] See *The General Theory of Employment, Interest and Money*, Keynes, 1936, p. 376.

deliver low inflation.

## Debt Management Policies

During the Great Depression, Keynes advocated a number of important practical policies designed to set borrowing cost more effectively across the whole spectrum of liquidity. The Liquidity Preference Theory implied that debt management policies should be used to influence market rates. Inappropriate debt issuance would undermine the ability of a central bank to target bond yields effectively. '... it is confidence in the future of short-term rates which is required to bring down long-term rates. Now the policy of the Treasury is not calculated to promote such confidence. They seem reluctant to issue bonds of from five to 10 years' maturity and anxious to reduce the short-term debt, in spite of the extraordinary cheapness with which it can be carried'.[125]

Setting the price of government securities - and therefore yields - at the optimal level for an economic recovery should be driven by the liquidity preference of lenders, not borrowers [i.e. the government]. If investors were reluctant to hold government debt with longer maturities, the authorities could - and should - modify their debt issuance accordingly. Indeed, according to

---

[125] See Keynes [CW XXI, p. 375], referenced in *Keynes's General Theory, The Rate Of Interest And 'Keynesian' Economics*, Tily, p. 75.

Tily, the authorities could 'set the rate of interest on long-term debt if they are willing to issue as much short-term debt as the public wishes to hold'.[126]

In this context, it was important to consider potential [adverse] signalling effects from debt management policies, which could make it harder for central banks to hold long-term rates down. Since the economic downturn of 2008 - 2009, governments have been encouraged to issue longer-term debt to 'lock in' cheaper borrowing costs. However, the motivation for this shift in debt issuance will not be lost on investors: by issuing more long-term debt, governments and central banks are implicitly assuming that borrowing costs will eventually rise. In this case, it will be more difficult to persuade investors to increase their exposure to long-term debt. Central banks and the government should be sending a strong, unequivocal message to investors that the rate of interest will remain low. Contrary to accepted wisdom, it might be preferable to shorten the maturity of debt issuance.

Of course, critics will argue that extending the maturity of government debt reduces the pressure at 'rollover'. If the borrowing is concentrated at shorter maturities, there might be a greater risk that investors will balk at refinancing government debt. In truth, this

---

[126] See *Keynes's General Theory, The Rate Of Interest And 'Keynesian' Economics*, Tily, p. 322.

argument is misconceived. Investors can sell or exit government bonds at any time, not just when it is being refinanced or at rollover. The notion that governments must lock in low borrowing rates for a longer period betrays a misunderstanding of the Liquidity Preference Theory and its importance to the economic recovery.

If governments are to be encouraged to increase the proportion of their funding on short-term debt, there will be even more reason for the monetary authorities to pursue tight money or quantitative regulation. The February 1937 Economic Advisory Council Report [UK] outlined the requisite policy framework. A higher share of floating or short-term debt implied that 'it may be much more possible and desirable for the financial authorities to exercise adequate control over the supply of credit without recourse to the manipulations of short-term interest rates which are traditionally associated with this objective'.[127]

## Tap Issues

Keynes wrote two articles for *The Times* in April 1939 urging the UK Chancellor of the Exchequer [Sir John Simon] to accept a large increase in the share of floating

---

[127] See *The Economic Advisory Council 1930 - 1939*, Howson and Winch, 1977, p. 352.

rate debt.[128] This would help to cap long-term interest rates and bring down borrowing costs across the board. Two more articles in *The Times* followed in July 1939, articulating debt management techniques that would buttress the policy of cheap money. After his return to the UK Treasury, Keynes promoted the *tap issue* policy for government debt issuance, which he had floated in *The General Theory* three years earlier:

'If the monetary authority were prepared to deal both ways on specified terms in debts of all maturities, and even more so if it were prepared to deal in debts of varying degrees of risk, the relationship between the complex of rates of interest and the quantity of money would be direct'.[129] Furthermore, 'a complex offer by the central bank to buy and sell at stated prices gilt-edged bonds of all maturities, in place of the single bank rate for short-term bills, is the most important practical improvement which can be made in the technique of monetary management'.[130] Keynes was arguing for central banks to use their undoubted clout [i.e. balance sheet] to target, even fix the price of government bonds. The quote is telling in one other important respect: central banks

---

[128] See *Keynes's General Theory, The Rate Of Interest And 'Keynesian' Economics*, Tily, p. 76.

[129] See *The General Theory of Employment, Interest and Money*, Keynes, 1936, p. 205.

[130] Ibid. p. 206.

*buying* bonds at a stated price is effectively a *reverse tap* [see Appendix I, Reverse Taps, page 153].

The tap issue led to a wider range of securities on offer. The tap of any bond was held open and investors could purchase when and whatever quantity they wished. This method was first introduced in June 1940 with the medium-term National War Bond, [2.5 per cent coupon] and subsequently for the 3 per cent long-term Savings Bonds. The policy of capping borrowing costs [the 'three per cent war'] was a success. Keynes's theory had been vindicated as the control of the rate of interest had been achieved against a difficult backdrop. Heavy military expenditure during the Second World War had pushed the budget deficit up to more than a quarter of GDP, but long-term interest rates remained low.[131]

However, it is important not to lose sight of the role of capital controls. According to Tily, the UK government's policy had been 'ad hoc and subject to change'.[132] Nevertheless, the War Loan conversion of 1932 was accompanied by an 'embargo on overseas loans'. For Keynes, capital controls were a prerequisite

---

[131] See *Historical Statistics of the United States, Colonial Times to 1970,* US Department of Commerce, Bureau of Census, Part 1, p. 224 and Part 2, p. 1105. The peak US deficit of 28.1 per cent of GDP was in 1943. Source: C.H. Feinstein, National Income, Expenditure & Output of the UK 1855 - 1965, Cambridge University Press, 1972, T10, T35. The peak UK deficit was 26.1 per cent of GDP in 1941.

[132] See *Keynes's General Theory, The Rate Of Interest And 'Keynesian' Economics,* Tily, p. 78.

to domestic monetary reform and the debt management policies required to bear down on long-term interest rates. Keynes formalised his case for capital controls in 1944 with the *International Clearing Union*, which was put forward as the UK Government's official proposal at the *Bretton Woods Agreement*.[133] Ultimately, they were watered down in favour of the rival plan from the US Treasury for a 'stabilisation' fund. The monetary reforms promoted by Keynes - to great affect from the early 1930s onwards - were diluted.

## Post-War Keynesian Economics and Fiscal Policy

Indeed, after his death in 1946, there was a broad retreat from the policies Keynes had supported during the 1930s and through the Second World War. The reversal culminated in a liberalisation of finance from 1969 onwards that he would surely have opposed. It was certainly contrary to the policies he promoted at Bretton Woods. By the early 1970s, the monetary reforms of the post-depression years were being systematically reversed. Keynes's theory was reinvented. Indeed, much of the post-1945 era was dominated by a post-war Keynesian agenda that lost sight of key messages from *The General Theory*.

Post-war Keynesians placed an exaggerated emphasis

---

[133] Ibid. p. 79.

on fiscal policy to control the economy and promote full employment. Monetary tools and control of the credit system were progressively diluted. Capital controls were dismantled and a policy of cheap, but tight money was replaced by the opposite - dear, but easy money - which had prevailed before 1929. The inflationary surge of the 1970s was not a failure of 'Keynes'. It represented the inevitable result of a collision between post-war Keynesians and liberalisation.

Today, capital flows freely. It is not realistic to imagine - in the current political climate - that governments or the monetary authorities would be able to affect an 'ad-hoc' embargo as seen in the 1930s, let alone the broader capital controls proposed in 1944. Capital flows necessarily compromise the management of domestic monetary policy, particularly when governments run large budget deficits. The policy dilemmas facing the authorities since 2008 have to be viewed through the prism of the free movement of capital.

Much of Keynes's analysis remains absolutely relevant. However, the Liquidity Preference Theory and the implications for monetary policy need to be adjusted for the political realities of a liberalised era. For Keynes, fiscal policy was secondary to monetary reflation. In the absence of capital controls, the case for fiscal stimulus will be relegated even further behind the control of the rate of interest.

# Appendix III

# The Demand for Money

Understanding the demand for money was critical to Keynes's Liquidity Preference Theory. Large shifts in liquidity preference could be an important consideration with respect to the conduct of monetary policy. It is, therefore, necessary to dissect the possible influences upon the demand for money, which are a 'composite result of a number of different motives'.[1] These were first discussed in the *Treatise* under the headings of income, business and savings deposits.[2] The divisions of liquidity preference were subsequently outlined in Chapter 13 and more formally in Chapter 15 of *The General Theory*.

In Chapter 13, Keynes introduces three motives for holding money - the transactions, precautionary and speculative demand. In Chapter 15, the transactions demand for money is further sub-divided into the income and business motives. In the former, cash may be required by an individual to 'bridge the interval between the

---

[1] See *The General Theory of Employment, Interest and Money*, John Maynard Keynes, p. 195.

[2] Ibid. p. 194-195.

receipt of income and its disbursement'. This demand for money will depend upon the level of income and 'the normal length of the interval between its receipt and its disbursement'. The business motive is similar. Cash will be required or 'held to bridge the interval between the time of incurring business costs and that of the receipt of the sale proceeds'.[3] The strength of this demand will be related to the value of current output and 'the number of hands (and hence on current income) through which output passes'.[4]

The income motive for transactions demand is closely connected with the income *velocity of money*. This measures the proportion of income that individuals hold in cash. An increase in income velocity may be seen as a symptom of a decline in liquidity preference. However, the two concepts are not the same: the individual can exercise his or her choice between liquidity and illiquidity for the stock of accumulated savings, not just income. Only a portion of the public's cash holdings can be related to income. As a result, the term income velocity of money is incomplete as it creates the 'misleading presumption' that the demand for money as a whole is proportionate to income.[5]

---

[3] Ibid. p. 195.

[4] Ibid. p. 195-196.

[5] Ibid. p. 194.

According to Keynes, the precautionary demand for money reflects cash held for 'contingencies requiring sudden expenditure and for unforeseen opportunities of advantageous purchases'. Individuals or businesses may also need to hold cash to meet 'a subsequent liability fixed in terms of money'.[6]

The transactions and precautionary demand for money will partly be influenced by the 'cheapness and reliability of obtaining cash'. They will also depend upon the opportunity or relative cost of holding cash. However, this is likely to be a 'minor factor where large changes in the cost of holding cash are in question'.[7] This qualification is important. In normal circumstances, the money needed to satisfy the transaction and the precautionary motives is mainly a result of the general activity of the economic system. It is typically irresponsive to interest rates.

The final motive is the speculative demand for money and this was central to Keynes's analysis of monetary policy. This is 'essentially the object of securing profit from knowing better than the market what the future will bring forth'.[8] Ironically, well-organised capital markets reduce the precautionary demand for money, as investors will be confident that they can dispose of

---

[6] Ibid. p. 196.

[7] Ibid.

[8] Ibid. p. 170.

assets. However, as already indicated on page 196, the existence of such a market with more buyers and sellers provides the opportunity for large, sometimes rapid shifts in liquidity preference.[9] Furthermore, the speculative motive for holding money is a 'continuous response to gradual changes in the rate of interest'.[10]

Keynes argues that the transactions and precautionary motives [M1] are largely independent of the speculative demand [M2]. Consequently, there are two liquidity functions L1 and L2. L1 mainly relates to income [Y]. L2 largely depends on the relation between the current rate of interest [r] and the state of expectation. Thus:

$$M \text{ [money supply outstanding]} = M1 + M2 = L1 \text{ [Y]} + L2 \text{ [r]}^{11}$$

Typically, a change in M would impact on Y by influencing r first. A change in r would lead to a new equilibrium through its impact on M2, but also by changing Y and thus M1.[12] A critical difference with the classical school [and monetarists] is the definition of the [income] velocity of money [V]. For the latter,

---

[9] Ibid. p. 170 - 171. 'For in the absence of an organised market, liquidity-preference due to the precautionary motive would be greatly increased; whereas the existence of an organised market gives rise to an opportunity for wide fluctuations in liquidity preference due to the speculative-motive'.

[10] Ibid. p. 197.

[11] Ibid. p. 199.

[12] Ibid. p. 200-201.

V is defined as the ratio of Y to M. Keynes proposed a different definition, where V is the ratio of Y to M1.[13] Over a short period of time, V can be treated as 'nearly enough constant'.[14]

Uncertainty over the future path of interest rates is the 'sole intelligible explanation' for L2, which leads to the public holding M2.[15] As a result, M2 will not depend on the absolute level of r, but the degree of divergence between r and what is regarded as a fairly safe level of r. Furthermore, M2 'will not have a definitive quantitative relationship to a given rate of interest of r'.[16] Hence, M will be endogenous and should not be the used as a target for central banks when conducting large-scale asset purchases.

---

[13] Ibid. p. 201.

[14] Ibid.

[15] Ibid.

[16] Ibid.

# Chapter 4

# Monetary Policy and The Great Depression

The economic collapse in the US from late 1929 onwards was aggravated by a failure of the Federal Reserve to adopt a more aggressive monetary policy. There were endless arguments and debates over how far to push *quantitative easing* in the US during the Great Depression. The policy was labelled *large-scale open market purchases*. When finally - under Congressional pressure - the Federal Reserve did respond, the economy stabilised. Nevertheless, large-scale open market purchases could have been much more effective if they had been implemented sooner. The number of bank failures and the economic downturn might have been smaller had the Federal Reserve pursued quantitative easing with an unwavering commitment.

Adherence to the gold standard through the first three-and-a-half years of the depression has been widely touted as a major cause of the severe economic contraction.[1] Interest rates did rise to defend the Dollar

---

[1] See for example, *Golden Fetters: The Gold Standard and the Great Depression, 1919-1939*, B. Eichengreen, Oxford University Press, 1992, p. 4.

on two separate occasions. Nonetheless, it is wrong to blame the gold standard entirely for the depth of the Great Depression. It would have been possible for the Federal Reserve to offset the deflationary impact by driving long-term interest rates lower through quantitative easing.[2] In addition, the US government could have abandoned the gold standard earlier. Britain left in September 1931 because the deflationary costs were too high. The US persevered, until finally under President Roosevelt, the costs were deemed unbearable too. Nevertheless, the US authorities had a chance to pursue a reflationary policy much earlier in the crisis, but there was deep resistance to the policy of cheap money advocated by Keynes.

Large numbers of banks defaulted a year after the stock market crash in the US in October 1929. The run began in November 1930 with the collapse of Caldwell and Company, a large Tennessee investment bank.[3] A

---

'The gold standard, then, is conventionally portrayed as synonymous with financial stability. Its downfall starting in 1929 is implicated in the global financial crisis and the worldwide depression. A central message of this book is that precisely the opposite was true. Far from being synonymous with stability, the gold standard itself was the principal threat to financial stability and economic prosperity between the wars ... we must show that the removal of the gold standard in the 1930s established the preconditions for recovery from the Great Depression'.

[2] See *A Monetary History of the United States, 1867-1960*, M. Friedman & A.J Schwartz, Princeton University Press, 1963, p. 395. 'The System took no active measures to ease the internal drain, as it could have done through open market purchases'.

[3] See *A History of the Federal Reserve*, Volume 1:1913-1951, A. Meltzer, University of Chicago Press, p. 323.

total of 256 banks failed in November. Another 352 banks folded in December 1932.[4] The New York State superintendent of banking closed the Bank of United States as 'more than half a million depositors found their deposits unavailable'.[5]

A second banking crisis from March 1931 onwards lasted longer and 'had far more severe effects on the stock of money'.[6] It also led to a 'more drastic rise in yields on lower-grade corporate bonds, as banks sought to realise on their portfolios'. The economic decline had 'seriously impaired the earning power of many [corporate] concerns and sharply raised the chances of default'.[7] Banks had accumulated a large exposure to corporate bonds during the boom of the late 1920s. As companies raced to expand, they issued bonds to fund growth. The risk of these companies defaulting grew during the long slump. The price on these bonds fell, pushing the yield up. As yields rose, banks were compelled to dump

---

[4] See A Monetary History of the United States, 1867-1960, M. Friedman & A.J Schwartz, Princeton University Press, 1963, p. 308. 'The failure of 256 banks with $180million deposits in November 1930 was followed by the failure of 352 with over $370million of deposits in December'.

[5] See A History of the Federal Reserve, Volume 1:1913-1951, Meltzer, University of Chicago Press, p. 323.

[6] See A Monetary History of the United States, 1867-1960, M. Friedman & A.J Schwartz, Princeton University Press, 1963, p. 314. 'In the six months from February to August 1931, commercial banks deposits fell by $2.7billion or nearly 7 per cent more than in the whole eighteen-month period from the cyclical peak in August 1929 to February 1931'.

[7] Ibid. p. 315.

their bonds, causing even bigger losses and more forced liquidations. Banks collapsed, the money supply shrank, the economy deteriorated, more companies went bust and unemployment soared. Corporate bond prices fell further.

The banking system was in meltdown. The only way out of the mire was for the Federal Reserve to intervene and reverse the rise in corporate borrowing costs, to stop companies defaulting. Under heavy Congressional pressure, the Federal Reserve started buying Treasuries more aggressively. There was nothing particularly radical about this policy. It had become an accepted instrument for central banks to use during periods of distress. Indeed, at the time, it was widely regarded as 'the most potent monetary tool' in the Federal Reserve's kit.[8]

There was an accepted logic behind the Federal Reserve's actions. By pushing down the so-called *risk-free* rate, the market could decide which companies could refinance at lower rates. If the Federal Reserve intervened directly in the corporate bond market, it would have been fostering moral hazard. By driving the baseline for all borrowing costs lower, the Federal Reserve would still allow the market to decide which companies would survive.

Within a month, the large-scale asset purchases had

---

[8] Ibid. p. 390.

started to drive down corporate bond yields. [See chart 4a] The average yield on corporate bonds for companies with a rating of Baa peaked at 11.6% in May 1932. Over the summer of that year, yields fell steadily, touching 7.6% four months later.[9]

The policy was not pursued anywhere near aggressively enough. The drop in corporate borrowing costs was inadequate because the Federal Reserve had been far from united in its pursuit of lower government bond yields. Nevertheless, in so much that it was tried, it stopped the rot. This important episode showed that quantitative easing was the *critical weapon* in the battle against asset deflation. The Federal Reserve turned the tide in 1932. US money supply still tumbled in the early months of 1933, but the impact of quantitative easing could be seen over the summer of 1932. Indeed, the decline in bank deposits reached a trough in July 1932, while money supply hit an interim low two months later. The improvements were modest, but by comparison with the hefty declines witnessed beforehand, 'the shift was major'.[10]

---

[9] Ibid. p. 323. 'In the first quarter of 1932 the rates had fallen from the peaks reached in December 1931 or January 1932. In the second quarter, however, the corporate Baa bond yield soared to a peak [11.63 per cent in May] - unmatched in the monthly record since 1919 - and the yield on long-term government bonds rose slightly. Commercial paper rates continued to decline in the second quarter, the reduction in the discount rate in New York on February 26 having led the commercial paper rate'.

[10] Ibid.

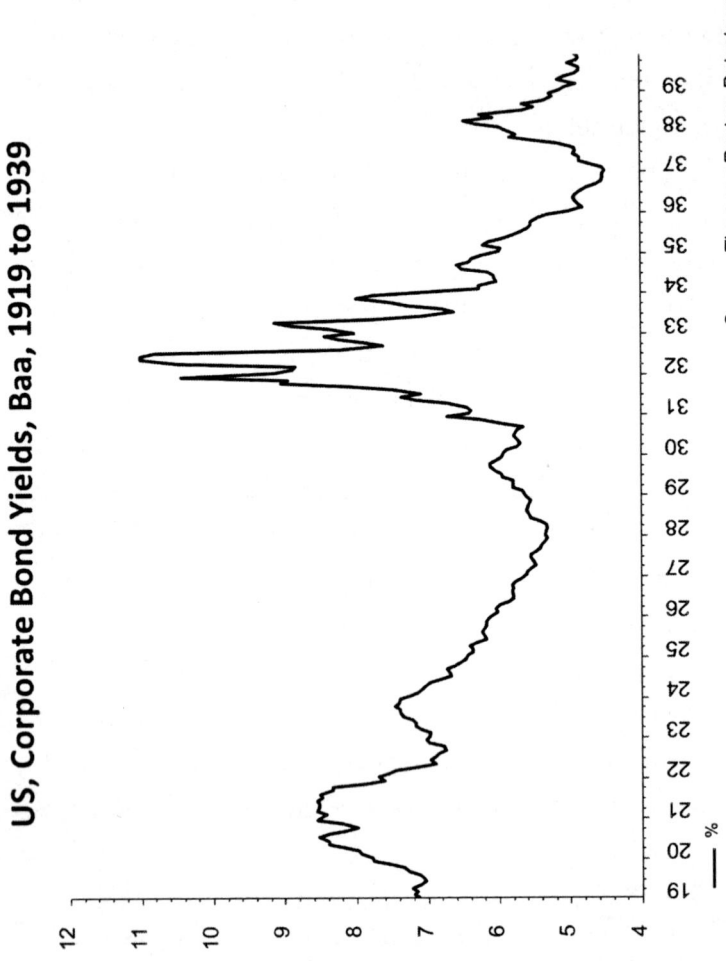

**US, Corporate Bond Yields, Baa, 1919 to 1939**

Source: Thomson Reuters Datastream

Chart 4a

The policy of large-scale open market purchases adopted in 1932 did not stop more banks failing. After its initial success with asset purchases, the Federal Reserve backtracked. During the final months of that year, a large number of banks collapsed in the Midwest and Far West, while 'there was a sharp spurt in January [1933] involving a wider area'.[11] The decision to raise interest rates to defend the Dollar in one last desperate attempt to prevent a collapse of the gold standard backfired too. The long fallout from the UK government's decision to abandon the gold standard in September 1931 was taking its toll. The subsequent decline in Sterling led the Federal Reserve to raise interest rates even as the economy contracted. Investors and depositors in a number of European countries began to anticipate that the US would leave the gold standard to reverse the gold drain. Interest rates went up, initially in the autumn of 1931 and again in early 1933.[12] Nevertheless, the crisis in early 1933 'was even more serious than in September 1931 because of all that had gone before ... the panic was far more widespread'.[13]

An important cause of this was 'the drastically

---

[11] Ibid. p. 324.

[12] Ibid. p. 326. 'The Federal Reserve System reacted to these events very much as it had in September 1931. It raised discount rates in February 1933 in reaction to the external drain, and it did not seek to counter either the external or internal drain by any extensive open market purchases'.

[13] Ibid.

weakened capital position of the commercial banks, which had made them vulnerable to even minor drains' of funds. Indeed, 'the recorded capital figures were widely recognised as overstating the available capital, because assets were being carried on the books at a value higher than their market value'.[14] Nevertheless, the vulnerability of banks in early 1933 underlined the folly of failing to deliver more aggressive quantitative easing earlier in the crisis. More substantive open market purchases in 1932 extending over a *longer* period 'would have improved the capital position [of banks] by raising market values [of corporate bonds]' reducing the probability of bank runs.[15]

## A Disunited Federal Reserve

The Federal Reserve was a reluctant convert to quantitative easing. There were deep schisms within the Federal Reserve that severely hampered the operation of monetary policy. At the time of the stock market crash in 1929, policy decisions were carried out by the *Open Market Investment Committee*. This was superseded by the *Open Market Policy Conference* in 1930.[16] Both were

---

[14] Ibid. p. 330.

[15] Ibid.

[16] Ibid. p. 368. 'That was the final meeting of the Open Market Investment Committee. It was replaced by the Open Market Policy Conference of all twelve bank governors, with an executive committee consisting initially of the same five governors who had constituted the Committee (New York, Boston, Chicago, Cleveland, Philadelphia). But the executive committee was in a

similar to the *Federal Open Market Committee* (FOMC), which today serves as the governing body for monetary policy decisions. As with the FOMC, governors from the regional or Federal Reserve banks had a vote on monetary policy matters.

The New York Fed Governor, George L. Harrison, was also chair of the Open Market Policy Conference. After share prices collapsed in October 1929, the New York Fed had few doubts about the steps that needed to be taken. It purchased $160million of government securities during the final months of 1929.[17] This was the first attempt to ameliorate the downturn through quantitative easing. Interest rates were also cut swiftly.[18]

However, other members of the Open Market Policy Conference were against quantitative easing. There was a power struggle within an organisation facing its first big test since its creation in 1913. There was resentment that the New York Fed had acted without consent, even

---

different position from the former committee. It was entrusted with executing policy decisions of the Conference; it did not, like the earlier Committee, both initiate and execute policy. The Conference itself remained a voluntary organisation of equals. Each bank was free to decide whether it would or would not participate in a purchase or sale recommended by the Conference, though dissenters were required to acquaint the Federal Reserve Board and the chairman of the executive committee with the reasons for not participating. Each bank also reserved the option to withdraw from the Conference'.

[17] Ibid. p. 339.

[18] Ibid. p. 341. 'The decline in discounts took place despite sharp reductions in discount rates - at the New York Bank - from 6 per cent [August 1929] to 2½ per cent in June 1930'.

though the bonds had been bought for the bank's own account. Indeed, the Federal Reserve Board 'was piqued at Mr Harrison and the New York bank for undertaking purchases without prior approval'.[19] The Governor of the New York Fed was advised that further purchases of government securities would 'probably lead to the eventual promulgation of a regulation on the subject' by the Federal Reserve Board.[20]

According to Allan Meltzer, the strong reaction of the Federal Reserve Board had 'a permanent effect on Mr Harrison and that thereafter he was reluctant to engage in open market operations without the consent of the Board or the Open Market Investment Committee'.[21] Other interpretations suggest 'that the Board members conceded Mr Harrison had been correct in making large-scale purchases of government securities'. However, 'they disliked New York's decision to act alone'.[22] The dispute was 'mainly about procedure, not about substance'.[23] These differences were not new. There had been disagreements over 'the division of responsibility and particularly the Board's role in open market policy from

---

[19] See *A History of the Federal Reserve*, Volume 1:1913-1951, Meltzer, University of Chicago Press, p. 284.

[20] Ibid. p. 285.

[21] Ibid. p. 288.

[22] Ibid. p. 289.

[23] Ibid.

the very first years of the system and particularly after 1923, when the importance of open market operations increased'.[24]

Nonetheless, on November 1929, Harrison wrote a letter highlighting the concerns of directors at the New York Federal Reserve, 'that there may be a greater danger of recession in business with consequent depression and unemployment, which we should do all in our power to prevent'.[25] However, repeated attempts by the New York Fed to pursue a more expansionary monetary policy were rejected by other members of the Open Market Policy Conference. In July 1930, three months before the first banking crisis, Mr Harrison wrote a long letter to all governors of the other Federal Reserve banks arguing for more quantitative easing, pleading that the 'Federal Reserve System do everything possible and within its power to facilitate a recovery of business'.[26]

Mr Harrison conceded that 'there may be no definite assurance that open market operations in government securities will of themselves promote any immediate recovery'. However, there was no 'appreciable harm' in trying, he claimed. The 'seriousness of the present depression is so great as to justify taking every possible

---

[24] Ibid.

[25] Ibid.

[26] See *A Monetary History of the United States, 1867-1960*, M. Friedman & A.J Schwartz, Princeton University Press, 1963, p. 370.

step to facilitate improvement'.[27]

The warning was ignored. The governor of the Chicago Fed, James McDougal, noted there was already an 'abundance of funds in the market'. Indeed, there was a danger that 'speculation might easily arise in some other direction'.[28] Mr McDougal even pushed for a reversal of the limited quantitative easing authorised at the previous meeting. John Calkins, head of the San Francisco Federal Reserve, argued that a recovery would not 'be accelerated by making credit cheaper', and urged the Open Market Policy Conference to wait for a more 'opportune moment' to take action.[29] It was wrong that 'artificial conditions should be created for the purposes of promoting a bond market ... We cannot see that this policy can be continuously followed without unfavourable results'.[30] Lynn Talley of the Dallas Federal Reserve was also against 'artificial methods' to reverse the effects of stock market speculation that had precipitated the crash. It is 'quite impossible to bring the patient back to life through the use of artificial respiration or injections of adrenalin', declared Mr Talley.[31] The head

---

[27] Ibid.

[28] Ibid. p. 371.

[29] Ibid. p. 372.

[30] See *A History of the Federal Reserve*, Volume 1:1913-1951, Meltzer, University of Chicago Press, p. 289.

[31] See *A Monetary History of the United States, 1867-1960*, M. Friedman &

of the Minneapolis Federal Reserve, William B. Geery was worried about the 'danger of stimulating financing'. Paradoxically, he fretted over the prospect of 'still more overproduction', while worrying about the effects of easier finance in promoting consumption.[32]

The Philadelphia Federal Reserve chief, George Norris, warned against 'attempting to depress still further the abnormally low interest rates now prevailing'. He added, 'We have been putting out credit in a period of depression, when it is not wanted, and could not be used, and will have to withdraw credit when it is wanted and can be used'.[33] Mr Norris 'opposed the purchase program because the recession was due to excess capacity and overproduction that had caused a fall in the price of commodities'. He added, 'easier money' or lower interest rates 'might lead to further increases in productive capacity and further overproduction'.[34] The problem was one of 'excess capacity and not one of underconsumption'.[35] Therefore, the 'correction must come about through reduced production, reduced

---

A.J Schwartz, Princeton University Press, 1963, p. 372.

[32] Ibid. 'There is danger of stimulating financing which will lead to still more overproduction while attempting to make it easy to do financing which will increase consumption'.

[33] Ibid. p. 372-373.

[34] See *A History of the Federal Reserve*, Volume 1:1913-1951, Meltzer, University of Chicago Press, p. 309.

[35] Ibid. p. 318.

inventories ... and the accumulation of savings through the exercise of thrift'.[36]

Mr Norris warned that he and the other members of the executive committee 'cannot bring themselves to believe that a further purchase of government securities would help'. Indeed, such purchases 'might be embarrassing at the time when business starts to pick up, at which time this System would find itself with a large amount of government securities and low discount rates'. In conclusion, the majority of the executive committee could not see any benefit from 'affirmative action'.[37]

According to Friedman and Schwartz, the contrast between the New York Fed and other Reserve Banks was due to 'extraordinary differences ... in the level of sophistication and understanding about monetary matters'. In part, this reflected the role of New York as the home of the country's money market, which had given the New York Fed a 'sensitive recognition of the effects of monetary policy actions'. By contrast, the regional reserve banks had been largely concerned with 'local and regional matters'.[38] They were inclined to view intervention as a sop to over-speculation.

Having initially tried to support the economy

---

[36] Ibid.

[37] Ibid. p. 310.

[38] See *A Monetary History of the United States, 1867-1960*, M. Friedman & A.J Schwartz, Princeton University Press, 1963, p. 374.

through quantitative easing, the Federal Reserve's policy became highly restrictive from December 1929. During the summer of 1930, the governor of the New York Fed pushed for more direct action, to no avail.[39] He was not alone. Another New York official warned that 'this deflation should now be aggressively combatted by additional purchases of Government securities', but he was ignored too.[40] The collapse of the Bank of the United States in December 1930 had forced the New York Fed to intervene on its own account, as it had in late 1929.[41] Other Federal Reserve Banks defiantly refused to support the New York Fed. Indeed, the Open Market Policy Conference in January 1931 voted to tighten policy, reversing the modest quantitative easing that had taken place.

---

[39] Ibid. p. 369. 'Early in June [1930], Harrison recommended that the [Federal Reserve] System undertake the purchase of $25million a week for a two-week trial period [...] the executive committee rejected the recommendation by a vote of 4 to 1'.

[40] Ibid. p. 374. 'A few days later, when Carl Snyder, at a meeting of the officers' council of the New York Bank, suggested that 'this deflation should now be aggressively combatted by additional purchases of Government securities ...', Harrison replied that 'from a System standpoint it is a practical impossibility to embark on such a program at the present time - to do so would mean an active division of System policy".

[41] Ibid. p. 376. 'The banking difficulties in New York following the failure of the Bank of United States in the second week of December necessitated purchase of $45million of government securities by the New York Reserve Bank for its own account. They were bought from two banks undergoing heavy withdrawals of currency in order to enable them to avoid borrowing. In addition, $80million of government securities were purchased for System account, as Harrison explained 'in order to avoid too great tightening of credit due to an unusual amount of 'window dressing".

Eugene Meyer, governor of the Federal Reserve Board, was aghast and warned of political repercussions, because 'The [Federal] Reserve System has been accused in a number of quarters of pursuing a deflationary policy in the past year, and a sale of government securities at this time is likely to draw fire'.[42] Despite this warning, the governors agreed unanimously that it 'would be desirable to dispose of some of the System holdings of government securities as and when the opportunity affords itself'.[43] Mr Harrison had also reported that 'European countries were planning to reduce imports from the United States' because of a shortage of gold. Britain, Germany and Italy had suffered a decline in gold reserves during 1930. The Smoot-Hawley Tariff had amplified the decline in world trade.[44] 'Despite these gloomy prospects', all members of the Open Market Policy Conference believed monetary policy was 'easy'.[45]

The lack of monetary policy action led inevitability to the banking crisis of March 1931. The governor of the New York Fed proposed that the Federal Reserve buy $100million of government securities in a belated

---

[42] Ibid. p. 377.

[43] Ibid.

[44] See *A History of the Federal Reserve*, Volume 1:1913-1951, Meltzer, University of Chicago Press, p. 328. 'The Smoot-Hawley Tariff had added to the decline in world trade and particularly to reduced exports and imports by the United States'.

[45] Ibid. p. 329.

attempt to ease the crisis. The resolution was passed 'with four reluctant supporters', and it was barely implemented.[46] By May 1931, the 'yields on Baa bonds were much higher than they had been at the peak of the economic cycle in August 1929, whereas Aaa yields were lower'.[47] The asset purchases did not begin until after a further meeting held on 22 June and then stopped on 16 July, with only $30million of securities purchased.[48] The minutes of the 6 July 1931 meeting of the Open Market Policy Conference had revealed that '222 banks were threatened with insolvency', but this had little impact on the Federal Reserve.[49] Indeed, Mr Harrison attributed the 'increased bank insolvency to bad management and more careful examination [of lower quality bonds]'.[50]

On 11 August 1931, Mr Harrison pressed for more authorisation to buy $300million of government

---

[46] See A Monetary History of the United States, 1867-1960, M. Friedman & A.J Schwartz, Princeton University Press, 1963, p. 378.

[47] See A History of the Federal Reserve, Volume 1:1913-1951, Meltzer, University of Chicago Press, p. 332.

[48] See A Monetary History of the United States, 1867-1960, M. Friedman & A.J Schwartz, Princeton University Press, 1963, p. 378-379. 'No purchases were made under that recommendation until after a June 22 meeting of the executive committee, at which Harrison urged purchases of $50million. […]. On July 9, the executive committee agreed to further purchase of $50million to complete the $100million authorized in April, but buying was stopped on July 16 at only $30million because of Harrison's concern over foreign developments and despite the remonstrances of Meyer'.

[49] See A History of the Federal Reserve, Volume 1:1913-1951, Meltzer, University of Chicago Press, p. 337.

[50] Ibid. p. 336-337.

securities. He was overruled and had to settle for a limit of $120million.[51] Another senior Federal Reserve official, agitating for stronger action, warned that this was an 'ineffective amount'.[52] Mr Harrison had outlined the 'economic, social, and political upheavals and of the high rate of unemployment expected in the winter'. The memorandum prepared for the 11 August Open Market Policy Conference meeting highlighted 166 bank failures in June 1931 alone, the highest number since January of the same year.[53] There is some debate over how far Mr Harrison pushed for the increase. The New York Fed governor had introduced a motion to buy up to $300million 'when they thought it was necessary'. However, according to Meltzer, Mr Harrison indicated that the time for purchases had not yet come because 'the attitude of the banks and investors was such that funds thus made available would be held idle'.[54] While Mr Harrison argued 'for a more expansive policy than the Open Market Policy Conference approved, he made

---

[51] See A Monetary History of the United States, 1867-1960, M. Friedman & A.J Schwartz, Princeton University Press, 1963, p. 379. 'Harrison proposed a program, to be put into effect when desirable, authorizing the executive committee to buy up to $300million of government securities. Other governors, except Black of Atlanta which joined Harrison in favour of it, were entirely negative in their reaction, and the Conference voted instead an authorization for the executive committee to buy or sell $120million'.

[52] Ibid. p. 380.

[53] See A History of the Federal Reserve, Volume 1:1913-1951, Meltzer, University of Chicago Press, p. 339.

[54] Ibid.

it clear that he did not plan to put the purchase plan into effect'. He was effectively arguing for a 'standby authority'.[55] Friedman and Schwartz offer a different interpretation, claiming Mr Harrison sought a 'more expansive policy,' but was unable to convince other members to support his position.[56]

According to Meltzer, Mr Harrison's laissez-faire approach to the banking crisis was 'very different from the response of Owen Young, one of his directors'. Indeed, at the 10 August 1931 meeting of the Open Market Policy Conference, Young noted that 'the country looked to the Federal Reserve System and not to the Comptroller of the Currency to assume leadership in banking crisis'. Pleas for a 'series of strong measures to assist the banks were ignored.[57]

Yields on lower-rated bonds rose during the autumn of 1931. The delays in implementing large-scale open market purchases allowed 'a large part of the banking system to fail'.[58] Even rates on Aaa bonds were now

---

[55] Ibid. p. 340.

[56] See A Monetary History of the United States, 1867-1960, Friedman & A.J Schwartz, Princeton University Press, 1963, p. 341. According to Meltzer, 'Harrison's statements at the (August 1931) meeting….show little interest in an expansive policy'.

[57] See A History of the Federal Reserve, Volume 1:1913-1951, Meltzer, University of Chicago Press, p. 337.

[58] Ibid. p. 352. 'In two months, September and October 1931, the deposits of suspended banks rose to $705million, as much as in the entire year 1932 yet to come. Nearly 30 percent of the banks suspensions between August 1929 and February 1933 came in the last four months of 1931'.

higher than the August 1929 level. By early 1932, New York Bank officials were once again pushing for radical intervention, and the Open Market Policy Conference was authorised to conduct $200million of open market purchases 'if necessary'.[59] The Federal Reserve failed even to exploit this limited agreement. Monetary policy remained too tight and the economy continued to slide deeper into depression.

An exasperated Congress was beginning to exert pressure on the Federal Reserve, threatening 'radical financial legislation'.[60] Treasury Secretary Ogden Mills spoke for the Hoover administration when he declared that the lack of action was 'almost inconceivable and almost unforgivable'. He pleaded for the policy options available to the Federal Reserve to 'be put to work on a scale commensurate with the existing emergency'.[61]

Between January 11 and February 24 1932, government security holdings declined by $11million. At the February meeting, there was a mild expansion in the authority of Open Market Policy Conference to buy up to $250million at the approximate rate of $25million a week. This 'modest program would very likely never have been expanded into a major one, or perhaps even

---

[59] See A Monetary History of the United States, 1867-1960, M. Friedman & A.J Schwartz, Princeton University Press, 1963, p. 384.

[60] Ibid.

[61] Ibid. p. 385.

carried out, if it had not been for direct and indirect pressure from Congress'.[62] The *Glass-Steagall Act*, passed on February 27 1932, sent a clear message to the Federal Reserve. The Act put the Hoover administration and Congress - including Senator Carter Glass - on record as favouring large scale purchases.[63]

## Turning The Tide, Reflation Begins

Eventually, the Federal Reserve voted on 12 April 1932 to expand quantitative easing. It would purchase $500million of government securities in addition to the unexpired authority agreed at the previous meeting [$250million]. The purchases were to be made 'as rapidly as practicable'.[64] This last provision was inserted after Mr Harrison had declared that 'he was scheduled to testify the next day before a subcommittee of the House on a bill that in effect would have directed the Reserve system to purchase [government securities or Treasuries] in the

---

[62] Ibid. p. 384.

[63] See *A History of the Federal Reserve*, Volume 1:1913-1951, Meltzer, University of Chicago Press, p. 358. 'The Glass-Steagall Act relaxed Federal Reserve collateral requirements in three ways. First, government securities became eligible as collateral for not issues, [...]. Second, reserve banks could lend on previously ineligible commercial paper at a rate of 1 percent above the discount rate. This provision permitted banks to borrow against a much broader range of assets. Third, groups of five or more banks could borrow on the group's credit. This provision permitted clearinghouses to borrow directly and encouraged the formation of county clearinghouses in rural areas'.

[64] See *A Monetary History of the United States, 1867-1960*, M. Friedman & A.J Schwartz, Princeton University Press, 1963, p. 385.

open market until wholesale prices had risen to their 1926 level'.[65] Mr Harrison warned that 'the only way to forestall some sort of radical financial legislation by Congress was an expanded program of [bonds] purchases'.[66]

At its next monthly meeting, the Federal Reserve voted to expand the open market purchases by a further $500million, but there were two dissenting voices - the Chicago and Boston Federal Reserve Banks. The Open Market Policy Conference also debated slowing the pace of buying. Over the five weeks since the previous meeting, the Federal Reserve had been buying government securities at the rate of $100million per week. Mr Harrison was furious, warning that 'The temper of Congress is not improving'.[67] However, the governor of the New York Fed was 'pulled in different directions' by conflict within Committee members. On May 5, Mr Harrison, seeking a compromise, opposed a proposal from one of his directors that the Federal Reserve should buy longer-term securities.[68]

The full authority agreed at the May meeting was utilised, and by the end of June the Federal Reserve had

---

[65] Ibid. p. 386.

[66] See *A History of the Federal Reserve*, Volume 1:1913-1951, Meltzer, University of Chicago Press, p. 360.

[67] See *A Monetary History of the United States, 1867-1960*, M. Friedman & A.J Schwartz, Princeton University Press, 1963, p. 386.

[68] See *A History of the Federal Reserve*, Volume 1:1913-1951, Meltzer, University of Chicago Press, p. 364.

bought $1,000million of government securities. Again, Chicago and Boston tried to stop quantitative easing. One official of the New York Fed complained bitterly, warning that the Federal Reserve had not gone far enough to 'stimulate an expansion of credit' to reflate the economy.[69] To stop now 'would be a ridiculous thing to do. We shall have no policy left if we do this'.[70] The Federal Reserve had reached a point where it was now able to apply the pressure quantitative easing was 'designed to produce'. The Federal Reserve was merely 'half way through' its programme.[71]

The head of the Chicago Fed countered that he could 'not see what the purchases have done anyway'. The Boston Fed chief was even more disingenuous. Further bank failures were inevitable, Governor Young warned, which would lead to more borrowing from the Federal Reserve. Therefore, he concluded, 'we are wasting our resources buying Government securities'.[72] The very point of large scale asset purchases - to forestall bank failure - was completely lost on Roy A. Young [Boston

---

[69] See *A Monetary History of the United States, 1867-1960*, M. Friedman & A.J Schwartz, Princeton University Press, 1963, p. 386. 'To Owen D. Young, this [the assets purchasing program] meant that 'most of our efforts had, in reality served to check a contraction of credit rather than to stimulate an expansion in credit".

[70] Ibid. p. 387.

[71] Ibid. p. 386.

[72] Ibid. p. 387.

Governor]. Owen D. Young [deputy chair of the New York Fed] travelled to Illinois in an attempt to persuade the directors of the Chicago Fed to change their minds, but he failed.

Boston and Chicago were in the minority, but their dissents influenced Mr Harrison. The Federal Reserve Governor was in favour of extending the purchases, but only if 'the program be made a real system program and that the Federal Reserve banks of Boston and Chicago, in particular, give it their affirmative support'.[73] Mr Harrison was concerned that proceeding without the support of reserve banks would compromise the unity of the Federal Reserve. At its next monthly meeting on 14 July 1932, the Federal Reserve decided to purchase government securities at a rate of just $5million to $15million a week.[74] That was not restrictive enough for the Boston or Chicago Feds, who were joined by the Richmond Fed in voting against the resolution.

Two days after the meeting, Congress adjourned. Freed from political pressure, the Federal Reserve conducted open market purchases at the minimum level consistent

---

[73] See A History of the Federal Reserve, Volume 1:1913-1951, Meltzer, University of Chicago Press, p. 367.

[74] See A Monetary History of the United States, 1867-1960, M. Friedman & A.J Schwartz, Princeton University Press, 1963, p. 389. 'For the guidance of the executive committee, the Conference recommended purchases not to exceed $15million a week - except in unusual of unforeseen circumstances - but not less than $5million a week for the next four weeks'.

with the July compromise, buying a mere $30million of government securities during the four weeks following the meeting. From 10 August until the end of 1932, monetary policy went neutral. Boston and Chicago refused to participate in any further efforts to support the economy and the head of New York 'was unwilling to proceed on his own'.[75]

By early January 1933, the Federal Reserve was coming under pressure again to relent. But the Open Market Policy Conference proceeded instead to vote for a tightening of policy at its 4 January meeting, reducing open market purchases by a maximum of $125million in the first month of the year, despite opposition from Treasury officials.[76] Having stabilised the economy during the summer of 1932, the Federal Reserve was reversing tack. Yet another banking crisis loomed. During February, the Federal Reserve did not even meet. Mr Harrison had given up trying to forge a consensus. Each Reserve Bank conducted individual actions to stem the gathering crisis. That merely added to the general atmosphere of panic. The Federal Reserve had fallen into disarray and the banking system imploded.

---

[75] Ibid.

[76] Ibid. p. 390. 'The sentiment of most governors was clearly in favour of reducing the portfolio, and the final motion reflected that sentiment. It gave the executive committee authority to reduce the System's holding of Treasury bills, the reduction in January not to exceed $125million and not to bring excess reserves below $500million'.

## The 'Final' Banking Crisis

The newly inaugurated President Roosevelt was forced to proclaim a nationwide bank holiday from 6–9 March.[77] The Emergency Banking Act of 1933 allowed banks to be reopened on a 'restricted' basis. Under previous laws, these banks would have been placed in receivership and liquidated. In a radio address on 12 March, the President announced a programme for reopening the banks. But over 2,000 out of 17,800 remained closed for good.[78]

The newly created Reconstruction Finance Corporation played a crucial role in the restoration of the banking system. It invested $1billion of taxpayers' money into 6,139 banks, equal to a third of the capital of all banks in 1933. The Reconstruction Finance Corporation also made loans totalling over $2billion.[79] It was an aggressive

---

[77] Ibid. p. 421. 'Title I of the [Emergency Banking Act] approved and confirmed the action taken by President Roosevelt in proclaiming a nationwide bank holiday from March 6 to March 9, inclusive, under the wartime measure of October 6, 1917, which conferred broad powers over banking and currency upon the President of the United States'.

[78] Ibid. p. 425.

[79] Ibid. p. 427-428. 'The RFC played a major role in the restoration of the banking system as it had in the futile attempts to shore it up before the banking holiday. It invested a total of over $1billion in bank capital - one third of the total capital of all banks in the United States in 1933 - and purchased capital issues of 6,139 banks, or almost one-half the number of banks. In addition, it made loans to open banks for distribution to depositors of $187million and to closed banks of over $900million, on the security of the best assets of those institutions. The loans, made after the banking panic, were in addition to loans of $951million to open banks and the $80million to closed banks made before the banking panic. In aggregate, 5,816 open banks and 2,773 closed banks obtained RFC loans totalling more than $2billion'.

programme of assistance, often seen as decisive in turning the tide. Without it, the banking crisis would have undoubtedly continued.

However, the impact of the Reconstruction Finance Corporation cannot be separated from the impetus provided by monetary policy. The Federal Reserve could and should have done much more, but it was pulling the levers, if reluctantly. Indeed, a closer inspection of the economic data testifies to the powerful impact of quantitative easing: had it been used more aggressively the banking crises of March 1933 might have been averted.

After November 1933, the Federal Reserve resisted any further extensive purchases, with officials claiming that the banks were awash with reserves.[80] Nevertheless, the increase in government securities held by the Federal Reserve during 1933 was still substantial.[81] The US Treasury continued to push for more aggressive monetary action in 1934. The size of the Federal Reserve's balance sheet did not change, but there was a dramatic shift in its

---

[80] Ibid. p. 518. 'This interpretation also explains the reason the System engaged in no extensive purchases of government securities after November 1933. Why add to excess reserves, which were being so rapidly expanded by gold inflows and which served no current economic function? It does not explain why the System kept its security holdings constant'.

[81] See *US Monetary Policy & Financial Markets*, A.M Meulendyke, Federal Reserve Bank of New York, 1998, p. 22. The Federal Reserve Total Holdings (of assets, including Government debt or securities) still rose 37.1 per cent between 1932 and 1933.

composition. The Federal Reserve sold short-term bonds and bought longer dated Treasuries. The objective was to drive the long-term interest rate down. This was the same as Operation Twist adopted in 2011 [see Chapter 2, page 105].[82]

## The Recovery Takes Hold

As the cost of borrowing fell, the pace of bankruptcies slowed and the recovery in the economy gained traction. US industrial output bottomed in 1932, having shrunk 47.9 per cent in three years. It clawed back nearly a fifth of the loss in 1933. Such was the scale of the contraction it was not until December 1936 that output had returned to the levels seen at the peak of 1929.[83] In broader terms, national income did not bottom until 1933, having collapsed by 30.5 per cent in real terms over four years.

[82] Ibid. p. 22. Federal Reserve Total Holdings fell 4.4 per cent in 1934 from 1933 to $2,430.4billion. However, holdings of Treasury Certificates fell from $425.1billion to $0.0billion. Holdings of Treasury Notes went up from $1,053.2billion to $1,507.1billion.

[83] See *Historical Statistics of the United States, Colonial Times to 1970, Part 2*, US Department of Commerce, Bureau of the Census, 1975, p. 667. The Index for US Industrial Production fell from 23 in 1929 to 12 in 1932, before rising to 14 in 1933. A less pessimistic assessment comes from the National Bureau of Economic Research, which shows that Manufacturing Output in Volume Terms fell 17.9 per cent between 1929 and 1932, before rising to a level in 1937 that was 17.9 per cent above the previous cyclical peak of 1929. Source: Federal Reserve, St Louis. The monthly data shows a bigger recovery from July 1932. The monthly Seasonally Adjusted Index for US Industrial Production (2002=100) rose from a low of 4.1179 in July 1932 to a high of 6.6728 a year later, a gain of 62.0 per cent. The Seasonally Adjusted Index for US Industrial Production (2002=100) peaked in July 1929 at 8.8670 and finally climbed back to 9.0173 in December 1936.

As prices had tumbled too, the drop in nominal terms was an astonishing 46.1 per cent.[84]

The yearly GDP data implies that the recovery did not really begin until after the final banking panic in early 1933. However, the more timely monthly data for industrial production suggests there was already some recovery underway in 1932 in response to the monetary easing witnessed that year. [See chart 4b]. Industrial output hit a low three months following the shift in Federal Reserve policy from April 1932. After quantitative easing stopped, the recovery stalled. As more banks failed, output tumbled again, nearly revisiting the lows of 1932. Nevertheless, while there was a renewed dip in 1933, July 1932 marks the trough of the Great Depression.[85]

Similarly, the decline in GDP in annual terms during 1933 was mild compared with the falls witnessed earlier in the first three years of the slump. In real terms, GDP dropped by just 1.9 per cent. It had fallen 9.9 per cent in

---

[84] See *Historical Statistics of the United States, Colonial Times to 1970*, *Part 1*, US Department of Commerce, Bureau of the Census, 1975, p. 224. Gross national product in nominal terms fell from $103.1billion in 1929 to $55.6billion in 1933.

[85] Source: Federal Reserve, St Louis. The Seasonally Adjusted Index for US Industrial Production (2002=100) fell to 4.1179 in July 1932, before recovering to 4.6589 in October and November 1932. It then fell again, to 4.2381 in March 1933, before rising swiftly to a high of 6.6728 for the year in July 1933. The July 1932 low was 2.8 per cent below the March 1933 trough.

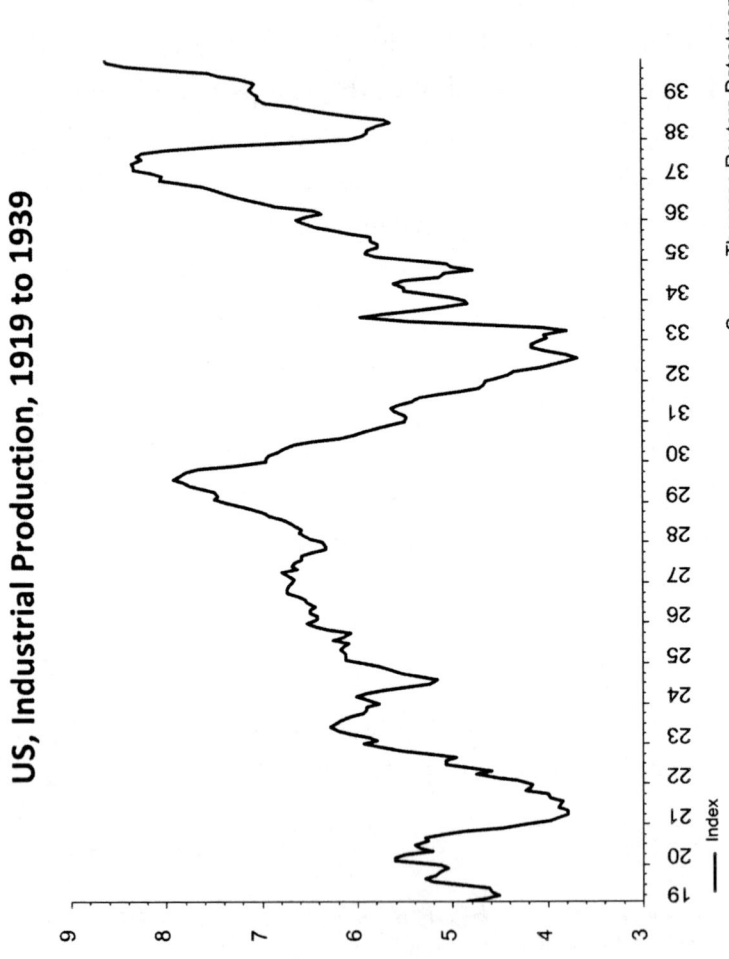

**US, Industrial Production, 1919 to 1939**

Source: Thomson Reuters Datastream

—— Index

Chart 4b

1930, 7.7 per cent in 1931 and 14.8 per cent in 1932.[86] The GDP data suggest that policy was starting to work in 1932, although it was clearly insufficient, as evident from the banking turmoil in early 1933.

Reflecting upon the impact of the shift in monetary policy Allan Meltzer concludes, 'It seems likely that had purchases continued, the collapse of the monetary system during the winter of 1933 might have been avoided'.[87] Indeed, 'The Federal Reserve recognised the improvement at the time'. Eugene Meyer, a director at the New York Fed, described 'the rise in commodity and security prices [in 1933] as the best in nearly three years'. He then dismissed 'those who think things are going too fast; they are not going fast enough'. A continued rise in commodity prices offered 'the chief hope for banks and the economy'.[88]

## Pulling the Trigger Too Soon

However, from 1934 onwards some Federal Reserve officials were beginning to fret over the risks of running a 'loose' monetary policy.[89] Banks were awash with

---

[86] See *Historical Statistics of the United States, Colonial Times to 1970, Part 1,* US Department of Commerce, Bureau of the Census, 1975, p. 228.

[87] See *A History of the Federal Reserve*, Volume 1:1913-1951, Meltzer, University of Chicago Press, p. 372-373.

[88] Ibid. p. 373.

[89] See *A Monetary History of the United States, 1867-1960*, M. Friedman & A.J Schwartz, Princeton University Press, 1963, p. 520. 'Beginning in

excess reserves, but only because they wanted the extra cushion this afforded after the tumult of recent years.[90] Furthermore, while the economy was recovering, the fall in unemployment was slow. The jobless rate was still 14.3 per cent in 1937.[91] Commodity prices were bouncing back after the sharp declines witnessed during the early years of the Great Depression. That did not stop the Federal Reserve panicking, fretting that its policy had engineered too much reflation. It prematurely turned the screw, with the first of three quick increases in bank reserve requirements beginning in August 1936.

The tighter monetary policy sent the economy spiralling back into recession.[92] The persistently high jobless rate showed the economy had failed to make a full recovery. The depth of the downturn in the early 1930s implied there was little chance of inflation 'pressures' becoming embedded. Commodity prices were rising, but wages had largely been supported by the New Deal.[93] As

---

early 1934, the Bank's staff prepared a series of internal memoranda, some circulated also to the Federal Open Market Committee, in which it examined the problem of excess reserves, emphasised potential dangers they raised, and considered alternative ways to control them'.

[90] Ibid. p. 458. 'When the rise in reserve requirements immobilized the accumulated cash, they [banks] proceeded rather promptly to accumulate additional cash for liquidity purposes'.

[91] See *Historical Statistics of the United States, Colonial Times to 1970, Part 1*, p. 126.

[92] Ibid. p. 224. Gross National Product at 1958 prices fell 5.1 per cent between 1937 and 1938.

[93] See *A Monetary History of the United States, 1867-1960*, M. Friedman

the higher bank reserve requirements started to bite, this underlying weakness in wages accelerated the slump. The jobless rate leapt to 19.1 per cent in 1938.[94] The economy was not strong enough to withstand such a severe jolt. The failure to distinguish between the weakness of wages and rising commodity prices was a mistake the Federal Reserve was to repeat in 2008 following the collapse of the investment bank Bear Stearns.[95]

A full economic recovery did not ultimately materialise until the onset of World War II. The outbreak of hostilities in Western Europe saw demand for military goods jump in the US, bringing the jobless rate down to 9.9 per cent in 1941. The Japanese attack on Pearl Harbour was the trigger for full-scale militarisation. The jobless rate dropped finally to a low of 1.2 per cent in 1944.[96] Nevertheless, the use of the Federal Reserve to fund the war effort holds important lessons. It

---

& A.J Schwartz, Princeton University Press, 1963, p. 493–495. Wage rises were initially promoted through the codes established under the National Industrial Recovery Act, passed on 16 June 1933. The codes were declared unconstitutional in 1935, but they still had some interim impact. Thereafter, wages were supported by the National Labour Relations Act and the enactment of minimum wage laws. Labour costs were also raised by laws introducing a range of new taxes, including social security taxes, from 1935. For more, see The Economics of Recession and Revival, K. Rose, Yale University Press, 1954, and FDR: The First Hundred Days, A. J. Badger, 2007.

[94] See Historical Statistics of the United States, Colonial Times to 1970, Part 1, p. 126.

[95] See Chapter 2, p. 83.

[96] See Historical Statistics of the United States, Colonial Times to 1970, Part 1, p. 126.

was nothing less than large-scale quantitative easing. Government spending nearly tripled between 1941 and 1942, and then rose a further 50 per cent in the following year. Tax receipts lagged, so the budget deficit exploded to unprecedented levels - to 28.1% of Gross National Product.[97]

This huge increase in defence spending was financed by the Federal Reserve buying government securities.[98] The Federal Reserve's holdings of government debt soared more than tenfold, from $2.3billion in 1941 to $24.3billion four years later.[99] After the war ended, the factories shifted back to producing consumer goods and aggressive quantitative easing came to an end.

## Ben Bernanke And The Great Depression

The former Federal Reserve chair Mr Bernanke built his academic reputation on studying the depression of the 1930s. He was also a vocal critic of Japan's inaction in the late 1990s, as the dotcom bubble imploded. Mr Bernanke's work may be revered in academic circles.

---

[97] See A Monetary History of the United States, 1867-1960, M. Friedman & A.J Schwartz, Princeton University Press, 1963, p. 556-557. See also Historical Statistics of the United States, Colonial Times to 1970, Part 1, p. 228 and Historical Statistics of the United States, Colonial Times to 1970, Part 2, p. 1105.

[98] Ibid. p. 561. 'In World War II, discounts were small throughout, and the Federal Reserve increased its credit outstanding by buying government securities'.

[99] See US Monetary Policy & Financial Markets, Meulendyke, p. 22.

In reality, the Fed chair spent less time analysing the policies of reflation adopted by the Federal Reserve during the early 1930s. His book *Essays on the Great Depression* published in 2000 contains few references to open market operations or quantitative easing.[100] His analysis of monetary policy is sketchy at best.

Mr Bernanke accepts that the contraction of money supply was the chief cause of the 1930s depression. However, he claimed this 'was itself the result of a poorly managed and technically flawed international monetary system' - in other words, the gold standard.[101] This view is too simplistic and misses the point. There were policy measures that could have been taken to counteract the deflationary bias of the gold standard. Keynes railed routinely against the gold standard. However, that did not stop Keynes advocating the implementation of aggressive large scale asset purchases to prevent economic contraction. Furthermore, as already noted, his sphere of influence stretched far beyond the UK.

Even if it is accepted that the gold standard was a constraint, it was abandoned in March 1933. The manufacturing sector hit the first of a double bottom in 1932. Indeed, as we have seen, 1932 marked the true low point, not the early 1933 relapse as Mr Bernanke

---

[100] See *Essays on the Great Depression*, Ben Bernanke, Princeton University Press, 2000, p. 77, 153.

[101] Ibid. p. viii.

and others claim. Any in-depth analysis of the Great Depression has to evaluate the role of open market purchases or quantitative easing, notably during 1932, in driving the recovery.

In his 2000 book, Mr Bernanke devoted far more time to the role of 'sticky wages' in an attempt to account for the persistence of unemployment. According to Mr Bernanke, the slow adjustment of wages in the face of unemployment was 'especially difficult' to reconcile or rationalise.[102]

Another chapter in Ben Bernanke's book explores 'non-manufacturing financial factors, such as banking panics and business failures'. He concludes, 'the malfunctioning of financial institutions during the early 1930s' had real effects'. Mr Bernanke also warned that 'Institutions which evolve and perform well in normal times may become counterproductive during periods when exogenous shocks or policy mistakes drive the economy off course'.[103] These unremarkable conclusions should have at least alerted Mr Bernanke to the risks of allowing so many mortgage lenders - and a major investment bank - to default during 2007 and 2008.

---

[102] Ibid. p. 6.

[103] Ibid. p. 66-67.

## Fate or Incorrect Diagnosis?

Along with Keynes, Milton Friedman and Anna Schwartz correctly identified the monetary policy mistakes made during the early 1930s, albeit with the benefit of hindsight and without giving Keynes the credit for reversing some of these errors. Friedman and Schwartz argue that *fate* determined the outcome. Benjamin Strong had been governor of the Federal Reserve Bank of New York from 1914 until 1928. Throughout his tenure at the New York Fed, Mr Strong had been a dominant figure. He 'had the confidence and backing of other financial leaders ... the personal force to make his own views prevail, and also the courage to act upon them'.[104] In August 1928, just before he died and more than a year before the stock market crash, Mr Strong had warned that a 'breaking point' would necessitate an easy monetary policy, but 'feared the consequences of hesitation or differences of opinion' within the Federal Reserve.[105] He was a strong advocate of quantitative easing and argued that 'if this power were used in a big way, it would stop any panic which might confront us'.[106]

Mr Strong died in 1928. Friedman and Schwartz

---

[104] See *A Monetary History of the United States, 1867-1960*, M. Friedman & A.J Schwartz, Princeton University Press, 1963, p. 412.

[105] Ibid.

[106] Ibid.

concluded that 'if Strong had still been alive and head of the New York Bank in the fall of 1930, he would very likely have recognised the oncoming liquidity crisis for what it was, would have been prepared by experience and conviction to take strenuous and appropriate measures to head it off'.[107] Their assessment has been shared by others, including Irving Fisher, who lamented 'I thoroughly believe that if he [Benjamin Strong] had lived and his policies had been continued, we might have had the stock market crash in a milder form, but after the crash there would have not have been the great industrial depression'.[108] The conclusion of Friedman and Schwartz is telling: 'The detailed story of every banking crisis in our history shows how much depends on the presence of one or more outstanding individuals willing to assume responsibility and leadership. It was a defect of the financial system that it was susceptible to crises resolvable only with such leadership'.[109]

As in the early 1930s, there were weapons at the disposal of central banks that could have mitigated much of the damage as the credit crunch ripped through the world economy in 2008. The policymakers misjudged the scale of the crisis. Similarly, the Federal

---

[107] Ibid. p. 412-413.

[108] Ibid. p. 413.

[109] Ibid. p. 418.

Reserve was found wanting during the early stages of the current housing debacle, notably in 2007, in almost identical circumstances to those prevailing in 1930 and 1931. Hundreds of mortgage lenders defaulted from late 2006 onwards without the Federal Reserve taking offsetting monetary action. The point was underlined by the collapse of Lehman Brothers. The neglect of the banking system was a critical factor in accelerating the depression during the early 1930s. Allowing a major US investment bank to default in September 2008 was surely a comparable mistake.

For much of 2008, the Federal Reserve stuck rigidly to a programme of liquidity injections, refusing to sanction a more direct 1930's style policy that might have mitigated some of the damage on the economy. However, once house prices start to slide, injecting liquidity is not a sufficient condition for a recovery. That was a critical lesson of the 1930s. Only after the Federal Reserve had aggressively driven down all borrowing costs to relieve debtors did the tide begin to turn in 1932. They were 'beholden' to the gold standard because it was considered to be the ultimate bulwark against inflation. Nevertheless, that left a number of weapons, including the policy option deployed eventually in the US in April 1932 - the purchase of Treasury bonds (Treasuries) or quantitative easing.

## New Deal in Perspective

Finally, contrary to popular assertion, the economic recovery from the Great Depression did not begin under President Roosevelt. The main impetus came earlier from the Congressional pressure exerted on the Federal Reserve during President Hoover's tenure. Indeed, it is worth emphasising that the Federal government's budget deficit was still only 4.7 per cent of GDP in 1932, the final year of President Hoover's administration. It rose to 5.1 per cent of GDP in 1934, which was also the peak deficit during the Great Depression.[110] However, the recovery was already well underway by 1934. The fiscal stimulus followed after monetary policy had been used to stabilise the economy and kick-start the turnaround from July 1932 onwards. This was a policy sequence more in line with Keynes's remedy, with monetary tools to the forefront and fiscal measures secondary.

It is also important to recognise the debt to GDP ratio was much lower in 1929 in comparison with 2009, when President Obama tried to use fiscal policy to secure an economic recovery. Federal government debt was just 16.4% of GDP in 1929. It rose during the economic

---

[110] See *Historical Statistics of the United States, Colonial Times to 1970, Part 1*, US Department of Commerce, Bureau of the Census, 1975, p. 224, and *See Historical Statistics of the United States, Colonial Times to 1970, Part 2*, US Department of Commerce, Bureau of the Census, 1975, p. 1105.

downturn, but was still only 40.5% in 1933.[111] The debt to GDP ratio was much higher in 2008 [72.6%].[112] This makes comparisons between the likely efficacy of fiscal stimulus in the Great Depression and during the Credit Crunch misplaced on a number of levels: the different debt burdens implies that the control of bond yields and the attempts to tighten fiscal policy from 2010 onwards were always going to be more important in securing the economic recovery.

---

[111] Ibid. See also *Historical Statistics of the United States, Colonial Times to 1970, Part 2*, US Department of Commerce, Bureau of the Census, 1975, p. 1104. Total Federal government debt outstanding as a share of GDP was 16.4% and 41.6% in 1929 and 1934 respectively.

[112] Source: Organisation of Economic Cooperation and Development. General government gross financial liabilities as a share of GDP rose to 72.6% in 2008.

## US Federal Government Finances

| Date | Federal Government Finances (as %GDP) Surplus/Deficit | Date | Federal Government Finances (as %GDP) Surplus/Deficit |
|------|------|------|------|
| 1929 | 0.87 | 2006 | -1.80 |
| 1930 | 1.00 | 2007 | -1.12 |
| 1931 | -1.32 | 2008 | -3.04 |
| 1932 | -4.66 | 2009 | -9.73 |
| 1933 | -4.68 | 2010 | -8.63 |
| 1934 | -5.07 | 2011 | -8.29 |
| 1935 | -3.32 | 2012 | -6.66 |
| 1936 | -4.24 | 2013 | -4.03 |

Table 4a

The U.S. Economic Recovery

# Index

# G

# N

# O

# P

# S

# T

# U

The U.S. Economic Recovery

Index

The U.S. Economic Recovery

Lightning Source UK Ltd.
Milton Keynes UK
UKOW04f1343040814

236331UK00002B/2/P